The Saga of Erik the Red
Original Text, Translations, and Word Lists
Translated by Matthew Leigh Embleton

Copyright ©2025 Matthew Leigh Embleton. All rights reserved.

The Saga of Erik the Red

The Saga of Erik the Red (*Old Norse*) 4
The Saga of Erik the Red (*Old Icelandic*) 52
Word List *(Norse to English)* 102
Word List *(English to Norse)* 145

Cover: Old Norse text over an outline of Iceland. Author's design.

The original Old Icelandic and Old Norse texts are in the public domain.
These translations ©2021 Matthew Leigh Embleton
©2025 Matthew Leigh Embleton (This Edition)

Acknowledgments

I have long been fascinated by languages and history, and I am very grateful to the special people in my life who have supported and encouraged me in my work. Thank you for believing in me. You know who you are.

Introduction

The Saga of Erik the Red (Eiríks Saga Rauða) is one of the two Icelandic Sagas which make up the Vínland Sagas (Vínlandingasögur), along with The Saga of the Greenlanders (Grœnlendinga Saga), which tell the story of the Norse discovery of North America. The rich tradition of Icelandic literature survived by oral tradition over several centuries before being written down in the 13th Century.

Old Norse is a North Germanic language spoken by inhabitants of Scandinavia from about the 7th to the 15th centuries. Old Icelandic is a variety of Old West Norse that emerged during the Norse settlement of Iceland in the second half of the 9th century.

The meaning of the word 'saga' (plural: 'sǫgur' or 'sögur') translates as 'that which is said', or more widely: a 'saying', 'statement', 'story', 'tale', or 'narrative'.

This book contains:
The Saga of Erik the Red (Eiríks Saga Rauða) (Old Norse Version)
The Saga of Erik the Red (Eiríks Saga Rauða) (Old Icelandic Version)

The texts are presented in their original Norse, with a literal word-for-word line-by-line translation, and a Modern English translation, all side-by-side. In this way, it is possible to see and feel how the Norse language worked and how it has evolved. Also included is a word list with 2,737 Norse words translated in to English, and 1,792 English words translated into Norse.

This book is designed to be of use and interest to anyone with a passion for the Old Norse or Old Icelandic language, Norse history, or languages and history in general.

The Saga of Erik the Red (*Old Norse*)

Old Norse	Literal	English
1	1	1
Óláfr hét herkonungr, er kallaðr var Óláfr hvíti.	Olaf was-named warrior-king, that called was Olaf the-White.	There was a warrior king named Olaf, that was called Olaf the White.
Hann var sonr Ingjalds konungs Helgasonar, Óláfssonar, Guðröðarsonar, Hálfdanarsonar hvítbeins Upplendingakonungs.	He was son-of Ingjald's the-king son-of-Helga, son-of-Olaf, son-of-Gudrod, son-of-Halfdan White-Leg Opplands-king.	He was the son of Ingjald, the son of Helga, the son of Olaf, the son of Gudrod, the son of Halfdan White Leg, the king of the Opplands.
Óláfr herjaði í vestrvíking ok vann Dyflinni á Írlandi ok Dyflinnarskíri.	Olaf harried to west-raiding and won Dublin in Ireland and Dublinshire.	Olaf harried on raids to the west and conquered Dublin in Ireland and Dublinshire.
Þar gerðist hann konungr yfir.	There made himself king over.	He made himself king there.
Hann fekk Auðar djúpúðgu, dóttur Ketils flatnefs, Bjarnarsonar bunu, ágæts manns ór Nóregi.	He married Aud the-Deep-Minded, daughter Ketil's Flat-Nose son-of-Bjorn Buna, excellent man from Norway.	He married Aud the Deep Minded, daughter of Ketil Flat Nose, the son of Bjorn Buna, an excellent man from Norway.
Þorsteinn rauðr hét sonr þeira.	Thorstein the-Red was-named son theirs.	Their son was named Thorstein the Red.
Óláfr fell á Írlandi í orrostu, en Auðr ok Þorsteinn fóru þá í Suðreyjar.	Olaf fell in Ireland in battle, then Aud and Thorstein went they to Sudreyar.	Olaf fell in Ireland in battle, then Aud and Thorstein went to the Southern Islands.
Þar fekk Þorsteinn Þuríðar, dóttur Eyvindar Austmanns, systur Helga ins magra.	There married Thorstein Thorid, daughter-of Eyvind the-Easternman sister-of Helga the Lean.	There Thorstein married Thorid, daughter of Eyvind the Easterner, sister of Helga the Lean.
Þau áttu mörg börn.	They had many children.	They had many children.
Þorsteinn gerðist herkonungr.	Thorstein became-a warrior-king.	Thorstein became a warrior king.
Hann réðst til lags með Sigurði jarli inum ríka, syni Eysteins glumru.	He appointed to position with Sigurd Earl the Rich, son-of Eystein Glumra.	He teamed up with Earl Sigurd the Rich, son of Eystein Glumra.
Þeir unnu Katanes ok Suðrland, Ross ok Meræfi ok meir en hálft Skotland.	They won Caithness and Sutherland, Ross and Moray and more than half-of Scotland.	They conquered Caithness, Sutherland, Ross, Moray, and more than half of Scotland.
Gerðist Þorsteinn þar konungr yfir, áðr Skotar sviku hann, ok fell hann þar í orrostu.	Became Thorstein there king over, until Scots betrayed him, and fell he there in battle.	Thorstein became king there until the Scots betrayed him and he fell in battle.

The Saga of Erik the Red (Old Norse)

Old Norse	Literal	English
Auðr var þá á Katanesi, er hon spurði fall Þorsteins.	Aud was then in Caithness, when she heard-of fall Thorstein's.	Aud was then at Caithness when she learned of Thorstein's falling.
Hon lét þá gera knörr í skógi á laun, ok er hon var búin, helt hon út í Orkneyjar.	She had then made ship in woods of hired, and when she was ready, held she out to Orkney.	She then hired a ship to be made in the woods, and when she was ready, she set out to Orkney.
Þar gifti hon Gró, dóttur Þorsteins rauðs.	There gave she Gro, daughter Thorstein the-Red's.	There she gave in marriage Gro, daughter of Thorstein the Red.
Hon var móðir Grélaðar, er Þorfinnr jarl hausakljúfr átti.	She was mother-of Grelod, who Thorfin Earl Scull-Cleaver married.	She was the mother of Grelod, who was married to Earl Thorfinn the Skull-Cleaver.
Eftir þat fór Auðr at leita Íslands.	After that went Aud to seek Iceland.	After that Aud went to seek Iceland.
Hon hafði á skipi tuttugu karla frjálsa.	She had in ship twenty men free.	She had twenty free men on her ship.
Auðr kom til Íslands ok var inn fyrsta vetr í Bjarnarhöfn með Birni, bróður sínum.	Aud came to Iceland and was the first winter in Bjarnarhofn with Bjorn, brother hers.	Aud came to Iceland and spent the first winter in Bjarnarhofn with her brother Bjorn.
Síðan nam Auðr öll Dalalönd milli Dögurðarár ok Skraumuhlaupsár.	Since took Aud all Dale-land between Dogurdara and Skraumuhlaupsa.	After that, Aud took all of the Dale land between Dogurdara and Skraumuhlapusa.
Hon bjó í Hvammi.	She settled at Hvamm.	She settled at Hvam.
Hon hafði bænahald í Krosshólum.	She had prayer-holdings at Krossholar.	She held prayers at Krossholar.
Þar lét hon reisa krossa, því at hon var skírð ok vel trúuð.	Where had she raise crosses, for that she was baptised and well religious.	There she had crosses raised, for she was baptised and a devout Christian.
Með henni kómu út margir göfgir menn, þeir er herteknir höfðu verit í vestrvíking ok váru kallaðir ánauðgir.	With her came out many noble people, they which war-taken had been among west-raiding and were called bondsmen.	Many noble people came with her, who had been taken prisoner in viking raids and they were called bondsmen.
Einn af þeim hét Vífill.	One of them was called Vifil.	One of them was called Vifil.
Hann var ættstórr maðr ok hafði verit hertekinn fyrir vestan haf ok var kallaðr ánauðigr, áðr Auðr leysti hann.	He was high-family man and had been war-taken before western sea and was-called bondsman, before Aud released him.	He was a man of noble birth and had been taken prisoner by the western sea and was called a bondsman until Aud gave him his freedom.
Ok er Auðr gaf bústaði skipverjum sínum, þá spurði Vífill, hví Auðr gæfi honum engan bústað sem öðrum mönnum.	And when Aud gave farms crew hers, then asked Vifil, why Aud gave him no abode as other people.	When Aud gave her crew farm sites, then Vifil asked why Aud had not given him a farm as she had other people.

The Saga of Erik the Red (Old Norse)

Old Norse	Literal	English
Auðr kvað þat eigi mundu skipta, kallaði hann þar göfgan mundu þykkja, sem hann væri.	Aud said that not would change, called he there esteemed would-be valued, wherever he was.	Aud said that it made no difference, as he would be considered a fine man, wherever he was.
Hon gaf honum Vífilsdal, ok bjó hann þar.	She gave him Vifilsdal, and settled he there.	She gave him Vifilsdal, and he settled there.
Hann átti þá konu, er hét -- --.	He married then wife, was called -- --.	He married a woman who was called -- --.
Þeira synir váru þeir Þorbjörn ok Þorgeirr.	Their sons were they Thorbjorn and Thorgeir.	Their sons were Thorbjorn and Thorgeir.
Þeir váru efniligir menn ok óxu upp með föður sínum.	They were promising men and grew up with father theirs.	They were promising men and grew up with their father.
2	2	2
Þorvaldr hét maðr.	Thorvald was-called a-man.	There was a man called Thorvald.
Hann var sonr Ásvalds Úlfssonar, Öxna-Þórissonar.	He was son Asvald's son-of-Ulf, son-of-Ox-Thorir	He was the son of Asvald, the son of Ulf, the son of Ox-Thorir.
Eiríkr rauði hét sonr hans.	Erik the-Red was-called son his	His son was called Erik the Red.
Þeir feðgar fóru af Jaðri til Íslands fyrir víga sakar ok námu land á Hornströndum ok bjuggu at Dröngum.	They father-and-son travelled from Jaeren to Iceland because-of killing conviction and took land in Hornstrandir and settled at Drangar.	Father and son travelled from Jaeran to Iceland because of a conviction for a slaying, and they took land at Hornstrandir and settled at Drangar.
Þar andaðist Þorvaldr.	There died Thorvald.	There Thorvald died.
Eiríkr fekk þá Þjóðhildar, dóttur Jörundar Úlfssonar ok Þorbjargar knarrarbringu, er þá átti Þorbjörn inn haukdælski.	Erik married then Thjodhild, daughter-of Jorund Ulfson and Thorbjorg Knarrarbringu, who then married Thorbjorn of Haukadal.	Erik then married Thjodhild, the daughter of Jorund Ulfson and Thorbjorn Knarrarbringu, who had since married Thorbjorn of Haukadal.
Réðst Eiríkr þá norðan ok ruddi land í Haukadal ok bjó á Eiríksstöðum hjá Vatnshorni.	Rode Erik then north and cleared land in Haukadal and settled at Eriksstadir near Vatnshorn.	Erik then rode north and cleared land in Haukadal and settled at Eriksstadir near Vatnshorn.
Þá felldu þrælar Eiríks skriðu á bæ Valþjófs á Valþjófsstöðum.	Then fell thralls Erik's landslide on farm Vallthjof at Vathjolfsstadr.	Then Erik's slaves caused a landslide to fall on the farm at Vallthjof at Vatnhjolfsstadr.
Eyjólfr saurr, frændi hans, drap þrælana hjá Skeiðsbrekkum upp frá Vatnshorni.	Eyolf the-Foul, kinsman his, killed thralls beside Skeidsbrekkur up from Vatnshorn.	His kinsman Eyolf the Foul killed the slaves near Skeidsbrekkur above Vatnshorn.

The Saga of Erik the Red (Old Norse)

Old Norse	Literal	English
Fyrir þat vá Eiríkr Eyjólf saur.	For that slew Erik Eyolf the-Foul.	For that Erik killed Eyolf the Foul.
Hann vá ok Hólmgöngu-Hrafn at Leikskálum.	He slew also Raven-the-Dueller at Leikskalar.	He also killed Raven the Dueller at Leikskalar.
Geirsteinn ok Oddr á Jörva, frændi Eyjólfs, mæltu eftir hann.	Gerstein and Odd of Jorfi, kinsman Eyolf's, spoke after him.	Gerstein and Odd of Jorvi, Eyolf's kinsmen sought judgement for his killing.
Þá var Eiríkr gerr brott ór Haukadal.	Then was Erik made out from Haukadal.	Then Erik was outlawed from Haukadal.
Hann nam þá Brokey ok Öxney ok bjó at Tröðum í Suðrey inn fyrsta vetr.	He took then Brokey and Oxney and settled at Tradir in Sudrey the first winter.	He took the islands Brokey and Oxney and settled at Tradir on Sudurey island that first winter.
Þá léði hann Þorgesti setstokka.	Then lent he Thorgest seat-posts.	Then he lent Thorgest bedstead boards.
Síðan fór Eiríkr í Öxney ok bjó á Eiríksstöðum.	Afterwards travelled Erik to Oxney and settled at Eriksstadir.	Afterwards Erik travelled to Oxney and settled at Eriksstadir.
Þá heimti hann setstokkana ok náði eigi.	Then claimed he seat-posts and got not.	Then he asked for the bedstead boards back, but did not get them.
Eiríkr sótti setstokkana á Breiðabólstað, en Þorgestr fór eftir honum.	Erik took seat-posts from Breidabolstad, but Thorgest went after him.	Erik went to Breidabolstad and took the bedstead boards, but Thorgest went after him.
Þeir börðust skammt frá garði at Dröngum.	There fought short from garden at Drangar.	They fought a short distance from the farm at Drangar.
Þar fellu tveir synir Þorgests ok nökkurir menn aðrir.	There fell two sons Thorgest's and some men other.	There Thorgest's two sons fell along with several other men.
Eftir þat höfðu hvárirtveggju setu fjölmenna.	After that had either-side sitting many-men.	After that, both sides kept a large following of many men.
Styrr veitti Eiríki ok Eyjólfr ór Svíney, Þorbjörn Vífilsson ok synir Þorbrands ór Álftafirði, en Þorgesti veittu synir Þórðar gellis ok Þorgeirr ór Hítardal, ok Áslákr ór Langadal ok Illugi, sonr hans.	Styrr supported Erik and Eyolf of Sviney, Thorbjorn Vifilson and sons Thorbrand's from Alftafjord, but Thorgest supported sons Thord Gellir and Thorgeir of Hitardal, and Aslak of Langadal and Illugi, son his.	Erik had the support of Styrr, Eyolf of Sviney, Thorbjorn Vifilsson, and the sons of Thorbrand of Alftafjord, while Thorgest was supported by Thord Bellower, Thorgeir of Hitardal, Aslak of Langdal, and his son Illugi.
Þeir Eiríkr urðu sekir á Þórsnessþingi.	They and Erik became outlawed at Thorsnes-Thing.	Erik and his companions became outlawed at the Thorsnes Assembly.

The Saga of Erik the Red (Old Norse)

Old Norse	Literal	English
Hann bjó skip í Eiríksvági, en Eyjólfr leyndi honum í Dímunarvági, meðan þeir Þorgestr leituðu hans um eyjarnar.	He prepared ship in Eriksvog, and Eyolf hid him in Dimunarvog, while they Thorgest sought him about islands.	He prepared a ship at Eriksvog, and Eyolf hid him in Dimunarvog while Thorgest and his men searched the islands for him.
Þeir Þorbjörn ok Eyjólfr ok Styrr fylgðu Eiríki út um eyjarnar, ok skilðust þeir með inni mestu vináttu.	There Thorbjorn and Eyolf and Styrr followed Erik back around islands, and separated they with the most friendship.	Thorbjorn, Eyolf, and Styrr followed Erik through the islands, and they separated with the most friendship.
Kveðst Eiríkr þeim skyldu verða at þvílíku trausti, ef hann mætti sér við koma ok kynni þeir hans at þurfa.	Said Erik to-them should be to likewise trust, if he may them with come and circumstance they him to need.	Erik said to them that they should trust that he would help them in any way if they ever needed him.
Hann sagði þeim, at hann ætlaði at leita lands þess, er Gunnbjörn, sonr Úlfs kráku, sá, er hann rak vestr um haf ok hann fann Gunnbjarnarsker.	He told them, that he intended to seek lands these, which Gunnbjorn, son-of Ulf Crow, saw, when he-was driven west about sea and he found Gunnbjarnarsker.	He said to them that he intended to search for the lands which Gunnbjorn son of Ulf Crow saw, when he was driven west at sea and found Gunnbjarbarsker.
Hann kveðst aftr mundu leita til vina sinna, ef hann fyndi landit.	He said return would seek to friends his, if he found land.	He said that he would return to seek them out if he found land.
Sigldi Eiríkr á haf undan Snæfellsjökli.	Sailed Erik to sea from Snaefellsjokli.	Erik sailed to sea from Snaefellsjokli.
Hann kom útan at jökli þeim, er heitir Bláserkr.	He came out of glacier that, was named Blaserkur.	He came out from a glacier that was named Blaserkr.
Hann fór þaðan suðr at leita, ef þar væri byggjanda.	He travelled from-there south to seek, if there was habitable.	He travelled south from there to see if there was any habitable land.
Hann var inn fyrsta vetr í Eiríksey nær miðri inni eystri byggð.	He was the first winter at Eriksey near the-middle of-the eastern settlement.	For the first winter he was at Eriksey, near the middle of the Eastern Settlement.
Um várit eftir fór hann til Eiríksfjarðar ok tók sér þar bústað.	About spring after travelled he to Eriksfjord and took he there settlement.	After about spring he travelled to Eriksfjord and took settlement there.
Hann fór þat sumar í ina vestri óbyggð ok gaf víða örnefni.	He travelled that summer into the western settlement and gave widely place-names.	That summer he travelled into the Western Settlement and gave place names widely.
Hann var annan vetr í Eiríkshólmum við Hvarfsgnípu en it þriðja sumar fór hann allt norðr til Snæfells ok inn í Hrafnsfjörð.	He was second winter at Eriksholmar off Hvarfsgnipu and the third summer went he altogether north to Snaefell and then into Hrafnsfjord.	The second winter he was at Eriksholmar near Hvarfsgnipu, and the third summer he travelled all the way north to Snaefell and into Hrafnsfjord.

The Saga of Erik the Red (Old Norse)

Old Norse	Literal	English
Þá þóttist hann kominn fyrir botn Eiríksfjarðar.	Then thought he came before the-bottom-of Eriksfjord.	There he thought he had reached the head of Eriksfjord.
Hverfr hann þá aftr ok var inn þriðja vetr í Eiríksey fyrir mynni Eiríksfjarðar.	Turned he then back and was in third winter at Eriksey before the-mouth-of Eriksfjord.	Then he returned to winter at Eriksey at the mouth of Eriksfjord.
En eftir um sumarit fór hann til Íslands ok kom í Breiðafjörð.	But afterwards about summer travelled he to Iceland and came to Breidafjord.	Then after about summer he travelled to Iceland and came to Breidafjord.
Hann var þann vetr með Ingólfi á Hólmlátri.	He was that winter with Ingolf at Holmlatr.	That winter he was with Ingolf at Holmlatr.
Um várit börðust þeir Þorgestr, ok fekk Eiríkr ósigr.	About spring fought they Thorgest, and got Erik defeat.	About spring Erik and Thorgest fought, and Erik was defeated.
Eftir þat váru þeir sættir.	After that were they reconciled.	After that they were reconciled.
Þat sumar fór Eiríkr at byggja land þat, er hann hafði fundit ok hann kallaði Grænland, því at hann kvað menn þat mjök mundu fýsa þangat, ef landit héti vel.	That summer went Erik to settle land that, which he had found and he called Greenland, because as he said people that much would desire there, if land named well.	That summer Erik went to settle the land that he had found, which he called Greenland, because as he said, people would be attracted if the land was named well.
[Svá segir Ari Þorgilsson, at þat sumar fór hálfr þriði tögr skipa til Grænlands ór Breiðafirði og Borgarfirði, en fjórtán kómust út.	So said Ari Thorgilson, by that summer came half-of thirty-and twenty ships to Greenland from Breidafjord and Borgafjord, and fourteen arrived from.	So said Ari Thorgilson, that summer thirty five ships travelled to Greenland from Breidafjord and Borgafjord, but fourteen arrived.
Sum rak aftr, en sum týndust.	Some driven back, but some lost.	Some were driven back, but some were lost.
Þat var fimmtán vetrum fyrr en kristni var í lög tekin á Íslandi.	That was fifteen winters before that Christianity was in law taken in Iceland.	That was fifteen winters before Christianity was taken into law in Iceland.
Eiríkr nam síðan Eiríksfjörð ok bjó í Brattahlíð.].	Erik took then Eriksfjord and settled in Brattahlid.	Erik then took Eriksfjord and settled in Brattahlid.
3	3	3
Þorgeirr Vífilsson kvángaðist ok fekk Arnóru, dóttur Einars frá Laugarbrekku, Sigmundarsonar, Ketilssonar þistils, er numit hafði Þistilsfjörð.	Thorgeir Vifilson married and got Arnora, daughter Einar's from Laugarbrekka, son-of-Sigmund, son-of-Ketil Thistle who taken had Thistilsfjord.	Thorgeir Vifilson took as his wife Arnora, daughter of Einar from Laugarbrekk, the son of Sigmund, the son of Ketil Thistle who had taken Thistilsfjord.
Önnur dóttir Einars hét Hallveig.	Second daughter Einar's was-named Hallveig.	Einar's second daughter was named Hallveig.

The Saga of Erik the Red (Old Norse)

Old Norse	Literal	English
Hennar fekk Þorbjörn Vífilsson ok tók með land á Laugarbrekku, á Hellisvöllum.	She married Thorbjorn Vifilson and took with land in Laugarbrekka, at Hellisvellir.	She married Thorbjorn Vifilson and took land at Laugarbrekku in Hellisvellir.
Réðst Þorbjörn þangat byggðum ok gerðist göfugmenni mikit.	Moved Thorbjorn there settlement and became noble much.	Thorbjorn moved his settlement there and became a great nobleman.
Hann var góðr bóndi ok hafði rausnarráð.	He was a-good farmer and had great-estate.	He was a good farmer and had a great estate.
Guðríðr hét dóttir Þorbjarnar.	Guthrid was-called daughter Thorbjorn's.	Thorbjorn's daughter was called Gudrid.
Hon var kvenna vænst ok inn mesti skörungr í öllu athæfi sínu.	She was woman fair and the most noble in all behaviour hers.	She was a fair woman and the most noble in all her behaviour.
Maðr hét Ormr, er bjó at Arnarstapa.	A-man was-called Orm, who settled at Arnarstapi.	There was a man called Orm who settled at Arnarstapi.
Hann átti konu, er Halldís hét.	He had a-wife, was Halldis named.	He had a wife who was named Halldis.
Ormr var góðr bóndi ok vinr Þorbjarnar mikill, ok var Guðríðr þar löngum at fóstri með honum.	Orm was a-good farmer and friend of-Thorbjorn great, and was Guthrid there long to foster with him.	Orm was a good farmer and a great friend of Thorbjorn, and Gudrid was fostered there and stayed for long periods of time with him.
Þorgeirr hét maðr.	Thorgeir was-named a-man.	There was a man named Thorgeir.
Hann bjó at Þorgeirsfelli.	He lived at Thorgeirsfell.	He lived at Thorgeirsfell.
Hann var auðigr at fé ok hafði verit leysingi.	He was wealthy in cattle and had-been made a-freed-man.	He was rich in cattle and had been made a free man.
Hann átti son, er Einarr hét.	He had a-son who-was Einar named.	He had a son who was named Einar.
Hann var vænn maðr ok vel mannaðr.	He was a-fair man and well mannered.	He was a fair man and well mannered.
Hann var ok skartsmaðr mikill.	He was also jewelled-man much.	He was also much bejewelled.
Einarr var í siglingum meðal landa, ok tókst honum þat vel.	Einar was among sailing between lands, and took him that well.	Einar was sailing between lands, and he took to it well.
Var hann jafnan sinn vetr hvárt á Íslandi eða í Nóregi.	Was he equally the winter either to Iceland or to Norway.	In winter he was equally in either Iceland or Norway.
Nú er frá því at segja eitt haust, þá er Einarr var á Íslandi, at hann fór með varning sinn út eftir Snæfellströnd ok vildi selja.	Now is from that to say one autumn, then that Einar was in Iceland, as he came with wares his out along Snaefellstrond and wished to-sell.	From that is there now to say that one autumn when Einar was in Iceland, he came with goods to Snaefellstrond wishing to sell.

The Saga of Erik the Red (Old Norse)

Old Norse	Literal	English
Hann kemr til Arnarstapa.	He came to Arnarstapi.	He came to Arnarstapi.
Ormr býðr honum þar at vera, ok þat þiggr Einarr, því at þar var vinátta við körin.	Orm invited him there to be, and that accepted Einar, because that there was friendship with chosen.	Orm invited him to be there, and Einar accepted, as friendship was also chosen.
Var borinn inn varningr hans í eitt útibúr.	Were carried in wares his into an out-house.	His goods were carried into an outhouse.
Einarr braut upp varning sinn ok sýndi Ormi ok heimamönnum ok bauð honum af at hafa slíkt er hann vildi.	Einar divided up wares his and showed Orm and housemen and invited him of to have such that he willed.	Einar divided up his goods and showed Orm and his housemen, inviting them to have whatever they wished.
Ormr þá þetta ok talði Einar vera góðan fardreng ok auðnumann mikinn.	Orm then that also told Einar was good traveller-generous and fortune much.	Orm accepted and told Einar that he was a good merchant, generous, and of great fortune.
En er þeir heldu á varninginum, gekk kona fyrir útibúrsdyrrin.	When were they busy of wares, walked woman before out-house-door.	While they were occupied with the goods, a woman walked in front of the outhouse door.
Einarr spurði Orm, hver væri sú in fagra kona, er þar gekk fyrir dyrrin, - "ek hefi eigi hana hér fyrr sét".	Einar asked Orm, who was that in fair woman, was there going before doorway, - "I have not her here before seen".	Einar asked Orm who that fair woman was who walked in front of the doorway: "I have not seen her here before".
Ormr svaraði: "Þat er Guðríðr, fóstra mín, dóttir Þorbjarnar at Laugarbrekku".	Orm answered: "That is Guthrid, foster-child mine, daughter Thorbjorn's from Laugarbrekka".	Orm answered: "That is Gudrid, my foster child, daughter of Thorbjorn from Laugarbrekka".
Einarr mælti: "Hon mun vera kostr góðr.	Einar said: "She would be choice good.	Einar said: "She would be a good choice.
Eða hafa nökkurir menn til komit at biðja hennar?"	Or have some men towards come to propose her?"	Or have any men come forward to propose to her?"
Ormr svarar: "Beðit hefir hennar víst verit, ok liggr þat eigi laust fyrir. Finnst þat á, at hon mun vera mannvönd ok svá faðir hennar".	Orm answered: "Proposals have for-her made been, and lies that not less for. Finding that of, that she should be husband and so father hers".	Orm answered: "Proposals have been made to her, but without success. She shall choose her husband, and so will her father".
"Svá, með því", sagði Einarr, "at hér er sú kona, er ek ætla mér at biðja, ok vilda ek, at þessa mála leitaðir þú við Þorbjörn, föður hennar, ok legðir allan hug á, at þetta mætti framgengt verða.	"So with therefore", said Einar, "That she is the woman, that I intend me to propose, and will I, to this matter seek you with Thorbjorn, father hers, and lay all thoughts to, that this may from-going be.	"So be it", said Einar, "she's the woman I intend to propose to, and I would like you to seek the matter with her father Thorbjorn, and give it your thoughts, how this may be so.

The Saga of Erik the Red (Old Norse)

Old Norse	Literal	English
Skal ek þér fullkomna vináttu fyrir gjalda, ef ek get táðit.	Shall I you full-come friendship for expenses, if I can say.	I will repay you with the fullest friendship, that I can say.
Má Þorbjörn bóndi þat sjá, at okkr væri vel hentar tengðir, því at hann er sómamaðr mikill ok á staðfestu góða, en lausafé hans er mér sagt heldr á förum.	May Thorbjorn farmer that see, to ours would-be well suits joined, for to he is famous-man great and of established good, but liquidity his is to-me said rather to going.	Thorbjorn the farmer may see we would be well joined, as he is a man of high regard with a good farm, but it is said that his means are rather depleting".
En mik skortir hvárki land né lausafé ok okkr feðga, ok myndi Þorbirni verða at þessu inn mesti styrkr, ef þetta tækist".	But my shortage neither land nor liquidity and us father-and-son, and should Thorbjorn be therefore this the most strength, if this takes".	But my father and I lack neither land or means, and would therefore give the most support, if this is concluded.
Ormr segir: "Víst þykkjumst ek vinr þinn vera, en þó em ek eigi við mitt ráð fúss, at vit berim þetta upp, því at Þorbjörn er skapstórr ok þó metnaðarmaðr mikill".	Orm said: "Knowing think-us I friend yours be, but though am I not with my advice willing, of to bring this up, because that Thorbjorn is temperamental and though ambitious-man much".	Orm said: "Knowing that I consider myself your friend, I am though not willing to bring up this discussion, because Thorbjorn is temperamental and a very ambitious man".
Einarr kveðst ekki vilja annat en upp væri borit bónorðit.	Einar said not willing another but up would-be carried proposal.	Einar said that he would not be satisfied unless the proposal was brought up.
Ormr kvað hann ráða skyldu.	Orm said his decision shall-be.	Orm said that his decision would be so.
Ferr Einarr suðr aftr, unz hann kemr heim.	Travelled Einar south back, until he came home.	Einar travelled back south until he came home.
Nökkuru síðar hafði Þorbjörn haustboð, sem hann átti vanða til, því at hann var stórmenni mikit.	Sometime since had Thorbjorn harvest-feast, that he had accustomed to, because to him were great-men much.	Sometime after Thorbjorn had a harvest feast, that was his custom, as he was a great man.
Kom þar Ormr frá Arnarstapa ok margir aðrir vinir Þorbjarnar.	Came there Orm from Arnarstapi and many other friends Thorbjorn's.	Orm came from Arnarstapi and many of Thorbjorn's other friends.
Ormr kom at máli við Þorbjörn ok sagði, at Einarr var þar skömmu, frá Þorgeirsfelli, ok gerðist inn efniligsti maðr.	Orm came to speak with Thorbjorn and said, that Einar was there recently, from Thorgeirsfell, and became the promising man.	Orm came to speak with Thorbjorn and said, that Einar from Thorgeirsfell had been there recently, and he had become a promising man.

The Saga of Erik the Red (Old Norse)

Old Norse	Literal	English
Hefr Ormr nú upp bónorðit fyrir hönd Einars ok segir þat vel hent fyrir sumra hluta sakar.	Had Orm now upped proposal for hand Einar's and said that well joined for some part's sake.	Orm now brought up Einar's marriage proposal and said that it would be well joined on several accounts.
"Má þér, bóndi, verða at styrkr mikill fyrir fjárkosta sakar".	"May to-you, farmer, be in strength much for financial-cost's sake".	"It may be to you be strong support in financial terms".
Þorbjörn svarar: "Eigi varði mik slíkra orða af þér, at ek mynda gifta þrælssyni dóttur mína.	Thorbjorn answered: "Not expected I such words from you, that I should give thrall's-son daughter mine.	Thorbjorn answered: "I did not expect to hear such words from you, that I should give my daughter to a slave's son.
Ok þat finnið þér nú, at fé mitt þverr, er slíkt ráð gefið mér.	And that find you now, that wealth mine decreases, is such counsel given to-me.	As you now suggest, that my wealth is decreasing, to give such advice to me.
Ok eigi skal hon með þér vera lengr, er þér þótti hon svá lítils gjaforðs verð".	And not shall she with you be longer, as you thought she such little marriage-offer deserve".	And no longer shall she be with you, as you thought she deserved such a lowly marriage offer".
Síðan fór Ormr heim ok hverr annarr boðsmanna til sins heimilis.	Afterwards went Orm home and each other guests to their households.	Afterwards Orm went home an each of the other guests went to their homes.
Guðríðr var eftir með föður sínum ok var heima þann vetr.	Guthrid was remained with father hers and stayed home that winter.	Gudrid stayed behind with her father and spent that winter at home.
En at vári hafði Þorbjörn vinaboð, ok kom þar margt manna, ok var in bezta veizla.	But in spring had Thorbjorn friend-invites, and came there many people, and was the best feast.	Then when spring came Thorbjorn invited his friends to come with many people, and there was the best feast.
Ok at veizlunni krafði Þorbjörn sér hljóðs ok mælti: "Hér hefi ek búit langa ævi, ok hefi ek reynt góðvilja manna við mik ok ástúð.	And at the-feast called Thorbjorn he be-heard and spoke: "Here have I lived long life, and have I experienced good-will men's to me and affection.	During the feast, Thorbjorn asked to be heard and spoke: "Here I have lived a long life, and I have enjoyed the good will and affection.
Kalla ek vel farit hafa vár skipti.	Call I well gone have been exchanges.	I call all our dealings well done.
En nú tekr hagr minn at óhægjast fyrir lausafjár sakar, en hér til hefir kallat verit heldr virðingarráð.	But now take benefits mine to maintain for liquidity's sake, that here until has called have-been rather worthiness.	But now my benefit begins to be uneasy for the sake of means, though so far it has been called worthy.
Nú vil ek fyrr búinu bregða en sæmðinni týna.	Now will I for settlement foreclose before honour lose.	Now I wish to foreclose before I lose my honour.

The Saga of Erik the Red (Old Norse)

Old Norse	Literal	English
Ætla ek fyrr af landi fara en ætt mína svívirða ok vitja heita Eiríks ins rauða, vinar míns, er hann hafði, þá er vit skilðum á Breiðafirði.	Intend I for of land travel but-for lineage mine shame and visit called Erik the Red, friend mine, that he had, then was with separated at Breidafjord.	I intend to travel from this land, rather than shame my lineage, and visit my friend Erik the Red who I was separated from at Breidafjord.
Ætla ek nú at fara til Grænlands í sumar, ef svá ferr sem ek vilda".	Intend I now to travel to Greenland in summer, if so goes as I wish".	I now intend to travel to Greenland I summer, if it goes as I wish".
Mönnum þótti mikil þessi ráðabreytni, því at Þorbjörn var vinsæll maðr, en þóttust vita, at Þorbjörn mundi svá fremi þetta upp hafa kveðit, at ekki myndi tjóa at letja hann.	People thought great this change, for that Thorbjorn was befriended man, but thought knowing, that Thorbjorn would so provide that up had declared, that not should avail to discourage him.	People thought this was a great change, because Thorbjorn was a popular man, but they thought that once Thorbjorn had declared this, it would be to no avail to discourage him.
Gaf Þorbjörn mönnum gjafar, ok var brugðit veizlunni.	Gave Thorbjorn people gifts, and was brought-out feast.	Thorbjorn gave people gifts, and a feast was brought out.
Síðan fór hverr til síns heima.	Afterwards went each to their homes.	Afterwards everyone went to their homes.
Þorbjörn selr lönd sín ok kaupir sér skip, er uppi stóð í Hraunhafnarósi.	Thorbjorn sold land his and bought himself ship, which up stood at Hraunhafnaros.	Thorbjorn sold his land and bought himself a ship, which stood at Hraunhafnaros.
Réðust til ferðar með honum þrír tigir manna.	Hired to travel with him three tens men.	He hired thirty men to travel with him.
Var þar í ferð Ormr frá Arnarstapa ok kona hans ok aðrir vinir Þorbjarnar, þeir er eigi vildu við hann skilja.	Was there to travel Orm from Arnarstapi and wife his and other friends Thorbjorn's, they were not willing with him separate.	There to travel with him was Orm from Arnarstapi, and his wife, and Thorbjorn's other friends, they were not willing to separate with him.
Síðan létu þeir í haf, ok er þeir váru í hafi, tók af byri.	Afterwards left they to sea, and then they were to sea, taken of fair-wind.	Afterwards they put to sea, and when they were at sea, the fair wind disappeared.
Fengu þeir hafvillur, ok fórst þeim ógreitt um sumarit.	Caught they open-sea, and went they not-without-obstacle about summer.	They were caught in the open sea, and they were not without obstacle all summer.
Því næst kom sótt í lið þeira, ok andaðist Ormr ok Halldís, kona hans, ok helmingr liðs þeira.	For next came sickness among team theirs, and died Orm and Halldis, wife his, and half team theirs.	Because next there came a sickness among their crew, and Orm died, and his wife Halldis, along with half of the crew.

The Saga of Erik the Red (Old Norse)

Old Norse	Literal	English
Sjó tók at stæra, ok þolðu menn it mesta vás ok vesölð á marga vega, en tóku þó Herjólfsnes á Grænlandi við vetr sjálfan.	Sea took to greatly, and endured men the most toil and misery in many ways, but took though Herjolfsnes to Greenland by winter itself.	The sea swelled, and people endured the most toil and misery in many ways, but they took land at Herjolfsnes in Greenland during the Winter Nights.
Sá maðr hét Þorkell, er bjó á Herjólfsnesi.	So a-man was-named Thorkell, who settled at Herjolfsnes.	There was a man named Thorkell, who lived at Herjolfsnes.
Hann var inn bezti bóndi.	He was the best farmer.	He was the best farmer.
Hann tók við Þorbirni ok öllum skipverjum hans um vetrinn.	He took with Thorbjorn and all crew his about winter.	He took with Thorbjorn and all his crew for the winter.
Þorkell veitti þeim sköruliga.	Thorkell provided-for them boldly.	Thorkell provided for them generously.
4	4	4
Í þann tíma var hallæri mikit á Grænlandi.	In that time was famine much in Greenland.	At that time there was much famine in Greenland.
Höfðu menn fengit lítit fang, þeir er í veiðiferðir höfðu farit, en sumir ekki aftr komnir.	Had people caught little, they which to hunting had been, and some not after returning.	People that had been hunting had caught little, and some of them had not returned.
Sú kona var þar í byggð, er Þorbjörg hét.	The woman was there in settlement, was Thorbjorg called.	There was a woman in the settlement who was named Thorbjorg.
Hon var spákona ok var kölluð lítilvölva.	She was prophetess and was called Little-Prophetess.	She was a prophetess, and was called Little Prophetess.
Hon hafði átt sér níu systr, ok váru allar spákonur, en hon ein var þá á lífi.	She had descendents hers nine sisters, and were all prophetesses, and she alone was then yet living.	Among her family were nine sisters, and all were prophetesses, and she was the only one yet living.
Þat var háttr Þorbjargar um vetrum, at hon fór at veizlum, ok buðu þeir menn henni mest heim, er forvitni var á at vita forlög sín eða árferð.	It was way Thorbjorg's about winter, that she went to feasts, and invited they people her most homes, that curious were for to know fortune theirs or season.	It was a custom of Thorbjorg's during winter, that she went to feasts, and to homes that people had invited her to, who were curious to know their fortune for the season.
Ok með því at Þorkell var þar mestr bóndi, þá þótti til hans koma at vita, hvé nær létta myndi óárani þessu, sem yfir stóð.	And with because that Thorkell was there greatest landowner, then thought to him came to know, how near relieve should scarcity this, which over stood.	And with Thorkell being the greatest landowner, it was thought that he should come to know when the scarcity that stood over them would be relieved.

The Saga of Erik the Red (Old Norse)

Old Norse	Literal	English
Býðr Þorkell spákonunni heim, ok er henni þar vel fagnat, sem siðr var til, þá er við þess háttar konum skyldi taka.	Invited Thorkell prophetess home, and was she there well welcomed, as custom was to, then was with this kind woman should take.	Thorkell invited the prophetess to his home, and she was well welcomed, as was the custom, when this kind of woman was received as a guest.
Var henni búit hásæti ok lagt undir hana hægendi.	Was she prepared a-high-seat and laid under her a-cushion.	A high seat was prepared for her, and under it a cushion.
Þar skyldi í vera hænsafiðri.	There should in be hen's-feathers.	This was to be filled with hen's feathers.
En er hon kom um kveldit ok sá maðr, er móti henni var sendr, þá var hon svá búin, at hon hafði yfir sér tuglamöttul blán, ok var settr steinum allt í skaut ofan.	Then when she came about evening and saw a-man, who meeting her was sent, then was she such ready, for she had over her mantle blue, and was set stones all in lap of.	Then when she arrived around evening, with the man who was sent to meet her when she was ready, she had over her a blue mantle, which was set with stones in the lap.
Hon hafði á hálsi sér glertölur, lambskinnskofra svartan á höfði ok við innan kattarskinn hvít.	She had on neck hers glass-beads, lamb-skin-hood black on head and with in cat-skin white.	She had glass beads on her neck, and on her head a hood of black lamb skin, lined with white cat skin.
Ok hon hafði staf í hendi, ok var á knappr.	And she had staff in hand, and was on a-knob	And she had in her hand a staff, which had a knob on the top.
Hann var búinn með messingu ok settr steinum ofan um knappinn.	It was set with brass and set stones on about knob.	It was set with brass and had stones set about the knob.
Hon hafði um sik hnjóskulinda, ok var þar á skjóðupungr mikill, ok varðveitti hon þar í töfr sín, þau er hon þurfti til fróðleiks at hafa.	She had about herself a-girdle and was there on skin-purse great, and kept she there in magic hers, those which she needed to knowledge of have.	She wore a girdle with a large skin purse, and she kept her magic in there, which she needed to have knowledge of.
Hon hafði á fótum kálfskinnsskúa loðna ok í þvengi langa ok á tinknappar miklir á endunum.	She had on feet calf-skin-shoes fur and in tied long and in pewter-buttons great on ends.	She had calf skin shoes lined with fur, with long laces with pewter knobs on the ends.
Hon hafði á höndum sér kattskinnsglófa, ok váru hvítir innan ok loðnir.	She had on hands hers cat-skin-gloves, and were white inside and furry.	She had cat skin gloves on her hands and they were white and furry inside.
En er hon kom inn, þótti öllum mönnum skylt at velja henni sæmiligar kveðjur.	Then when she came in, thought all people should to will her honourable greetings.	When she came in, everyone was supposed to give her honourable greetings.
Hon tók því sem henni váru menn geðjaðir til.	She received therefore as she was people agreeable to.	She responded to people according to how the person appealed to her.

The Saga of Erik the Red (Old Norse)

Old Norse	Literal	English
Tók Þorkell bóndi í hönd henni ok leiddi hana til þess sætis, sem henni var búit.	Took Thorkell the-Farmer in hand hers and led her to this seat, which she was prepared.	Thorkell the Farmer took her hand and led her to the seat which was prepared for her.
Þorkell bað hana þá renna þar augum yfir hjú ok hjörð ok svá híbýli.	Thorkell asked her then run there eyes over herd and hearth and so settlement.	Thorkell asked her to run her eyes over the herd, the hearth, and the settlement.
Hon var fámálug um allt.	She was silent about all.	She was silent about all of it.
Borð váru upp tekin um kveldit, ok er frá því at segja, hvat spákonunni var matbúit.	Tables were up taken about evening, and was from since to say, what prophetess was food-prepared.	That evening tables were set up, and afterwards it was to say, what food was prepared for the prophetess.
Henni var gerr grautr af kiðjamjólk ok matbúin hjörtu ór öllum kykvendum, þeim er þar váru til.	She was made porridge of kid's-milk and food-prepared hearts of all creatures, they that there were to.	She was made a porridge of kid's milk and hearts of all animals available there.
Hon hafði messingarspón ok hníf tannskeftan, tvíhólkaðan af eiri, ok var brotinn af oddrinn.	She had brass-spoon and knife walrus-tusk, two-ringed of bronze, and was broken of tip.	She had a brass spoon and a knife with a walrus tusk, two halves ringed with bronze, and the tip had been broken off.
En er borð váru upp tekin, þá gengr Þorkell bóndi fyrir Þorbjörgu ok spyrr, hversu henni þykki þar um at lítast eða hversu skapfelld henni eru þar híbýli eða hættir manna eða hversu fljótliga hon mun vís verða þess, er hann hefir spurt hana ok mönnum er mest forvitni at vita.	Then when table was up taken, then went Thorkell farmer before Thorbjorg and asked, how she thought there about it looked or how agreeable to-her were there settlements or manner people's or how soon she could aware be this, that he had asked her and men were most curious to know.	And when the tables were taken up, then Thorkell the Farmer went before Thorbjorg and asked her what she thought of the conduct of the household, the manner of people, and how soon she would know what he had asked her, and what people were most curious to know.
Hon kallast ekki mundu segja fyrr en um morgininn eftir, er hon hafði áðr sofit um nóttina.	She considered not would say before that about morning after, when she had after slept for night.	She said that she would not say before the following morning, when she had slept about the night.
En um morgininn at áliðnum degi var henni veittr sá umbúningr, sem hon þurfti at hafa til at fremja seiðinn.	Then from morning to following day was she given that clothing, which she needed to have for to perform enchantments.	Then the following morning she was given the clothing that she needed to have to perform her enchantments.
Hon bað ok fá sér konur þær, er kynni fræði þat, sem til seiðsins þarf ok Varðlokur hétu.	She asked also get the women there, who knew wisdom that, which for enchantments needed and warlock-songs called.	She asked for women who had the wisdom of the enchantments needed, which were called warlock songs.
En þær konur fundust eigi.	But those women were-found not.	But those women were not found.

The Saga of Erik the Red (Old Norse)

Old Norse	Literal	English
Þá var at leitat at um bæinn, ef nökkurr kynni.	They were to seek to about household, if anyone knew.	The people of the household searched for anyone who knew.
Þá segir Guðríðr: "Hvárki em ek fjölkunnig né vísendakona, en þó kenndi Halldís, fóstra mín, mér á Íslandi þat kvæði, er hon kallaði Varðlokur".	Then said Guthrid: "Neither am I of-magic nor fore-knowing-woman, but though taught Halldis, foster mine, to-me in Iceland that poem, that she called warlock-songs".	Then Gudrid said: "I am neither of magic nor prophecy, but my foster mother, Halldis, taught me chants that she called warlock songs.
Þorkell segir: "Þá ertu happfróð".	Thorkell said: "Then are-you lucky-wise".	Thorkell said: "Then you are luckily wise".
Hon segir: "Þetta er þat eitt atferli, er ek ætla í engum atbeina at vera, því at ek em kristin kona".	She said: "That is the one ceremony, that I intend to no assistance in being, because that I am Christian woman".	She said: "That is one ceremony that I do not intend to be assisting because I am a Christian woman".
Þorbjörg segir: "Svá mætti verða, at þú yrðir mönnum at liði hér um, en þú værir þá kona ekki verri en áðr.	Thorbjorg said: "So may be, that you become people to help here about, but you would-be then woman not worse than before.	Thorbjorg said: "So it may be that you may come to help here, but you would be no worse a woman than before.
En við Þorkel mun ek meta at fá þá hluti til, er hafa þarf".	But with Thorkell should I evaluate to get the things for, which have need".	But I will appreciate getting the things from Thorkell that are needed".
Þorkell herðir nú at Guðríði, en hon kveðst gera mundu sem hann vildi.	Thorkell hardened now to Guthrid, but she said do would as he wished.	Thorkell now hardened towards Gudrid, and said that she should do as he wished.
Slógu þá konur hring um hjallinn, en Þorbjörg sat á uppi.	Formed then women a-ring around the-platform, while Thorbjorg sat on up.	The women then formed a ring around the platform, while Thorbjorg sat above.
Kvað Guðríðr þá kvæðit svá fagrt ok vel, at engi þóttist heyrt hafa með fegri rödd kvæði kveðit, sá er þar var hjá.	Said Guthrid then recited so beautiful and well, that none thought heard had with more-beautiful voice poem sung, so as there was heard.	Gudrid then recited so beautifully and so well, that no one thought they had head a poem sung with more beautiful a voice, than that which they heard.

The Saga of Erik the Red (Old Norse)

Old Norse	Literal	English
Spákonan þakkar henni kvæðit ok kvað margar þær náttúrur nú til hafa sótt ok þykkja fagrt at heyra, er kvæðit var svá vel flutt, - "er áðr vildu við oss skiljast ok enga hlýðni oss veita.	Prophetess thanked her poem and said many they spirits now to have attended and think beautiful to hear, that poem was so well performed, - "Who before would by us separate and none homage us grant.	The prophetess thanked her for the poem and said that the many spirits have now attended who thought it beautiful to hear, as it was so well performed: "those who before turned their backs on us and refused to grant us assistance.
En mér eru nú margir þeir hlutir auðsýnir, er áðr var ek duldið, ok margir aðrir.	And to-me are now many those things shown, which before were I hidden, and many others.	And there are now many things shown to me which before were hidden from me and others.
En ek kann þér þat at segja, Þorkell, at hallæri þetta mun ekki haldast lengr en í vetr, ok mun batna árangr, sem várar.	And I can to-you that to say, Thorkell, to famine this should not hold longer than to winter, and should better harvest, then spring.	And I can now say to you, Thorkell, that this famine should not hold longer than to winter, and there should be a better harvest in the spring.
Sóttarfar þat, sem á hefir legit, mun ok batna vánu bráðara.	Sickness that, which to has laid, should also better-than hope sooner.	That sickness which has happened, should hopefully be better sooner.
En þér, Guðríðr, skal ek launa í hönd liðsinni þat, er oss hefir af þér staðit, því at þín forlög eru mér nú allglöggsæ.	And you, Guthrid, shall I reward in hand assistance that, for us have of you stood, because that your fortunes are to-me now clear.	And you, Gudrid, I shall reward in hand for the assistance that you placed, because to me your fortunes are now clear.
Þú munt gjaforð fá hér á Grænlandi, þat er sæmiligast er, þó at þér verði þat eigi til langæðar, því at vegir þínir liggja út til Íslands, ok mun þar koma frá þér bæði mikill ætt ok góð, ok yfir þínum kynkvíslum skína bjartari geislar en ek hafa megin til at geta slíkt vandliga sét.	You shall married be here in Greenland, that which honourable is, though for you will-be that not for long, because the way yours lies out to Iceland, and shall there come from you both great descendents and good, and over your family shine bright rays but I have most towards that can such closely seen.	You shall be married here in Greenland, and honourably, though you will not be married for long, because your way lies out to Iceland, and there shall come from you good descendents, and bright rays will shine over your family, towards that I can clearly see.
Enda far þú nú heil ok vel, dóttir".	End go you now whole and well, daughter".	After all, travel you now whole and well, daughter".
Síðan gengu menn at vísendakonunni, ok frétti þá hverr þess, er mest forvitni var á at vita.	Afterwards went people to wise-woman, and heard then each these, were most curious was of to know.	Afterwards people went to the wise woman, and then each heard that which they were most curious to know.
Hon var ok góð af frásögnum. Gekk þat ok lítt í tauma, er hon sagði.	She was also good of account. Went that also little of reins, that she said.	She gave a good answer. Things went little from the reins of what she had said.

The Saga of Erik the Red (Old Norse)

Old Norse	Literal	English
Þessu næst var komit eftir henni af öðrum bæ.	This next were come after her from another farm.	Following this, someone came for her from another farm.
Fór hon þá þangat.	Went she then from-there.	She then went from there.
Þá var sent eftir Þorbirni, því at hann vildi eigi heima vera, meðan slík hindrvitni var framið.	Then was sent after Thorbjorn, because that she willed not home be, while such hindered-knowledge was committed.	Then Thorbjorn was sent for, because she did not want to be at home while such hindered knowledge was committed.
Veðrátta batnaði skjótt, sem Þorbjörg hafði sagt.	Weather bettered shortly, as Thorbjorg had said.	The weather soon bettered, as Thorbjorg had said.
Býr Þorbjörn skip sitt ok ferr þar til, er hann kemr í Brattahlíð.	Prepared Thorbjorn ship his and travelled there to, that he came to Brattahlid.	Thorbjorn prepared his ship and travelled until he came to Brattahlid.
Eiríkr tekr vel við honum með blíðu ok kvað þat vel, er hann var þar kominn.	Erik took well with him with friendliness and saying that well, that he was there coming.	Erik received him well with friendliness and said how good it was that he had come.
Var Þorbjörn með honum um vetrinn ok skuldalið hans, en þeir vistuðu háseta með bóndum.	Was Thorbjorn with him about winter and household his, then they sheltered men among farms.	Thorbjorn was with him over the winter and his household was sheltered among the farms.
Eftir um várit gaf Eiríkr Þorbirni land á Stokkanesi, ok var þar gerr sæmiligr bær, ok bjó hann þar síðan.	After about spring gave Erik Thorbjorn land in Stokkanes, and was there made honourable farm, and settled he there since.	After about spring, Erik gave Thorbjorn land in Stokkanes, and there was made an honourable farm, and he settled there since.
5	5	5
Eiríkr átti þá konu, er Þjóðhildr hét, ok við henni tvá sonu.	Erik had then a-wife, was Thjodhild named, and with her two sons.	Erik had then a wife, who was named Thjodhild, and with her two sons.
Hét annarr Þorsteinn, en annarr Leifr.	Was called-one Thorstein, and another Leif.	One was called Thorstein, and another Leif.
Þeir váru báðir efniligir menn.	They were both promising men.	They were both promising men.
Var Þorsteinn heima með föður sínum, ok var eigi sá maðr á Grænlandi, er jafnmannvænn þótti sem hann.	Was Thorstein home with father his, and was not so a-man in Greenland, as equally-handsome thought as he.	Thorstein lived at home with his father, and there was no man in Greenland thought as equally handsome as him.
Leifr hafði siglt til Nóregs ok var með Óláfi konungi Tryggvasyni.	Leif had sailed to Norway and was with Olaf king Tryggvason.	Leif had sailed to Norway and was with King Olaf Tryggvason.
En er Leifr sigldi af Grænlandi um sumarit, urðu þeir sæhafa til Suðreyja.	But when Leif sailed from Greenland about summer, became they sea-scattered to Sudreyar.	But when Leif sailed from Greenland that summer, the ship was driven off course to Sudreyar.

The Saga of Erik the Red (Old Norse)

Old Norse	Literal	English
Þaðan byrjaði þeim seint, ok dvölðust þeir þar lengi um sumarit.	From-there began they late, and dwelled they there long about summer.	From there they began late, and they dwelled there a long time through the summer.
Leifr lagði þokka á konu þá, er Þórgunna hét.	Leif laid thoughts to a-woman there, was Thorgun called.	Leif fell in love with a woman there, who was named Thorgun.
Hon var kona ættstór, ok skilði Leifr, at hon mundi vera margkunnig.	She was woman noble, and understood Leif, that she would be many-knowing.	She was a noble woman, and Leif understood that she knew much.
En er Leifr bjóst brott, beiddist Þórgunna at fara með honum.	When was Leif prepared away, asked Thorgun to travel with him.	When Leif was preparing to leave, Thorgun asked to travel with him.
Leifr spurði, hvárt þat væri nökkut vili frænda hennar.	Leif asked, if that was something wished kinsmen hers.	Leif asked if that was something her kinsmen would agree to.
Hon kveðst þat ekki hirða.	She said that not consider.	She said that she did not care.
Leifr kveðst eigi þat kunna at sjá at sínu ráði at gera hertekna svá stórættaða konu í ókunnu landi, - "en vér liðfáir".	Leif said not that know-how to see of her advice to make captive such noble woman in unknown land, - "as we-are few".	Leif said that he did not know how to see to it that he make a captive such a noble woman in an unknown land - "as we have few troops".
Þórgunna mælti: "Eigi er víst, at þér þykki því betr ráðit".	Thorgun spoke: "Not is certain, that to-you seems therefore better decision".	Thorgun spoke: "I am not sure there is for you a better choice".
"Á þat mun ek þó hætta", sagði Leifr.	"At that should I though stop", said Leif.	"I will stop at that", said Leif.
"Þá segi ek þér", sagði Þórgunna, "at ek mun fara kona eigi ein saman, ok em ek með barni.	"Then say I to-you", said Thorgun, "That I should travel as-a-woman not alone together, and am I with child.	"Then I say to you", said Thorgun, "That I travel not alone, and I am with child.
Segi ek þat af þínum völdum. Get ek, at þat muni vera sveinbarn, þá er fæðist.	Say I this of your doing. Guess I, of that shall be boy, then to born.	And I say that this is your doing. I guess that a boy shall be born.
En þóttú vilir engan gaum at gefa, þá mun ek upp fæða sveininn ok þér senda til Grænlands, þegar fara má með öðrum mönnum.	But though will-you no heed of give, then shall I up feed boy and to-you send to Greenland, when travel may with other people.	But though you will not heed him, I shall bring the boy up and send him to you in Greenland, when he may travel with other people.

The Saga of Erik the Red (Old Norse)

Old Norse	Literal	English
En ek get, at þér verði at þvílíkum nytjum sonareignin sem nú verðr skilnaðr okkarr til.	But I guess, that you will-be as for-like use son's-property as now worth parting ours to.	But I guess that he will serve you as well as you have served me with your departure.
En koma ætla ek mér til Grænlands, áðr lýkr".	But come intend I myself to Greenland, before it-ends".	But I intend to come to Greenland myself, before it all ends".
Leifr gaf henni fingrgull ok vaðmálsmöttul grænlenzkan ok tannbelti.	Leif gave her finger-gold and mantle Greenland-skin and tusk-belt.	He gave her gold for her finger and a mantle of Greenland-skin and a belt with ivory.
Þessi sveinn kom til Grænlands ok nefndist Þorgils.	This boy came to Greenland and named Thorgils.	The boy came to Greenland and was named Thorgils.
Leifr tók við honum at faðerni.	Leif took with him to paternity.	Leif recognised him as his son.
Ok er þat sumra manna sögn, at þessi Þorgils hafi komit til Íslands fyrir Fróðárundr um sumarit.	And was that summer people said, that this Thorgils had come to Iceland before hauntings about summer.	And that summer people said that Thorgils had come to Iceland before the hauntings in summer.
En sjá Þorgils var síðan á Grænlandi, ok þótti þar enn eigi kynjalaust um hann verða, áðr lauk.	Then seen Thorgils was since in Greenland, and thought there yet not extraordinary about him to-be, before end.	Then Thorgils was seen afterwards in Greenland, and it was thought that there was something unusual about him before it ended.
Þeir Leifr sigldu brott ór Suðreyjum ok tóku Nóreg um haustit.	There Leif sailed away from Sudreyar and took-to Norway about autumn.	There Leif sailed away from Sudreyar and took to land in Norway about autumn.
Fór Leifr til hirðar Óláfs konungs Tryggvasonar.	Travelled Leif to court Olaf king Tryggvason's.	Leif travelled to the court of King Olaf Tryggvason.
Lagði konungr á hann góða virðing ok þóttist sjá, at hann mundi vera vel menntr maðr.	Had the-king towards him good honour and thought saw, that he would be a well-educated man.	The King had good honour towards him, and thought that he was a well educated man.
Eitt sinn kom konungr at máli við Leif ok sagði: "Ætlar þú til Grænlands í sumar?"	Once he came king to speak to Leif and said: "Intend you to Greenland in summer?".	One time, the king spoke to Leif and said: "Do you intend to go to Greenland in summer?".
"Þat ætla ek", sagði Leifr, "ef þat er yðvarr vili".	"That intend I", said Leif, "If that is your will".	"That I do intend", said Leif, "If that is your will".
Konungr svarar: "Ek get, at þat muni vel vera, ok skaltu þangat fara með erendum mínum, at boða þar kristni".	King answered: "I do, for that should well be, and shall-you there travel with errand mine, to preach there Christianity".	The king answered: "I do, for that will be well, and you shall travel there with my purpose, to preach there Christianity".

The Saga of Erik the Red (Old Norse)

Old Norse	Literal	English
Leifr kvað hann ráða skyldu, en kveðst hyggja, at þat erendi myndi torflutt á Grænlandi.	Leif said he decide should, but said thought, it that errand would difficult-be in Greenland.	Leif said that the king should decide that, but that he thought the errand would be difficult in Greenland.
Konungr kveðst eigi þann mann sjá, er betr væri til fallinn en hann, - "ok muntu giftu til bera".	King said none that men seen, were better would-be to fall than he, - "And should luck towards carry".	The king said there was no one better for the task to fall to than him, "and luck shall carry you towards".
"Þat mun því at eins", segir Leifr, "ef ek nýt yðvar við".	"That should therefore by likewise", said Leif, "If I benefit yours with".	"That it should be", said Leif, "if I travel with your luck also".
Lætr Leifr í haf ok er lengi úti ok hitti á lönd þau, er hann vissi áðr enga ván til.	Put Leif to sea and was long out and met to lands those, that he knew before none looked to.	Leif put to sea when he was ready and after a long time at sea, he met lands that he knew none had seen before.
Váru þar hveitiakrar sjálfsánir ok vínviðr vaxinn.	Were there wheat-acres self-sowing and vine-trees growing.	There were acres of wheat that were self-sowing, and vine trees growing.
Þar váru þau tré, er mösurr heita, ok höfðu þeir af þessu öllu nökkur merki, sum tré svá mikil, at í hús váru lögð.	There were there trees, were maple called, and had they from this all some imprint, some trees so great, that to houses were laid.	There were trees there known as burl, and they took some specimens of all of them, and some trees were so large that houses could be laid in them.
Leifr fann menn á skipflaki ok flutti heim með sér.	Leif found people on shipwreck and brought home with him.	Leif found people on a shipwreck and brought them home with him.
Sýndi hann í því ina mestu stórmennsku ok drengskap sem mörgu öðru, er hann kom kristni á landit, ok var jafnan síðan kallaðr Leifr inn heppni.	Showed he to therefore the most greatness and honour as many other, as he came Christianity to land, and was ever after called Leif the lucky.	He showed his greatness and honour and boyishness, so as many others, when he brought Christianity to the land, and was ever after called Leif the Lucky.
Leifr tók land í Eiríksfirði ok fór heim síðan í Brattahlíð.	Leif took land in Eriksfjord and went home afterwards to Brattahlid.	Leif took land in Eriksfjord and went home afterwards to Brattahlid.
Tóku þar allir menn vel við honum.	Took there all people well with him.	People there all received him warmly.

The Saga of Erik the Red (Old Norse)

Old Norse	Literal	English
Hann boðaði brátt kristni um landit ok almenniliga trú ok sýndi mönnum orðsending Óláfs konungs Tryggvasonar ok sagði, hversu mörg ágæti ok mikil dýrð fylgði þessum sið.	He preached soon Christianity about land and properly faith and showed people message Olaf king Tryggvason's and said, how much excellent and great glory followed this tradition.	He soon preached the faith of Christianity throughout the land and showed people the message that King Olaf Tryggvason who said how much excellence and glory followed this tradition.
Eiríkr tók því máli seint, at láta sið sinn, en Þjóðhildr gekk skjótt undir ok lét gera kirkju eigi allnær húsunum.	Erik took since matter late, to leave tradition his, but Thjodhild went quickly behind and had made church not all-near the-house.	Erik was reluctant to take to it and leave his tradition, but Thjodhild was quick to follow and had a church made a distance away from the house.
Þat hús var kallat Þjóðhildarkirkja.	That house was called Thjodhildakirkja.	That house was called Thjodhildakirkja.
Hafði hon þar fram bænir sínar ok þeir menn, sem við kristni tóku.	Had she there from prayers hers and they people, since with Christianity took.	She held her prayers there, and with people who had since converted to Christianity.
Þjóðhildr vildi ekki samræði við Eirík, síðan hon tók trú, en honum var þat mjök móti skapi.	Thjodhild willed not intercourse with Erik, since she took faith, but he was that much against mood.	Thjodhild did not want to have intercourse with Erik since she had taken the faith, which went very much against his mood.
Á því gerðist orð mikit, at menn myndi leita lands þess, er Leifr hafði fundit.	Then therefore made words much, to people would search lands these, that Leif had found.	Then there were many words about people searching these lands that Leif had found.
Var þar formaðr at Þorsteinn Eiríksson, fróðr maðr ok vinsæll.	Was there chief to Thorstein Eriksson, wise man and popular.	Chief among them was Thorstein Eriksson, a wise and popular man.
Eiríkr var ok til beðinn, ok trúðu menn hans gæfu framast ok forsjá.	Erik was and to asked, and believed people his gifted foremost and foresight.	Erik was also asked, and people believed he was gifted and a man of foresight.
Hann var lengi fyrir, en kvað eigi nei við, er vinir hans báðu hann til, bjuggu síðan skip þat, er Þorbjörn hafði út haft, ok váru til ráðnir tuttugu menn, ok höfðu lítit fé, eigi meir en vápn ok vistir.	He was long before, that saying not no with, then friends his asked him to, prepared since then ship that, Thorbjorn had out had, and were to appointed twenty people, and had little cattle, not more than weapons and provisions.	For a long time he was against going, but his friends bid him to go, and then a ship was prepared, which Thorbjorn had sailed out on, and twenty men were hired, and some cattle, not more than weapons and provisions.
Þann myrgin, er Eiríkr reið heiman, tók hann einn kistil, ok var þar í gull ok silfr.	That morning, was Erik riding home, took he one chest, and was there of gold and silver.	That morning, Erik was rode home, he took a chest, and therein was gold and silver.

The Saga of Erik the Red (Old Norse)

Old Norse	Literal	English
Fal hann þat ok fór síðan leiðar sinnar, ok bar svá til, at hann fell af baki, ok brotna rifin í síðunni, en lesti höndina í axlarliðnum.	Hid he that and went afterwards way his, and carrying such until, that he fell from back, and broke rib among his, and gripped hand to shoulder.	He hid that and then travelled his way, and carried such until, he fell back from the horse, and broke one of his ribs, and gripped his hand to his shoulder.
Af þeim atburð sagði hann Þjóðhildi, konu sinni, at hon tæki féit á brott, lézt þess hafa at goldit, er hann hafði féit fólgit.	Of these events said he Thjodhild, wife his, that she take treasure to away, should this have of gold, that he had wealth hidden.	He said to his wife Thjodhild what had happened, and asked her to take the treasure hidden away, and have this gold that he had hidden.
Síðan sigldu þeir út ór Eiríksfirði með gleði mikilli.	Since sailed they out from Eriksfjord with gladness much.	Afterwards they sailed out of Eriksfjord with much gladness.
Þótti þeim allvænt um sitt efni.	Thought they expected about their prospects.	They thought expectantly about their prospects.
Þá velkði úti lengi í hafi, ok kómu þeir ekki á þær slóðir, sem þeir vildu.	Then drove about long at sea, and came they not to those routes, which they willed.	Then they were driven about at sea for a long time, and did not come to those routes which they had wished.
Þeir kómu í sýn við Ísland, ok svá höfðu þeir fugl af Írlandi.	They came it seemed to Iceland, and so had they birds of Ireland.	They came in sight of what seemed like Iceland they had birds of Ireland.
Rak þá skip þeira um haf innan, fóru aftr um haustit ok váru allmjök væstir ok þrekaðir, koma við vetr sjálfan á Eiríksfjörð.	Driven then ship theirs about sea within, travelled back about autumn and were all-very worn and exhausted, came in winter itself to Eriksfjord.	Their ship was driven about the sea, and they travelled back about autumn, and all were very weary and exhausted, as winter was coming to Eriksfjord.
Þá mælti Eiríkr: "Kátari sigldum vér í sumar út ór firðinum en nú erum vér, ok eru nú þó enn mörg góð at".	Then said Erik: "Merrier sailed we this summer out from fjord than now are we, and are now though still many good to".	Then Erik said: "We sailed more merrily in the summer out of this fjord than we now return to it, but there is still much good".
Þorsteinn svarar: "Þat er nú höfðingligt bragð at sjá nökkut gott ráð fyrir þeim mönnum öllum, sem hér eru nú ráðstafalausir, ok fá þeim vist í vetr".	Thorstein answered: "That is now having-like solution to see some good proposal for those people all, which here are now disposed, and get they provisions to winter".	Thorstein answered: "Now we should propose that these people here are given provisions for the winter".
Eiríkr svarar: "Þat er jafnan satt, sem mælt er, at eigi veit, fyrr en svarat er, ok svá mun hér fara.	Erik answered: "That is equally true, which said was, to not know, before but answered is, and so should here go.	Erik answered: "That is equally true, as is said, you can't know a question before it is answered, and so it will be here.

The Saga of Erik the Red (Old Norse)

Old Norse	Literal	English
Skal nú hafa ráð þín um þetta".	Shall now have discussion with-you about that".	Now shall we have a discussion with you about that".
Fóru nú allir þeir, er eigi höfðu aðrar vistir, með þeim feðgum.	Went now all they, who not had other supplies, with they father-and-son.	All those who had no provisions with the father and son.
Síðan fóru þeir heim í Brattahlíð ok váru þar um vetrinn.	Afterwards travelled they home to Brattahlid and were there about winter.	Afterwards they travelled hoe to Brattahlid and were there for the winter.
6	6	6
Nú er frá því at segja, at Þorsteinn Eiríksson vakði bónorð við Guðríði, ok var því máli vel svarat bæði af henni ok af föður hennar.	Now is from accordingly to say, that Thorstein Eriksson awoke proposal to Guthrid, and was accordingly the-matter well answered both from her and of father hers.	Now following this is to say that Thorstein Eriksson brought up a marriage proposal to Gudrid, and accordingly the matter was well answered from both her and her father.
Er þetta at ráði gert.	Then that as advised was-done.	Then that which was planned was done.
Þorsteinn gengr at eiga Guðríði, ok var þetta brúðkaup í Brattahlíð um haustit.	Thorstein went to marry Guthrid, and was this wedding in Brattahlid about autumn.	Thorstein went to marry Gudrid, and this wedding was in Brattahlid around autumn.
Fór sjá veizla vel fram, ok var allfjölmennt.	Went seen the-feast well from, and were many-people.	The feast was well witnessed, and there were many people there.
Þorsteinn átti bú í Vestribyggð á bæ þeim, er heitir í Lýsufirði.	Thorstein had a-farm in Vestribyggd in town theirs, was named it Lysufjord.	Thorstein had a farm in the Western Settlement in the worn, which was named Lysufjord.
En sá maðr átti þar helming í búi, er Þorsteinn hét.	But so a-man had there half a farm, was Thorstein called.	There was a man there that had a half share of a farm, who was named Thorstein.
Sigríðr hét kona hans.	Sigrid was-called wife his.	His wife was named Sigrid.
Fór Þorsteinn í Lýsufjörð um haustit til nafna síns ok þau Guðríðr bæði.	Went Thorstein to Lysufjord about autumn to namesake his and they Guthrid both.	They went to Lysufjord around autumn to both his namesake and Gudrid.
Var þar við þeim vel tekit.	Were there with them well taken.	They were well received by them.
Váru þau þar um vetrinn.	Were they there about winter.	They were there around winter.
Þat gerðist til tíðenda, at sótt kom í bæ þeira, er lítit var af vetri.	That happened until news, that sickness came among settlement theirs, that little was from winter.	Then came the news, that sickness came among their settlement, shortly after the beginning of winter.

The Saga of Erik the Red (Old Norse)

Old Norse	Literal	English
Garðarr hét þar verkstjóri.	Gardi was-called there a-foreman.	There was a foreman there who was named Gardi.
Hann var ekki vinsæll maðr.	He was not popular a-man.	He was not a popular man.
Hann tók fyrst sótt ok andaðist.	He took first sickness and died.	He was the first to become ill, and he died.
Síðan var skammt at bíða, at hverr lézt at öðrum.	Since was short to wait, that each died the others.	It was not long after that, that each of the others died.
Þá tók sótt Þorsteinn Eiríksson ok Sigríðr, kona Þorsteins, nafna hans.	Then took sickness Thorstein Eriksson and Sigrid, wife Thorstein's, namesake his.	Then the sickness took Thorstein Eriksson, and his namesake's wife Sigrid.
Ok eitt kveld fýstist Sigríðr at ganga til náðahúss, er stóð í gegnt útidurum.	And one evening desired Sigrid to go to outhouse, which stood about opposite the-out-door.	And one evening, Sigrid wanted to go to the outhouse, which stood opposite the farmhouse door.
Guðríðr fylgði henni, ok horfðu þær móti útidurunum.	Guthrid followed her, and looked they towards the-out-door.	Gudrid followed her, and they looked towards the farmhouse door.
Þá kvað hon við hátt, Sigríðr.	Then cried-out she with loud, Sigrid.	Then Sigrid cried out loudly.
Guðríðr mælti: "Vit höfum óvarliga farit, ok áttu engan stað við, at kalt komi á þik, ok förum vit heim sem skjótast".	Guthrid said: "We have unwisely gone, and have-you none stand with, that cold comes to you, and go into home then quickly".	Gudrid said: "We have acted carelessly, you should not stand in the cold, and we must go inside quickly".
Sigríðr svarar: "Eigi er fært at svá búnu.	Sigrid answered: "Not am-i going-out as so are.	Sigrid answered: "I won't go out with things as they are.
Hér er nú liðit þat allt it dauða fyrir durunum ok Þorsteinn, bóndi þinn, ok þar kenni ek mik.	Here is now company that all to death before the-door and Thorstein, husband yours, and there recognise I me.	Here are now all the companions that died standing there before the door, and Thorstein your husband, and there I recognise myself.
Ok er slíkt hörmung at sjá".	And is such horrible to see".	And it is such a horrible thing to see".
Ok er þetta leið af, mælti hon: "Förum vit nú, Guðríðr.	And when that passed out-of, spoke she: "Gone known now, Guthrid.	And when it had passed, she spoke: "They are gone now Gudrid".
Nú sé ek ekki liðit".	Now see I not company".	Now I don't see those companions".
Var þá Þorsteinn horfinn.	Was then Thorstein disappeared.	It was then that Thorstein had disappeared.

The Saga of Erik the Red (Old Norse)

Old Norse	Literal	English
Henni þótti hann áðr haft hafa svipu í hendi ok vilja berja liðit.	She thought he returned had having whip in hand and willing to-bear the-company.	She thought he had returned with a whip in hand ready and willing to strike those companions.
Síðan gengu þær inn, ok áðr morginn kæmi, þá var hon látin, ok var ger kista at líkinu.	Afterwards went they in, and before morning came, then was she dead, and was made coffin for body.	Afterwards they went inside, and before the morning came, she was dead, and a coffin was made for her body.
Ok þenna sama dag ætluðu menn at róa, ok leiddi Þorsteinn þá til vara, ok í annan lit fór hann at sjá veiðiskap þeira.	And then same day intended people to row, and led Thorstein then to wares, and to others the-team went he to see fishing there.	And then that same day people intended to row and go fishing, and led Thorstein to where the goods were kept, and to the others in the company he went to see how the fishing was going.
Þá sendi Þorsteinn Eiríksson nafna sínum orð, at hann kæmi til hans, ok sagði svá, at þar væri varla kyrrt ok húsfreyja vildi færast á fætr ok vildi undir klæðin hjá honum.	Then sent Thorstein Eriksson namesake his word, that he come to him, and said such, that there was hardly peace and housewife willed move to feet and willing under bed-clothes by him.	Then Thorstein Eriksson sent his namesake his word to come to him, and said that there was no peace at home and his housewife was trying to rise up and get into bed with him.
Ok er hann kom inn, var hon komin upp á rekkjustokkinn.	And when he came in, was she coming up to sideboards.	And when he came in, she had reached the sideboards of the bed.
Þá tók hann hana höndum ok lagði bolöxi fyrir brjóst henni.	Then took he her hand and laid a-pole-axe for breast hers.	Then he took her hand and drove an axe into her breast.
Þorsteinn Eiríksson andaðist nær dagsetri.	Thorstein Eriksson died near day-setting.	Thorstein Eriksson died close to sunset.
Þorsteinn bóndi bað Guðríði leggjast niðr ok sofa, en hann kveðst vaka mundu um nóttina yfir líkinu.	Thorstein farmer asked Guthrid ti-lie down and sleep, and he said awake would-be about night over the-bodies.	Thorstein the Farmer told Gudrid to lie down and sleep, and he said that he would keep watch over the bodies.
Hon gerir svá.	She did so.	She did so.
Ok er skammt leið á nóttina, settist Þorsteinn Eiríksson upp ok mælti, kveðst vilja, at Guðríðr væri þangat kölluð, ok kveðst vilja tala við hana: "Guð vill, at þessi stund sé mér gefin til leyfis ok umbótar míns ráðs".	And that short way in night, sat Thorstein Eriksson up and spoke, saying willed, that Guthrid was there called, and saying he-willed to-speak with her: "God wills, that this time so me given to leave and offer my plans".	A short way into the night, Thorstein Eriksson sat up and spoke, saying that he wished for Gudrid to be called, as he willed to speak with her. "God wills that this time has been given to me to better my prospects".

The Saga of Erik the Red (Old Norse)

Old Norse	Literal	English
Þorsteinn bóndi gengr á fund Guðríðar ok vakði hana, biðr hana signa sik ok biðja sér guð hjálpar ok segir, hvat Þorsteinn Eiríksson hafði talat við hann, - "ok hann vill finna þik.	Thorstein the-farmer went to find Guthrid and woke her, asked her to-sign herself and ask herself God's help and said, what Thorstein Eriksson had told to him, - "And he wills find you.	Thorstein the Farmer went to find Gudrid and woke her, asking her to sign herself with the cross, and to ask for God's help, telling her what Thorstein Eriksson had told him: "And he wishes to meet you.
Verðr þú ráð fyrir at sjá, hvat þú vill upp taka, því at ek kann hér um hvárkis at fýsa".	Become you obliged for to see, what you will up take, because that I know here about neither to desire".	Are you obliged to see what you will learn from this?, for I will not advise you either way".
Hon svaraði: "Vera kann, at þetta sé ætlat til nökkurra þeira hluta, er síðan sé í minni hafðir, þessi inn undarligi hlutr, en ek vænti, at guðs gæzla mun yfir mér standa.	She answered: "Be it possible that this intends to something part there which afterwards are to mine have, this the strange lot, but I expect that God's herding shall over me stand.	She answered: "Could it possibly be that there is some purpose to this, which afterwards will have consequences for me, this strange occurrence, but I hope that God will shepherd over me".
Mun ek ok á hætta með guðs miskunn at fara til móts við hann ok vita, hvat hann vill tala, því at ek mun eigi forðast mega, ef mér skal mein at verða.	Should I to danger with God's mercy to speak with him because that I may now not avoid harm to mine.	I will to chance, with God's mercy, to speak with him, because I may not escape any threat to myself.
Vil ek síðr, at hann gangi víðara.	Will I less that he go far-and-wide.	I do not wish for him to have to go further and wider.
En mik grunar, at þat mun á liggja".	But I suspect that it so to other choice".	And I suspect that it would be the alternative choice".
Nú fór Guðríðr ok hittir Þorstein.	Now came Guthrid and met Thorstein.	Now Gudrid came and met Thorstein.
Sýndist henni sem hann felldi tár.	Seemed to-her that he shed tears.	It seemed to her that he had shed tears.
Hann mælti í eyra henni nökkur orð hljótt, svá at hon ein vissi, en þat mælti hann, svá at allir heyrðu, at þeir menn væri sælir, er trúna heldu, ok henni fylgði öll hjálp ok miskunn, ok sagði þó, at margir heldi hana illa.	He spoke in ear hers some words quietly, so that she alone knew, and that spoke he, so as all heard, that they men were happy, that faith held, and him followed all help and mercy, and said though, that many held it badly.	He spoke some words in her ear quietly, so that she alone knew, and he said that those men who had kept their faith well rejoiced as it brought them mercy and salvation, but he said that some had kept their faith badly though.

The Saga of Erik the Red (Old Norse)

Old Norse	Literal	English
"Er þat engi háttr, sem hér hefir verit á Grænlandi, síðan kristni kom hér, at setja menn niðr í óvígða mold við litla yfirsöngva.	"Is that no way, which here has been in Greenland, after Christianity came here, to set people down among unconsecrated dust with little burial-service.	"It is no way to set people down among unconsecrated dust with little burial service, which people have done here in Greenland since Christianity came here.
Vil ek mik láta flytja til kirkju ok aðra þá menn, sem hér hafa andazt, en Garðar vil ek brenna láta á báli sem skjótast, því at hann veldr öllum aftrgöngum þeim, sem hér hafa verit í vetr".	Will I me laid carried to church and others they people, which here have died, but Gardar will I burn let to fire that quickly, because that he caused all hauntings those, which here have been in winter".	I wish that I be carried to church, along with the other people who have died here, but Gardi should be burned on a pyre straight away, because he caused all those hauntings which were here in winter".
Hann sagði henni ok um sína hagi ok kvað hennar forlög mikil mundu verða, en bað hana varast at giftast grænlenzkum mönnum, bað, at hon legði fé þeira til kirkju ok sumt fátækum mönnum.	He told her and about his state and said her fortune great would be, but asked she avoid to marry Greenlander men, asked, that she leave wealth theirs to the-church and some poor people.	He told her about his situation and said that her fortune would be great, but warned her against marrying a Greenlander, he also asked that she donate their wealth to the church, and to the poor.
Ok þá hné hann aftr öðru sinni.	And then knee he back second his.	And then he sank back down for the second time.
Sá hafði háttr verit á Grænlandi, síðan kristni kom þangat, at menn váru grafnir á bæjum, þar sem önduðust, í óvígðri moldu.	So had the-way been in Greenland, since Christianity came there, that people were buried in farms, there which died, in unconsecrated ground.	So had been the way in Greenland, since Christianity arrived there, that people were buried in farms where they died in unconsecrated ground.
Skyldi setja staur upp af brjósti inum dauða, en síðan, er kennimenn kómu til, þá skyldi upp kippa staurinum ok hella þar í vígðu vatni ok veita þar yfirsöngva, þótt þat væri miklu síðar.	As-should-be set poles up on breast in the-dead, then after, a priest came to, then should-be up pulled poles and flat-stones there among ground water and supplied there burial-service, though that was much later.	A pole was set up on the breast of each corpse, then afterwards there came a priest, then the poles were pulled up, and flat stones placed on the ground, and consecrated water poured into the hole with a burial service, even though this was done much later.
Lík þeira Þorsteins váru færð til kirkju í Eiríksfjörð ok veittir þar yfirsöngvar af kennimönnum.	Body there Thorstein's was taken to church in Eriksfjord and supplied there burial-service from priests.	There Thorstein's body was taken to church in Eriksfjord and priests held burial services for them.
Tók Eiríkr við Guðríði ok var henni í föður stað.	Took Erik with Guthrid and was she at father's place.	Erik received Gudrid and she stayed at her father's place.

The Saga of Erik the Red (Old Norse)

Old Norse	Literal	English
Litlu síðar andaðist Þorbjörn. Bar þá fé allt undir Guðríði.	Little later died Thorbjorn. Bore then wealth all up-to Guthrid.	A little later Thorbjorn died. All of his wealth was given up to Gudrid.
Tók Eiríkr hana til sín ok sá vel um hennar kost.	Took Erik her to his and saw well about her provided.	Erik invited her to live with him, and saw that she was well provided for.
7	7	7
Þórðr hét maðr, er bjó at Höfða á Höfðaströnd.	Thord was-called a-man who lived at Hofda in Hofdastrond.	There was a man called Thord who lived at Hofda in Hofdastrond.
Hann átti Þorgerði, dóttur Þóris hímu ok Friðgerðar, dóttur Kjarvals Írakonungs.	He married Thorgerd, daughter-of Thori's aunt and Fridgerdar, daughter-of Kjarval Ireland-King.	He married Thorgerd, daughter of Thori's aunt and Fridgerar, the daughter of King Kjarval of Ireland.
Þórðr var sonr Bjarnar byrðusmjörs Hróaldssonar hryggs, Áslákssonar, Bjarnarsonar járnsíðu, Ragnarssonar loðbrókar.	Thord was son-of Bjarn Byrdusmjors Roaldsson the-Sad, son-of-Aslak, son-of-Bjorn Ironside son-of-Ragnar Lothbrok	Thord was the son of Bjarn Byrdusmjors, the son of Roald the Sad, the son of Aslak, the son of Bjorn Ironside, the son of Ragnar Lothbrok.
Þau áttu son, er Snorri hét.	They had a-son who-was Snorri named.	They had a son who was named Snorri.
Hann átti Þórhildi rjúpu, dóttur Þórðar gellis.	He married Thorhild Rjupa, daughter-of Thord Gellis.	He married Thorhild Rjupa, the daughter of Thord Gellis.
Þeira sonr var Þórðr hesthöfði.	Their son was Thord Horse-head.	Their son was Thord Horse-Head.
Þorfinnr karlsefni hét sonr Þórðar.	Thorfin Karlsefni was-called son-of Thord.	Thord's son was called Thorfin Karlsefni.
Móðir Þorfinns hét Þórunn.	Mother Thorfin's was-called Thorun.	Thorfin's mother was called Thorun.
Þorfinnr var í kaupferðum ok þótti góðr fardrengr.	Thorfin was on trading-journeys and thought a-good travelling-companion.	Thorfin went on trading journeys and was thought of as a good travelling companion.
Eitt sumar býr Karlsefni skip sitt ok ætlar til Grænlands.	One summer prepared Karlsefni ship his and intended to Greenland.	One summer Karlsefni intended to go to Greenland and prepared his ship.
Snorri Þorbrandsson ferr með honum, ór Álftafirði, ok váru fjórir tigir manna á skipi.	Snorri Thorbrandson travelled with him, from Alftafjord, and was four tens men on ship.	Snorri Thorbrandson travelled with him from Alftafjord, and there were forty men on his ship.
Maðr hét Bjarni Grímólfsson, breiðfirzkr at ætt.	A-man was-called Bjarni Grimolfson, Breidafjord man ancestry.	There was a man called Bjarni Grimolfson, a man from Breidafjord by ancestry.

The Saga of Erik the Red (Old Norse)

Old Norse	Literal	English
Annarr hét Þórhallr Gamlason, austfirzkr maðr.	Another was-called Thorhall Gamlason, east-fjords man.	Another was called Thorhall Gamlason, a man from the East Fjords.
Þeir bjuggu it sama sumar skip sitt ok ætluðu til Grænlands.	There prepared the same summer ship his and intended to Greenland.	There they prepared their ship that summer, intending to go to Greenland.
Þeir váru ok fjórir tigir manna á skipi.	They were and four tens men on ship.	There were forty men on the ship.
Láta þeir Karlsefni í haf þessum tveim skipum, þegar þeir váru búnir.	Had they Karlsefni to sea these two ships, as-soon-as they were ready.	Karlsefni had these two ships put to sea as soon as they were ready.
Ekki er um þat getit, hversu langa útivist þeir höfðu, en frá því er at segja, at bæði þessi skip kómu á Eríksfjörð um haustit.	Not is about that told-of, how long out-journey they had, but from since was to say, that both these ships came to Eriksfjord about autumn.	Not much was said about how long a journey they had, but since was said that both these ships came to Eriksfjord about autumn.
Eiríkr reið til skips ok aðrir landsmenn.	Erik rode to ships and other landsmen.	Erik rode to the ships along with other men of the land.
Tókst með þeim greiðlig kaupstefna.	Took with them promptly trading-posts.	They promptly took trading posts with them.
Buðu stýrimenn Eiríki at hafa slíkt af varningi sem hann vildi.	Invited steersmen Erik to have such of wares that he willed.	The captains invited Erik to have whatever goods he wanted.
En Eiríkr sýnir þeim stórmennsku af sér í móti, því at hann bauð þessum tveim skipshöfnum til sín heim um vetrinn í Brattahlíð.	Then Erik showed them great-man-ness of him among towards, for that he invited these two ships-ports to his home about winter to Brattahlid.	Erik then showed them great generosity, as he invited these two ships to his home for the winter at Brattahlid.
Þetta þágu kaupmenn ok þökkuðu honum.	This accepted trading-men and thanked him.	The traders accepted this and thanked him.
Síðan var fluttr heim varningr þeira í Brattahlíð.	Then were transported home goods theirs to Brattahlid.	Later their goods were transported to Brattahlid.
Skorti þar eigi útibú stór til at varðveita í varning þeira.	Shortage there was-not outhouses great for in supplies to wares theirs.	There was no shortage of large outhouses for the to store their goods in.
Skorti þar ekki margt þat, er hafa þurfti, ok líkaði kaupmönnum vel um vetrinn.	Shortage there not many that, were had needed, and liked trading-men well about winter.	There no shortage of anything that they needed, and the traders very much enjoyed their winter.
En er dró at jólum, tók Eiríkr fæð mikla ok var óglaðari en hann átti vana til.	But as drew to Yule, took Erik sadness much and was without-gladness that he had custom to.	But as it drew closer to Yule, Erik became sad and was without the cheerfulness that he usually had.

The Saga of Erik the Red (Old Norse)

Old Norse	Literal	English
Eitt sinn kom Karlsefni at máli við Eirík ok mælti: "Er þér þungt, Eiríkr bóndi? Menn þykkjast finna, at þú ert óglaðari en þú átt vana til.	Along then came Karlsefni to speak with Erik and said: "Are you unhappy, Erik farmer people think find, that you are un-glad than you have custom to.	Then along came Karlsefni to talk to Erik and said: "Are you unhappy, Erik the farmer? People seem to find that you are unhappier than usual.
Þú hefir veitt oss með inni mestu rausn, ok erum vér skyldir til at launa þér slíku góðu sem vér höfum föng á.	You have given us well the most generosity, and are we obliged to that repay you such good as we have possessions of.	You have provided for us most generously, and we are obliged to repay you as best we can with everything we have.
Nú segðu, hvat ógleði þinni veldr".	Now say, what sadness yours brought-about".	Now tell me, what is it that makes you sad?".
Eiríkr svarar: "Þér þiggið vel ok góðmannliga.	Erik answered: "You accepted well and good-man-like.	Erik answered: "You have accepted with gratitude and respect.
Nú leikr mér þat eigi í hug, at á yðr verði hallat um vár skipti.	Now like I that not in mind, that for you have-been inclined about what-was exchanged.	To my mind, you have not been lacking in our exchanges.
Hitt er heldr, at mér þykkir uggligt, þá er þér komið annars staðar, at þat flytist, at þér hafið engi jól verri haft en þessi, er nú koma ok Eiríkr inn rauði veitti yðr í Brattahlíð á Grænlandi".	I find rather, that to-me seems fearful, then that you come to-another place, by that flows, that you have not Yule worse had than this, when now came and Erik the Red supported you in Brattahlid in Greenland".	I worry to think that it will get around that you have not had a Yule worse than this, when Erik the Red came and supported you in Brattahlid in Greenland".
"Þat mun eigi svá fara, bóndi", segir Karlsefni.	"That shall not so go, farmer", said Karlsefni.	"It shall not be that way, farmer", said Karlsefni.
Vér höfum á skipi váru bæði malt ok korn, hafið þar af slíkt er þér vilið ok gerið veizlu svá stórmannliga sem yðr líkar fyrir því".	"We have in ships ours both malt and corn, have there of such that you will and make feast such great-man-ness as you like for according".	"We have malt and flour and grain aboard our ships, and you will have whatever you wish to make such a great feast according to your generosity".
Þetta þiggr Eiríkr, ok var þá búit til jólaveizlu, ok var hon in sæmiligsta, svá at menn þóttust trautt þvílíka rausn sét hafa í fátæku landi.	This accepted Erik, and were then preparations for Yule-feast, and was it in honourable, such that people thought scarcely spectacular generous seen had among poor land.	Erik accepted this, and then the preparations were made for the Yule feast, and it was honourable, so much so that people thought the had scarcely seen such spectacular generosity in such a poor land.

The Saga of Erik the Red (Old Norse)

Old Norse	Literal	English
Ok eftir jólin vekr Karlsefni bónorð fyrir Eiríki um Guðríði, því at honum leizt sem hann mundi forræði á hafa.	And after Yule awoke Karlsefni proposal to Erik about Guthrid, because to him looked-like that he would power of have.	And after Yule, Karlsefni brought up a marriage proposal about Gudrid, as it seemed to him that Erik had protection of her.
Eiríkr svaraði vel ok segir, at hon mun sínum forlögum verða at fylgja, ok kveðst góða eina frétt af honum hafa.	Erik answered well and said, that she could her fortune be to follow, and said good only news of him had.	Erik answered favourably and said that she could follow her fortune, and said only good things about him.
Ok lauk svá, at Þorfinnr festi Guðríði, ok var þá aukin veizlan ok drukkit brullaup þeira, ok váru þau í Brattahlíð um vetrinn.	And ended so, that Thorfin joined Guthrid, and was then increased the-feast and drink wedding theirs, and were they in Brattahlid about winter.	And so it concluded, that Thorfin and Gudrid joined in marriage, and the feast was expanded to include toasting their wedding, and they were in Brattahlid over the winter.
8	8	8
Í Brattahlíð hófust miklar umræður, at menn skyldi leita Vínlands ins góða, ok var sagt, at þangat myndi vera at vitja góðra landkosta.	In Brattahlid began much discussion, that people should seek Vinland the good, and was said, that there would be to visit good land-benefits.	There began much discussion in Brattahlid about people seeking Vinland the good, and it was said that there would be good benefits.
Ok þar kom, at Karlsefni ok Snorri bjuggu skip sitt at leita landsins um várit.	And there came, that Karlsefni and Snorri prepared ship theirs to seek lands about spring.	And then it came, that Karlsefni and Snorri prepared their ship to seek lands during the spring.
Til þeirar ferðar réðust þeir Bjarni ok Þórhallr með skip sitt ok þat föruneyti, er þeim hafði fylgt.	To their travel appointed they Bjarni and Thorhall with ship theirs and that companions, that they had followed.	For their voyage, they hired Bjarni and Thorhall with their own ship, and their companions who followed them.
Maðr hét Þorvarðr.	A-man was-called Thorvard.	There was a man called Thorvard.
Hann átti Freydísi, dóttur Eiríks rauða, laungetna.	He married Freydis, daughter Erik the-Red's, illegitimate.	He married Freydis, the illegitimate daughter of Erik the Red.
Hann fór ok með þeim ok Þorvaldr, sonr Eiríks, ok Þórhallr, er kallaðr var veiðimaðr.	He went also with them and Thorvald, son Erik's, and Thorhall, who called was hunter.	He also travelled with them, along with Thorvald, Erik's son, and Thorhall, who was called the hunter.
Hann hafði lengi verit með Eiríki, veiðimaðr hans um sumrum, en bryti um vetrum.	He had long been with Erik, hunter his about summer, but breaks about winter.	He had long been with Erik, hunting during the summer, and breaks during the winter.

The Saga of Erik the Red (Old Norse)

Old Norse	Literal	English
Hann var mikill maðr ok sterkr ok svartr ok þursligr, hljóðlyndr ok illorðr, þat er hann mælti, ok eggjaði jafnan Eirík ins verra.	He was great man and strong and dark and giant, quiet and difficult-of-words, that when he spoke, and urged ever Erik the worse.	He was a great and strong man, dark and giant, a man of few words, but when he spoke, he usually desired to make trouble.
Hann var illa kristinn.	He was a-bad Christian.	He was a bad Christian.
Honum var víða kunnigt í óbyggðum.	He was widely known to unsettled-land.	He knew the unsettled land widely.
Hann var á skipi með Þorvarði ok Þorvaldi.	He was in ship with Thorvard and Thorvald.	He was in a ship with Thorvard and Thorvald.
Þeir höfðu þat skip, er Þorbjörn hafði út haft.	They had that ship, which Thorbjorn had back had.	They had the ship which Thorbjorn had brought back.
Þeir höfðu alls fjóra tigu manna ok hundrað, er þeir sigldu til Vestribyggðar ok þaðan til Bjarneyjar.	They had all forty ten men and hundred, when they sailed to Vestribyggd and there to Bjarney.	They had among all a hundred and forty men, then they sailed to the Western Settlement and from there to Bjarney.
Þaðan sigldu þeir tvau dægr suðr.	From-there sailed they two days south.	From there they sailed south for two days.
Þá sá þeir land ok skutu báti ok könnuðu landit, fundu þar hellur stórar ok margar tólf álna víðar.	Then saw they land and launched boat and explore land, found they slabs large and as-much-as twelve cubits wide.	Then they saw land and launched a boat to explore the land, and they found large slabs as wide as twelve cubits.
Fjölði var þar melrakka.	Many were there melrakka.	There were many melrakka.
Þeir gáfu þar nafn ok kölluðu Helluland.	They gave there name and called Helluland.	They gave there a name and called it Helluland.
Þaðan sildu þeir tvau dægr, ok brá þá landsuðrs ór suðri, ok fundu land skógvaxit ok mörg dýr á.	From-there sailed they two days, and drew they south-east from south, and found land forest-grown and many wild-animals on.	From there they sailed for two days, and drew southeast and south, and found forested land with many wild animals on.
Ey lá þar undan í landsuðr.	Island lay there from among south-east.	An island lay south east from there.
Þar drápu þeir einn björn ok kölluðu þar síðan Bjarney, en landit Markland.	There killed they a bear and called they since Bjarney, and land Markland.	They killed a bear there and afterwards they called it Bjarney, and called the land Markland.
Þaðan silgdu þeir suðr með landinu langa stund ok kómu at nesi einu.	From-there sailed they south along land long while and came to headland one.	From there they sailed south along the land, and after a long while they came to a headland.
Lá landit á stjórn.	Lay land to stern.	They kept the land to their stern.
Váru þar strandir langar ok sandar.	Were there beaches long and sandy.	The beaches were long and sandy.

The Saga of Erik the Red (Old Norse)

Old Norse	Literal	English
Þeir reru til lands ok fundu þar á nesinu kjöl af skipi ok kölluðu þar Kjalarnes.	They rowed towards land and found there on headland keel from ship and called they Kjalarnes.	They rowed towards the land and found that there on the headland was the keep from a ship, and they called it Kjalarnes.
Þeir kölluðu ok strandirnar Furðustrandir, því at langt var með at sigla.	They called and beaches Furdustrandir, because by long was along to sail.	The called the beaches Furdustrandir because they were long to sail by.
Þá gerðist landit vágskorit.	Then became land creek-indented.	Then the land became indented with creeks.
Þeir heldu skipunum í einn vág.	They held ship into one inlet.	They kept the ship in an inlet.
Óláfr konungr Tryggvason hafði gefit Leifi tvá menn skozka.	Olaf king Tryggvason had given Leif two men Scottish.	King Olaf Tryggvason had given Leif two Scottish people.
Hét karlmaðrinn Haki, en konan Hekja.	Called servants Haki, and woman Hekja.	The servants were called Haki, and a woman Hekja.
Þau váru dýrum skjótari.	They were wild-animals faster-than.	They were faster than wild animals.
Þessir menn váru á skipi með Karlsefni.	These people were on the-ship with Karlsefni.	They were on the ship with Karlsefni.
En er þeir höfðu siglt fyrir Furðustrandir, þá létu þeir ina skozku menn á land ok báðu þau hlaupa suðr á landit at leita landskosta ok koma aftr, áðr þrjú dægr væru liðin.	Then when they had sailed for Furdustrandir, they let they the Scottish people to land and asked them run south of land to seek land-benefits and coming back, before three days would-be passed.	Then when they had sailed along Furdustrandir, the put the Scottish people on land and asked them to run southwards and explore the land and come back before three days were passed.
Þau höfðu þat klæði, er þau kölluðu kjafal.	They had the clothes, that they called kjafal.	They had clothing which was called a kjafal.
Þat var svá gert, at höttr var á upp ok opit at hliðunum ok engar ermar á ok kneppt saman milli fóta með knappi ok nezlu, en ber váru þau annars staðar.	That was so made, that hood was for up and opened at sides and no sleeves of and fastened together between feet with fastening and nettle, but bare were they other places.	It was made with a hood at the top, with an opening at the sides and no sleeves, and fastened together between the feet, with a button and a loop, they were bare in other places.
Þeir biðuðu þar þá stund.	Then settled they then awhile.	Then they settled there awhile.
En er þau kómu aftr, hafði annat í hendi vínbejaköngul, en annat hveitiax sjálfsáit.	Then when they came back, had one in hand grape-vines, and another wheat self-sowing.	Then when they came back, one had grape vines in hand, and the other self-sowing wheat.
Gengu þau á skip út, ok silgdu þeir síðan leiðar sinnar.	Went they to ship back, and sailed they since route theirs.	They went back to their ship and then sailed on their way.

The Saga of Erik the Red (Old Norse)

Old Norse	Literal	English
Þeir silgdu inn á fjörð einn.	They sailed the to fjord one.	They sailed to a fjord.
Þar lá ein ey fyrir útan.	There lay an island before out-of.	There lay before it an island.
Þar um váru straumar miklir.	There about were streams great.	There were great streams surrounding it.
Því kölluðu þeir hana Straumey.	Therefore called they it Straumsey.	Therefore they called it Straumsey.
Svá var mörg æðr í eynni, at varla mátti ganga fyrir eggjum.	So was many eider-birds on island, that rarely may walk for eggs.	There were so many eider-birds on the island, that they could hardly walk for eggs.
Þeir kölluðu þar Straumfjörð.	There called they Straumfjord.	There they called Straumfjord.
Þeir báru þar farm af skipum sínum ok bjuggust þar um.	They carried there from out-of ships theirs and settled there about.	They carried there cargo from their ship and settled thereabouts.
Þeir höfðu með sér alls konar fénað.	They had with them all kinds livestock.	They had with them all kinds of livestock.
Þar var fagrt landsleg.	There was beautiful landscape.	There the landscape was beautiful.
Þeir gáðu einskis útan at kanna landit.	They heeded nothing outside-of to explore land.	They observed nothing other than exploring the land.
Þeir váru þar um vetrinn, ok var ekki fyrir unnit um sumarit.	They were there about winter, and was not before spared about summer.	They were there during the winter, and nothing had been done in preparation during summer.
Tókust af veiðarnar, ok gerðist illt til matar.	Taken of fishing, and became disorderly for food.	They took to hunting, but became bad for food.
Þá hvarf brott Þórhallr veiðimaðr.	Then disappeared away Thorhall the-Hunter.	Then Thorhall the Hunter disappeared.
Þeir höfðu áðr heitit á guð til matar, ok varð eigi við svá skjótt sem sem þeir þóttust þurfa.	They had before called to God for food, and was not with so quickly that which they thought needed.	They had afterwards prayed to God for food, and it was not as quick in arriving as they needed.
Þeir leituðu Þórhalls um þrjú dægr ok fundu hann á hamargnípu einni.	They sought Thorhall about three days and found him on cliff-top alone.	They looked for Thorhall for three days and found him on top of a cliff.
Hann lá þar ok horfði í loft upp ok gapði bæði munni ok nösum ok þulði nökkut.	He lay there and looking to sky up and gaping both mouth and nose and rattling-off something.	He lay there looking up to the sky with his mouth and nose gaping, and he was reciting something.
Þeir spurðu, hví hann var þar kominn.	They asked, why he was there come.	They asked why he had come there.
Hann kvað þá engu þat varða.	He said to-them nothing that concerned.	He said to them that it was nothing of any concern.
Þeir báðu hann fara heim með sér, ok hann gerði svá.	They asked him travel home with them, and he did so.	They asked him to travel home with them, and he did so.

The Saga of Erik the Red (Old Norse)

Old Norse	Literal	English
Litlu síðar kom þar hvalr, ok fóru þeir til ok skáru, ok kenndi engi maðr, hvat hvala var.	Little afterwards came there a-whale, and went they to and cut, and knew no man, what whale was.	Shortly afterwards there came a whale, and they went to it and carve it, and no man knew what kind of whale it was.
Ok er matsveinar suðu, þá átu þeir, ok varð öllum illt af.	And when ship's-cook boiled, then ate they, and were all ill from.	And when the ship's cook boiled it, they ate it, and everyone was then from it.
Þá mælti Þórhallr: "Drjúgari varð inn rauðskeggjaði nú en Kristr yðvarr.	Then spoke Thorhall: "Ample was the Redbeard now than Christ yours.	Thorhall then spoke: "Ampler was the Red-Beard now than your Christ.
Hefi ek þetta nú fyrir skáldskap minn, er ek orta um Þór, fulltrúann.	Have I that now for poetry mine, that I wrote about Thor, patron.	I had this now for my poem, which I wrote about Thor, my guardian.
Sjaldan hefir hann mér brugðizt".	Seldom has he me broken".	Seldom has he broken me".
Ok er menn vissu þetta, báru þeir hvalinn allan á kaf ok skutu sínu máli til guðs.	And when people knew this, carried they whale all to submerge and launched they the-matter to God.	And when people knew this, they carried the whale to cast to sea, and threw themselves on God's mercy.
Batnaði þá veðrátta, ok gaf þeim útróðra, ok skorti þá síðan eigi föng, því at þá var dýraveiðr á landinu, en eggver í eynni, en fiski ór sjónum.	Bettered then weather, and gave they out-rowing, and shortage then since not supplies, because that then were animal-hunting to land, and eggs on island, and fishing from sea.	The weather improved, and they were given to rowing, and since then they had no shortage in supplies, because they hunted animals on land, gathered eggs on the island, and caught fish from the sea.
9	9	9
Svá er sagt, at Þórhallr veiðimaðr vill fara norðr fyrir Furðustrandir ok fyrir Kjalarnes at leita Vínlands, en Karlsefni vill fara suðr fyrir landit.	So was said, that Thorhall the-hunter willed travel north for Furdustrandir and for Kjalarnes to seek Vinland, but Karlsefni willed travel south along land.	So it was said that Thorhall the Hunter wished to travel north for Furdustrandir and for Kjalarnes to seek Vinland, but Karlsefni wished to travel south along the land.
Býst Þórhallr út undir eynni, ok verða þeir eigi fleiri saman en níu menn, en allt annat lið fór með Karlsefni.	Prepared Thorhall out under island, and were there not more together than nine people, and all other company went with Karlsefni.	Thorhall prepared his ship close to the island, and there were not more than nine people together, and all the other group went with Karlsefni.

The Saga of Erik the Red (Old Norse)

Old Norse	Literal	English
En er Þórhallr bar vatn á skip sitt ok drakk, þá kvað hann vísu:	And was Thorhall carrying water to ship his and drank, then said he verse:	And as Thorhall was carrying water to their ship, he drank from it and said this verse:
Hafa kváðu mik meiðar malmþings, es komk hingat,	Shores sang me hurt metal-assemblied, when coming here,	The shores sang me hurt Metal assembled, when I came here,
mér samir láð fyr lýðum	To-me same invited for people	I have the same advice for the people
lasta, drykk inn bazta Bílds hattar verðr byttu beiði-Týr at reiða.	Load, drink the best. Axe hoods become replaced Bids-Tyr to ruling.	Loaded, drink the best. Axe hoods will be replaced Asking for Tyr's ruling.
Heldr's svát krýpk at keldu.	Rather is so that I creep to the well,	It is rather that I creep to the well,
Komat vín á grön mína.	Come wine to green mine.	Bring green wine to me.
Ok er þeir váru búnir, undu þeir upp segl. Þá kvað Þórhallr:	And when they were ready, hoisted they up sails. Then said Thorhall:	And when they were ready, they hoisted up the sails. Then Thorhall said:
Förum aftr, þar es órir	Travel-we back, there where others	We travel back to where the others
eru, sandhimins, landar,	are, sand-heaven's, land,	Are, the heavens of the sands, land,
látum kenni-Val kanna	let-us know-choose explore	Let us knowing choose to explore
knarrar skeið in breiðu, meðan bilstyggvir byggva bellendr ok hval vella Laufa veðrs, þeirs leyfa lönd, á Furðuströndum.	Ship sheathed-sword in wide, while space settle partakers and whale boil leaf weathered, they have land, to Furdustrandir.	Ship of swords in the wide, Among the space settle. Participants and boil the whale Leaf weathered, they have Land, in Furdustrandir.
Síðan sigldu þeir norðr fyrir Furðuströndir ok Kjalarnes ok vildu beita vestr fyrir.	Then sailed they north along Furdustrandir and Kjalarnes and willed applied west for.	Then they sailed north along Furdustrandir and Kjalarnes, and wished to head for the west.
Þá kom móti þeim vestanveðr, ok rak þá upp á Írlandi, ok váru þeir þar barðir ok þjáðir, ok lét Þórhallr þar líf sitt, eftir því sem kaupmenn hafa sagt.	Then came towards them west-wind, and driven they up to Ireland, and were they there beaten and enslaved, and lost Thorhall there life his, after for so trading-men have said.	Then the west wind came towards them, and they were driven up to Ireland, and there they were beaten and enslaved, and there Thorhall lost his life, so the trading men have said.

The Saga of Erik the Red (Old Norse)

Old Norse	Literal	English
Nú er at segja af Karlsefni, at hann fór suðr fyrir landit ok Snorri ok Bjarni með sínu fólki.	Now is it said of Karlsefni, that he went south along land and Snorri and Bjarni with their folk.	Now it is said of Karlsefni, that he went south along the land, with Snorri and Bjarni and the rest of their company.
Þeir fóru lengi ok allt þar til, er þeir kómu at á einni, er fell af landi ofan ok í vatn eitt til sjóvar.	They travelled along and all there until, then they came to river one, which fell from land off and into lake single to sea.	They travelled along the land until they came to a river which fell from the land into a lake, and into the sea.
Eyrar váru þar miklar, ok mátti eigi komast inn í ána útan at háflæðum.	Islands were there great, and may not come in to river out of high-tide.	There were large islands there, and they could not come into the river outside of high tide.
Þeir Karlsefni silgdu í ósinn ok kölluðu í Hópi.	There Karlsefni sailed to inlet and called it Hop.	There Karlsefni sailed to the inlet and called it Hop.
Þeir fundu þar á landi sjálfsána hveitiakra, þar sem lægðir váru, en vínvið allt þar, sem holta vissi.	There found they of land self-sowing wheat-acres, there where low-ground was, and vines all there, which hills knew.	There they found acres of self-sowing wheat, where the low ground was, and vines growing on the hills.
Hverr lækr var þar fullr af fiskum.	Every stream was there full of fish.	Every stream there was full of fish.
Þeir gerðu grafar, þar sem mættist landit ok flóðit gekk ofast, ok þá er út fell sjórinn, váru helgir fiskar í gröfunum.	They made trenches, there which may land and tide went highest, and then when back fell sea, were flat fish in trenches.	They made trenches in the land where the tide reached its highest, and then when the sea fell back, there were flat fish in the trenches.
Þar var mikill fjölði dýra á skóginum með öllu móti.	There were great many animals in forest with all met.	There were a great many wild animals of all kinds in the forest.
Þeir váru þar hálfan mánuð ok skemmtuðu sér ok urðu við ekki varir.	They were there half month and entertained themselves and became with nothing aware.	They were there half a month and entertained themselves and were not aware of anything unusual.
Fé sitt höfðu þeir með sér.	Cattle theirs had they with them.	They had their livestock with them.
Ok einn morgin snemma, er þeir lituðust um, sá þeir mikinn fjölða húðkeipa, ok var veift trjám á skipunum, ok lét því líkast sem í hálmþúst, ok var veift sólarsinnis.	And one morning early, when they looked about, saw they great many skin-boats, and were waving poles from boats, and had accordingly like as to straw-staves, and were waved sun-wise-motion.	And early one morning, when they looked about, they saw a great many hide-boats, and there were poles waving from the boats, which made a sound like a straw man, and they were waved in a sun-wise motion.
Þá mælti Karlsefni: "Hvað mun þetta hafa at teikna?"	Then spoke Karlsefni: "What could this have to betoken?"	Then spoke Karlsefni: "What could this mean?"

The Saga of Erik the Red (Old Norse)

Old Norse	Literal	English
Snorri Þorbrandsson svaraði honum: "Vera kann, at þetta sé friðarmark, ok tökum skjöld hvítan ok berum at móti".	Snorri Thorbrandson answered he: "Be-it can, that this so peace-mark, and take shield white and bear it towards".	Snorri Thorbrandson answered: "Maybe it can be a peace sign, and we should take a white shield and show it to them".
Ok svá gerðu þeir.	And so did they.	And so they did.
Þá reru þeir í mót ok undruðust þá, sem fyrir váru, ok gengu á land upp.	Then rowed they to meet and astonished they, as present were, and went to land up.	Then they rowed to meet them, and they were astonished as they came up on land to meet them.
Þeir váru svartir menn ok illiligir ok höfðu illt hár á höfði.	They were dark men and ill-looking and had disorderly hair on heads.	They were dark men, and looked threatening, with tangled hair on their heads.
Þeir váru mjök eygðir ok breiðir í kinnum.	They were much eyed and broad in cheeks.	They had large eyes and broad cheeks.
Dvölðust þeir of stund ok undruðust þá, sem fyrir váru, ok reru síðan brott ok suðr fyrir nesit.	Dwelled they about awhile and marvelled they, which present were, and rowed then away and south for headland.	They stayed around awhile and marvelled at those who were present, and then they rowed away and headed south around the headland.
Þeir Karlsefni höfðu gert búðir sínar upp frá vatninu, ok váru sumir skálarnir nær vatninu, en sumir firr.	They Karlsefni had made booths theirs up from lake, and were some cabins near lake, but some further.	Karlsefni's group made their booths up from the lake, and there were some cabins near the lake, but some further inland.
Nú váru þeir þar þann vetr.	Now were they there then winter.	They were there for the winter.
Þar kom enginn snjór, ok allt gekk fé þeira sjálfala fram.	There came no snow, and all going cattle they themselves from.	There was no snow there, and all the livestock could fend for themselves outside.
11	11	11
En er vára tók, sá þeir einn morgin snemma, at fjölði húðkeipa reri sunnan fyrir nesit, svá margt sem kolum væri sáit fyrir Hópit.	Then when spring took, saw they one morning early, that many skin-boats rowing south for headland, so many as coal were seen for group.	Then when spring came, early one morning they saw many hide boats rowing up from the south around the headland, so many that it looked like coal had been thrown across the water.
Var þá ok veift af hverju skipi trjánum.	Was then and waved of each ship poles.	They were also waving poles from each ship.

The Saga of Erik the Red (Old Norse)

Old Norse	Literal	English
Þeir Karlsefni brugðu þá skjöldum upp, ok er þeir fundust, tóku þeir kaupstefnu sín á milli, ok vildi þat fólk helzt hafa rautt skrúð.	Then Karlsefni brought then shields up, and were they met, taken their trading-posts theirs in between, and willed that people preferably have red cloth.	Then Karlsefni's company brought up their shields, and when they met them, they set up trading posts, and the people wanted to buy red cloth.
Þeir höfðu móti at gefa skinnavöru ok algrá skinn.	They had met to give skin-wares and grey skins.	They had met them with skins and gray skins.
Þeir vildu ok kaupa sverð ok spjót, en þat bönnuðu þeir Karlsefni ok Snorri.	They willed also purchase swords and spears, but that banned them Karlsefni and Snorri.	They also wanted to purchase swords and spears, but Karlsefni and Snorri banned them from purchasing them.
Þeir Skrælingar tóku spannarlangt rautt skrúð fyrir ófölvan belg ok bundu um höfuð sér.	They Skraelings took long-spanning red cloth for dark pelts and bound about heads theirs.	They Skraelings took spans of red cloth in return for dark pelts and tied the cloth around their heads.
Gekk svá kaupstefna þeira um hríð.	Went so trading-posts theirs about awhile.	And so the trading went on in this way for a while.
Þá tók at fættast skrúðit með þeim Karlsefni, ok skáru þeir þá svá smátt í sundr, at eigi var breiðara en þvers fingrar, ok gáfu Skrælingar þó jafnmikit fyrir sem áðr eða meira.	Then took to carry cloth with them Karlsefni, and cut they then so small to distribute, that not was broad but across finger, and gave Skraelings though equal for which before or more.	Then as the cloth was carried with them, Karlsefni's company cut the cloth smaller to distribute it further, so that it was narrower, about a finger's width, and the Skraelings paid just as much for it, or even more.
Þat bar til, at griðungr hljóp ór skógi, er þeir Karlsefni áttu, ok gellr hátt.	That bore towards, a bull ran from woods, which they Karlsefni owned, and bellowed loudly.	Then a bull that Karlsefni owned ran out of the woods and towards them, bellowing loudly.
Þetta fælast Skrælingar ok hlaupa út á keipana ok reru síðan suðr fyrir landit.	This frightened Skraelings and ran out of trading and rowed then south for land.	This frightened the Skraelings and they ran away from the trading posts and rowed away south around the headland.
Verðr þá ekki vart við þá þrjár vikur í samt.	Were they not noticed by them three weeks at together.	They did not notice them again for another three weeks.
En er sjá stund var liðin, sjá þeir fara sunnan mikinn fjölða Skrælingaskipa, svá sem straumr stæði.	And when seen awhile was company, saw there travelling south great many Skraelings, so as stream steady.	Then after a while their company saw travelling from the south, a great many Skraelings, like a steady stream.
Var þá trjánum öllum veift andsælis, ok ýla upp allir mjök hátt.	Were they poles all waving anti-sun-wise, and howling up all very loudly.	They were all waving their poles anti-sunwise now, and all were howling very loudly.

The Saga of Erik the Red (Old Norse)

Old Norse	Literal	English
Þá tóku þeir Karlsefni rauðan skjöld ok báru at móti.	Then took they Karlsefni red shields and bore to meet.	Then Karlsefni's company took their red shields and carried them up to meet them.
Skrælingar hlupu af skipum, ok síðan gengu þeir saman ok börðust.	Skraelings running from ship, and then went they together and battled.	The Skraelings ran from their ships, and then they went together to battle.
Varð þar skothríð hörð, því at Skrælingar höfðu valslöngur.	Were they launching hard, because the Skraelings had war-slings.	They were launching hard, because the Skraelings had catapults.
Þat sá þeir Karlsefni, at Skrælingar færðu upp á stöng knött stundar mikinn, því nær til at jafna sem sauðarvömb, ok helzt blán at lit, ok fleygðu af stönginni upp á landit yfir lið þeira Karlsefnis, ok lét illiliga við, þar sem niðr kom.	That saw they Karlsefni, that Skraelings went up to poles balls around as-big, as nearly to from equal that sheep's-stomach, and rather blue that around, and flew off poles up to land over team theirs Karlsefni's, and lay badly to, there where down came.	Karlsefni's company saw the Skraelings raised large round objects up on poles, about the size of a sheep's stomach, and blue all over, and they flew from the poles to land over Karlsefni's company, and landed terribly when they came down.
Við þetta sló ótta miklum á Karlsefni ok allt lið hans, svá at þá fýsti einskis annars en flýja ok halda undan upp með ánni, því at þeim þótti lið Skrælinga drífa at sér öllum megin, ok létta eigi fyrr en þeir koma til hamra nökkurra ok veittu þar viðtöku harða.	With that struck fear much in Karlsefni and all team his, such that they desired nothing else than fleeing and holding away up with river, because that they thought company Skraelings drove at them all ways, and let not before that they came to crags some and gave there resistance hard.	This struck great fear into Karlsefni and his men, so much so that they wanted nothing else but to flee up the river, since the Skraelings seemed to be attacking from all angles, and not stop until they reached a cliff where they could give a stiffer resistance.
Freydís kom út ok sá, at þeir Karlsefni heldu undan, ok kallaði: "Hví rennið þér undan þessum auvirðismönnum, svá gildir menn sem þér eruð, er mér þætti sem þér mættið drepa niðr svá sem búfé? Ok ef ek hefða vápn, þætti mér sem ek skylda betr berjast en einnhverr yðvar".	Freydis came out and saw, that they Karlsefni held ahead, and called: "Why run you away these un-worthy-men, so thick men that you are, that to-me seems that you may kill down such as livestock and if I had weapon, seems to-me that I should better fight than any-of you".	Freydis came out and saw that Karlsefni's company were fleeing, and called out: "Why are you running away from such unworthy opponents? such men that you are, who look to me like you could kill them as easily as livestock, and if I had a weapon I would fight them better than any of you".
Þeir gáfu engan gaum hennar orðum.	They gave no heed her words.	They paid no attention to what she said.

The Saga of Erik the Red (Old Norse)

Old Norse	Literal	English
Freydís vildi fylgja þeim ok varð seinni, því at hon var eigi heil.	Freydis willed follow them and became behind, because that she was not well.	Freydis wanted to follow them, and fell behind, because she was with child.
Gekk hon þó eftir þeim í skóginn, en Skrælingar sækja at henni.	Went she though after them into woods, but Skraelings sought towards her.	She went after them into the forest, but the Skraelings reached her.
Hon fann fyrir sér mann dauðan.	She found before their man dead.	She found in front of her one of their men who had died.
Þar var Þorbrandr Snorrason, ok stóð hellusteinn í höfði honum.	There was Thorbrand Snorrason, and stood slab-stone in head his.	It was Thorbrand Snorrason, and a stone slab was buried in his head.
Sverðit lá bert í hjá honum.	Sword lay uncovered to by him.	A sword lay unsheathed next to him.
Tók hon þat upp ok býst at verja sik.	Took she that up and prepared to protect herself.	She took that sword and prepared to protect herself.
Þá kómu Skrælingar at henni.	Then came Skraelings to her.	Then the Skraelings came to her.
Hon dró þá út brjóstit undan klæðunum ok slettir á beru sverðinu.	She pulled then out breast from clothes and slapped on open sword.	She pulled out one of her breasts from her clothes, and slapped the sword against it.
Við þetta óttast Skrælingar ok hljópu undan á skip sín ok reru í brott.	With that feared Skraelings and ran away to ships theirs and rowed to away.	With that the Skraelings became afraid and they ran away to their ships and rowed away.
Þeir Karlsefni finna hana ok lofa happ hennar.	There Karlsefni found her and praised zeal hers.	Here Karlsefni found her and praised her bravery.
Tveir menn fellu af þeim Karlsefni, en fjölði af þeim Skrælingum.	Two men fell of theirs Karlsefni, but many of them Skraelings.	Two men from Karlsefni's company fell and many of the Skraelings.
Urðu þeir Karlsefni ofrliði bornir ok fóru nú heim eftir þetta til búða sinna ok bundu sár sín ok íhuga, hvat fjölmenni þat mundi verit hafa, er at þeim sótti af landinu ofan.	Became they Karlsefni outnumbered borne and went now home after that to settlement theirs and bound wounds theirs and thought, what many that would been have, that which they encountered of land on.	Karlsefni's men were outnumbered, and they returned home to their settlement and bound their wounds, and thought what had been, which they encountered on the land.
Sýnist þeim nú sem þat eina mun liðit verit hafa, er af skipunum kom, en hitt fólkit mun verit hafa sjónhverfingar.	Seemed that now then that one could team have-been at-sea, where out-of ships came, but other people could been have illusions.	It seemed now that there could have been one team at sea where the ships came, but other people could have been illusions.
Þeir Skrælingar fundu ok mann dauðan, ok lá öx í hjá.	Then Skraelings found also man dead, and laying axe to near.	The Skraelings also found a man dead, and an axe laying near to him.

The Saga of Erik the Red (Old Norse)

Old Norse	Literal	English
Einn þeira tók upp öxina ok höggr með tré ok þá hverr at öðrum, ok þótti þeim vera gersimi ok bíta vel.	One there took up axe and hewed with tree and then each to other, and thought they was treasure and bit well.	One of them there took up the axe and hewed at a tree, and then each of them took turns trying it, and they thought it was a treasure that cut so well.
Síðan tók einn ok hjó í stein, svá at brotnaði öxin, ok þá þótti þeim engu nýt, er eigi stóðst grjótit, ok köstuðu niðr.	Then took one and struck at stone, so that broke axe, and then thought they none use, was not withstood stones, and cast down.	Then one of them took up the axe and struck at stone with it, and the axe broke, and then they thought it was of no use, as it did not withstand stone, and they threw it down.
Þeir Karlsefni þóttust nú sjá, þótt þar væri landskostir góðir, at þar myndi jafnan ótti og ófriðr á liggja af þeim, er fyrir bjuggu.	There Karlsefni thought now looked, thought there was land-benefits good, but there should equal fear and without-peace to lay of them, as before inhabitants.	There Karlsefni's company thought that although there were many benefits in that land, they would always be without peace, fearing attack by the inhabitants.
Síðan bjuggust þeir á brottu ok ætluðu til síns lands ok sigldu norðr fyrir landit ok fundu fimm Skrælinga í skinnhjúpum, sofnaða, nær sjó.	Afterwards prepared they to leave and intended towards they land and sailed north along the land and found five Skraelings in skin-sacks, sleeping, near sea.	Afterwards they prepared to leave and intended to sail north around the land, and they found five Skraelings in skin sacks sleeping near the sea.
Þeir höfðu með sér stokka ok í dýramerg, dreyra blandinn.	They had with them stock of in animal-marrow, blood mixed.	They had with them a stock made of animal marrow mixed with blood.
Þóttust þeir Karlsefni þat skilja, at þessir menn myndi hafa verit gervir brott af landinu.	Thought they Karlsefni that separated, which these people would have been made away from land.	Karlsefni's company thought that they must have been outlaws.
Þeir drápu þá.	They killed then.	They then killed them.
Síðan fundu þeir Karlsefni nes eitt ok á fjölða dýra.	Afterwards found they Karlsefni headland one and of many animals.	Afterwards Karlsefni's company found a headland that had many wild animals.
Var nesit at sjá sem mykiskán væri, af því at dýrin lágu þar um nætrnar.	Was headland to see which muck-encrusted was, of therefore were wild-animals laying there about night.	The headland looked like it was covered with dung, as the deer gathered there at night to sleep.
Nú koma þeir Karlsefni aftr í Straumfjörð, ok váru þar fyrir alls gnóttir þess, er þeir þurftu at hafa.	Now came they Karlsefni back to Straumfjord, and were there before all abundance this, as they needed to have.	Now Karlsefni's company came back to Straumfjord, where they found all in abundance, everything that they needed.

The Saga of Erik the Red (Old Norse)

Old Norse	Literal	English
Þat er sumra manna sögn, at þau Bjarni ok Guðríðr hafi þar eftir verit ok tíu tigir manna með þeim ok hafi eigi farit lengra, en þeir Karlsefni ok Snorri hafi suðr farit ok fjórir tigir manna með þeim ok hafi eigi lengr verit í Hópi en vart tvá mánuði ok hafi sama sumar aftr komit.	It was some men said, that those Bjarni and Guthrid had there after been and ten tens men with them and had not travelled further, but there Karlsefni and Snorri had south travelled and four ten men with them and have no longer been in tidal-pool but hardly two months and had the-same summer returned come.	Some say that Bjarni and Gudrid had remained behind with a hundred men and had not travelled further, and that it was Karlsefni and Snorri who went further south with forty men, stayed at Hop for not longer than two months, and returned that same summer.
Karlsefni fór þá einu skipi at leita Þórhalls veiðimanns, en annat liðit var eftir, ok fóru þeir norðr fyrir Kjalarnes, ok berr þá fyrir vestan fram, ok var landit á bakborða þeim.	Karlsefni travelled then one ship to seek Thorhall the-Hunter, but another team were remained, and travelled they north for Kjalarnes, and bore they for west from, and was the-land to larboard-side theirs.	Karlsefni then travelled with one ship to find Thorhall the Hunter, while the other tem stayed behind, and they travelled north around Kjalarnes, and they then bore west, and the land was to their port side.
Þar váru þá eyðimerkr einar allt at sjá fyrir þeim ok nær hvergi rjóðr í.	There was then deserted-forest only all to see before them and near neither clearing among.	There was then nothing to see except deserted forest before them, with no clearing among them.
Ok er þeir höfðu lengi farit, fellr á af landi ofan ór austri ok í vestr.	And were they had long travelled, falls to out-of land above out east and to west.	And after they had travelled for a long time, they reached a river flowing from east to west.
Þeir lögðu inn í árósinn ok lágu við inn syðra bakkann.	They laid in to river-mouth and laid to in southern bank.	They sailed into the mouth of the river and lay to near the south bank.
12	12	12
Þat var einn morgin, er þeir Karlsefni sá fyrir ofan rjóðrit flekk nökkurn, sem glitraði við þeim, ok æpðu þeir á þat.	It was one morning, that they Karlsefni saw before above clearing speck certain, that glittered by them, and shouted they at that.	It was one morning that Karlsefni's company saw a clearing before them, and a speck of light that glittered before them, and they shouted at it.
Þat hrærðist, ok var þat einfætingr ok skauzt ofan á þann árbakkann, sem þeir lágu við.	It stirred, and was it a-one-footer and launched down towards the river-bank, where they lay by.	It stirred, and it was a one legged creature, and it launched down towards the river bank there the ship was laid.
Þorvaldr Eiríksson rauða sat við stýri, ok skaut einfætingr ör í smáþarma honum.	Thorvald son-of-Erik the-Red sat by steering, and shot one-footer arrow into small-intestine his.	Thorvald, son of Erik the Red, sat at the helm, and the one legged creature shot an arrow into his intestine.

The Saga of Erik the Red (Old Norse)

Old Norse	Literal	English
Þorvaldr dró út örina ok mælti: "Feitt er um ístruna.	Thorvald dragged out arrow and spoke: "Bold is around belly-fat.	Thorvald dragged out the arrow and spoke: "Bold it is around the belly.
Gott land höfum vér fengit kostum, en þó megum vér varla njóta".	Good land have we found benefit, but though may we barely enjoy".	We have found good benefit from this land here, but we may scarcely be able to enjoy it".
Þorvaldr dó af sári þessu litlu síðar.	Thorvald died of wound his a-little later.	Thorvald died of his wound a little later.
Þá hleypr einfætingr á braut ok suðr aftr.	Then ran the-one-footer to away and south returning.	Then the one legged creature ran away and returned south.
Þeir Karlsefni fóru eftir honum ok sá hann stundum.	They Karlsefni went after him and saw him sometimes.	Karlsefni's company went after him and saw him sometimes.
Þat sá þeir síðast til hans, at hann hljóp á vág nökkurn.	That saw they last towards him, that he ran to inlet some.	The last time they saw him, he ran into an inlet.
Þá hurfu þeir Karlsefni aftr.	Then disappeared they Karlsefni returned.	Then he disappeared, and Karlsefni's company returned.
Þá kvað einn maðr kviðling þenna:	Then said one man verse this:	Then one man said this verse:
Eltu seggir, allsatt vas þat, einn einfæting ofan til strandar, en kynligr maðr kostaði rásar hart of stopir. Heyr, Karlsefni.	"Pursued said, true was that, a one-footer down to shore, but uncanny man exerted rushed rough about stopped. Hear, Karlsefni".	"Pursued it was said true it was a one-footer down to the shore, but the uncanny man rushed away hard of stopping. Hear us, Karlsefni".
Þeir fóru þá í brott ok norðr aftr ok þóttust sjá Einfætingaland.	They went then to away and north returning and thought saw One-Footer-Land.	Then they went away and headed back north and thought they saw One Footer Land.
Vildu þeir þá eigi hætta liði sínu lengra.	Willed they then not danger team theirs further.	They did not wish to put themselves in any further danger.
Þeir ætluðu öll ein fjöll, þau, er í Hópi váru, ok þessi, er nú fundu þeir, ok þat stæðist mjök svá á ok væri jafnlangt ór Straumfirði beggja vegna.	They supposed all same mountains, these, were among Hop was, and this, was now found they, and that place much so that also was equal-long from Straumfjord both ways.	They supposed that the mountains they saw were the same as the ones at Hop, and so that place was equally distant from Straumfjord.
Inn þriðja vetr váru þeir í Straumfirði.	The third winter were they in Straumfjord.	They spent the third winter in Straumfjord.

The Saga of Erik the Red (Old Norse)

Old Norse	Literal	English
Gengu menn þá mjök í sveitir, ok varð þeim til um konur, ok vildu þeir, er ókvæntir váru, sækja til í hendr þeim, sem kvæntir váru, ok stóð af því in mesta óró.	Went people then much to fighting, and became they to around women, and willed they, who unmarried were, seek to into hand that, who married were, and stood of therefore in most uneasiness.	Then there was much fighting among the men, as those that were not married sought after the women that were married, and there became the worst uneasiness.
Þar kom til it fyrsta haust Snorri, sonr Karlsefnis, ok var hann þá þrévetr, er þeir fóru brott.	There came to the first autumn Snorri, son Karlsefni's, and was he then three-winters, when they went away.	Karlsefni's son Snorri was born there the first autumn, and he was three winters old when they left.
Þá er þeir silgdu af Vínlandi, tóku þeir suðræn veðr ok hittu þá Markland ok fundu þar Skrælinga fimm, ok var einn skeggjaðr, konur váru tvær ok börn tvau.	Then when they sailed from Vinland, took they southern wind and met then Markland and found there Skraelings five, and was one bearded, women were two and children two.	Then they sailed from Vinland, and they were taken by a southerly wind and reached Markland, and found there five Skraelings, and one of them was bearded, two were women, and two were children.
Tóku þeir Karlsefni sveinana, en hinir kómust undan, ok sukku þeir Skrælingar í jörð niðr.	Took they Karlsefni young-men, and others went away, and sank they Skraelings among land down.	Karlsefni's company took the two boys, and the others went away, and then the Skraelings disappeared into the earth.
Sveina þessa tvá höfðu þeir með sér.	Young-men these two had they with them.	They kept these two with them.
Þeir kenndu þeim mál, ok váru skírðir.	They taught them language, and were baptised.	They taught them their language, and they were baptised.
Þeir nefndu móður sína Vethildi ok föður Óvægi.	They named mother theirs Vethild and father Ovaegi.	Their mother was named Vethildi and their father Ovaegi.
Þeir sögðu, at konungar stjórnuðu Skrælingum, ok hét annarr þeira Avaldamon, en annarr Avaldidida.	They said, that kings greatly-ruled-over Skraelings, and called one theirs Avaldamon, and another Valdidida.	They said that there were great kings who ruled over the Skraelings, one of them was called Avaldamon, and the other Valdidida.
Þeir kváðu þar engin hús.	They said there no houses.	They said they had no houses.
Lágu menn þar í hellum eða holum.	Laid people there in caves or holes.	The people slept in caves or holes.

The Saga of Erik the Red (Old Norse)

Old Norse	Literal	English
Þeir sögðu þar liggja land öðrum megin gagnvart sínu landi, er þeir menn byggðu, er váru í hvítum klæðum ok báru stangir fyrir sér, ok váru festar við flíkr ok æpðu hátt, ok ætla menn, at þat hafi verit Hvítramannaland eða Írland it mikla.	They said there lying land other side going-from their land, were their people settled, where were among white clothes and bore poles before them, and were fixed with banners and shouted loudly, and supposed people, that that had been White-man-land or Ireland the great.	The said there was another land across from theirs, where there were people settled, and they wore white clothes and carried poles before them, fixed with banners, and they shouted loudly, and they supposed that this was White Man Land or Great Ireland.
Nú kómu þeir til Grænlands ok eru með Eiríki rauða um vetrinn.	Now came they to Greenland and were with Erik the-Red about winter.	Now they came to Greenland and were with Erik the Red by about winter.
13	13	13
Þá Bjarna Grímólfsson bar í Írlandshaf ok kómu í maðksjó, ok sökk drjúgum skipit undir þeim.	Then Bjarni Grimolfson was-carried to the-Irish-Sea and came into ship-worms, and sank greatly ship under them.	Then Bjarni Grimolfson was carried to the Irish Sea and the ship was beset by worms, and the ship sank greatly beneath them.
Þeir höfðu bát þann, er bræddr var með seltjöru, því at þar fær eigi sjómaðkr á.	They had boat then, which spread was with seal-fat, because to there go not sea-worms to.	They had a boat, which had been spread with seal fat, so that the sea worms did not eat into it.
Þeir gengu í bátinn, ok sá þeir þá, at þeim mátti hann eigi öllum vinnast.	They went into the-boat, and saw they then, that they may it not all go-on.	They went into the boat, and realised that they could not all go aboard it.
Þá mælti Bjarni: "Af því at bátrinn tekr eigi meira en helming manna várra, þá er þat mitt ráð, at menn sé hlutaðir í bátinn, því at þetta skal ekki fara at mannvirðingu".	Then spoke Bjarni: "Of since the boat takes not more than half people ours, then is this my advice, that men see lots in boat, accordingly that this shall not go to rank".	Then Bjarni spoke: "Since the boat does not take more than half of our people, then I advise that we draw lots to enter the boat, and therefore this will not be decided by rank".
Þetta þótti öllum svá drengiliga boðit, at engi vildi móti mæla.	This thought all such bravely bid, that no-one willed against speak.	Everyone thought this was such a brave idea, that no one wanted to speak against it.
Gerðu þeir svá, at þeir hlutuðu mennina, ok hlaut Bjarni at fara í bátinn ok helmingr manna með honum, því at bátrinn tók ekki meira.	Did they so, to their lots men, and lot Bjarni to travel in the-boat and half the-men with him, because the boat took not more.	They did so, the people's lots were drawn, and it was Bjarni's lot to travel in the boat with half the men with him, because the boat would not take any more.

The Saga of Erik the Red (Old Norse)

Old Norse	Literal	English
En er þeir váru komnir í bátinn, þá mælti einn íslenzkr maðr, er þá var í skipinu ok Bjarna hafði fylgt af Íslandi: "Ætlar þú, Bjarni, hér at skiljast við mik?"	But as they were coming into the-boat, then spoke one Icelander man, who then was in ship and Bjarni had followed from Iceland: "Intend you, Bjarni, here to separate with me?"	But as they were coming into the boat, then an Icelander who was in the ship spoke, who Bjarni had followed from Iceland: "Do you intend to separate with me now Bjarni?".
Bjarni svaraði: "Svá verðr nú at vera".	Bjarni answered: "So becomes now to be".	Bjarni answered: "So it has now come to be".
Hann svaraði: "Öðru hézt þú föður mínum, þá er ek fór af Íslandi með þér, en skiljast svá við mik, þá er þú sagðir, at eitt skyldi ganga yfir okkr báða".	He answered: "Otherwise promised you father mine, when as I travelled from Iceland with you, than separate so with me, then as you said, that one should go over us both".	He answered: "It dos not go with what you promised my father, then I travelled from Iceland with you, that you separate with me, for then you said that we would both go as one".
Bjarni svaraði: "Eigi skal ok svá vera. Gakk þú hingat í bátinn, en ek mun upp fara í skipit, því at ek sé, at þú ert svá fúss til fjörsins".	Bjarni answered: "Not shall and so be. Go you here in boat, and I will up go to ship, because that I see, that you are so willing to live".	Bjarni answered: "It shall not be so. You go here in the boat, and I will go up to the ship, because I see that you are so willing to live".
Gekk Bjarni þá upp í skipit, en þessi maðr í bátinn, ok fóru þeir síðan leiðar sinnar, til þess er þeir kómu til Dyflinnar í Írlandi, ok sögðu þar þessa sögu.	Went Bjarni then up into ship, while this man into boat, and went they afterwards way theirs, until this when they came to Dublin in Ireland, and told they this saga.	Bjarni then went up into the ship, while this man went into the boat, and afterwards they went their way, until they came to Dublin in Ireland, and they told this story.
En þat er flestra manna ætlan, at Bjarni ok þeir menn, sem í skipinu váru með honum, hafi látizt í maðksjónum, því at ekki spurðist til þeira síðan.	And that was most people's supposing, that Bjarni and those men, which in the-ship were with him, had died in the-worm-sea, because of nothing heard for they since.	And most people supposed that Bjarni and those men who were on the ship with him had died in the worm sea, because they were not heard of since.
14	14	14
Annat sumar eftir fór Karlsefni til Íslands ok Guðríðr með honum ok fór heim í Reynines.	Next summer after went Karlsefni to Iceland and Guthrid with him and went home to Reynines.	The next summer Karlsefni went to Iceland with Gudrid and went home to Reynines.

The Saga of Erik the Red (Old Norse)

Old Norse	Literal	English
Móður hans þótti sem hann hefði lítt til kostar tekit, ok var hon eigi heima inn fyrsta vetr.	Mother his thought that he had little for choice taken, and was she not home the first winter.	His mother thought she had made a bad choice, and she did not stay at their home for the first winter.
En er hon reyndi, at Guðríðr var kvenskörungr mikill, fór hon heim, ok váru samfarar þeira góðar.	But when she experienced, that Guthrid was noble much, went she home, and was interaction theirs good.	But when she experienced that Gudrid was very noble, she went home, and their relationship was good.
Dóttir Snorra Karlsefnissonar var Hallfríðr, móðir Þorláks byskups Runólfssonar.	Daughter-of Snorri Karlsefnison was Hallfrid, Mother Thorlak's the-Bishop son-of-Runolf.	Snorri Karlsefnison's daughter was Hallfrid, mother to Thorlak the Bishop, son of Runolf.
Þau áttu son, er Þorbjörn hét.	They had a-son, was Thorbjorn named.	They had a son who was named Thorbjorn.
Hans dóttir hét Þórunn, móðir Bjarnar byskups.	His daughter was-called Thorun, mother Bjarn's the-Bishop.	His daughter was named Thorun, the mother of Bishop Bjarn.
Þorgeirr hét sonr Snorra Karlsefnissonar, faðir Yngvildar, móður Brands byskups ins fyrra.	Thorgeir was-called of Snorri son-of-Karlsefni, father-of Yngvild, mother-of Brand's Bishop the first.	Snorri Karlsefnison's son was named Thorgeir, he was the father of Yngvild, the mother of the first Bishop Brand.
Ok lýkr hér þessi sögu.	And ends here this saga.	And here ends this saga.

The Saga of Erik the Red (*Old Icelandic*)

Old Icelandic	Literal	English
1	1	1
Óleifur hét herkonungur er kallaður var Óleifur hvíti.	Olaf was-named warrior-king, that called was Olaf the-White.	There was a warrior king named Olaf, that was called Olaf the White.
Hann var son Ingjalds konungs Helgasonar, Ólafssonar, Guðröðarsonar, Hálfdanarsonar hvítbeins Upplendingakonungs.	He was son-of Ingjald's the-king son-of-Helga, son-of-Olaf, son-of-Gudrod, son-of-Halfdan White-Leg Opplands-king.	He was the son of Ingjald, the son of Helga, the son of Olaf, the son of Gudrod, the son of Halfdan White Leg, the king of the Opplands.
Óleifur herjaði í vesturvíking og vann Dyflinni á Írlandi og Dyflinnarskíri og gerðist konungur yfir.	Olaf harried to west-raiding and won Dublin in Ireland and Dublinshire and became king over.	Olaf harried on raids to the west and conquered Dublin in Ireland and Dublinshire, and made himself king there.
Hann fékk Auðar djúpúðgu dóttur Ketils Flatnefs Bjarnarsonar bunu, ágæts manns úr Noregi.	He married Aud the-Deep-Minded, daughter Ketil's Flat-Nose son-of-Bjorn Buna, excellent man from Norway.	He married Aud the Deep Minded, daughter of Ketil Flat Nose, the son of Bjorn Buna, an excellent man from Norway.
Þorsteinn rauður hét son þeirra.	Thorstein the-Red was-named son theirs.	Their son was named Thorstein the Red.
Óleifur féll á Írlandi í orustu en Auður og Þorsteinn fóru þá í Suðureyjar.	Olaf fell in Ireland in battle, then Aud and Thorstein went they to Sudreyar.	Olaf fell in Ireland in battle, then Aud and Thorstein went to the Southern Islands.
Þar fékk Þorsteinn Þuríðar dóttur Eyvindar austmanns, systur Helga hins magra.	There married Thorstein Thorid, daughter-of Eyvind the-Easternman sister-of Helga the Lean.	There Thorstein married Thorid, daughter of Eyvind the Easterner, sister of Helga the Lean.
Þau áttu mörg börn.	They had many children.	They had many children.
Þorsteinn gerðist herkonungur.	Thorstein became-a warrior-king.	Thorstein became a warrior king.
Hann réðst til lags með Sigurði jarli hinum ríka syni Eysteins glumru.	He appointed to position with Sigurd Earl the Rich, son-of Eystein Glumra.	He teamed up with Earl Sigurd the Rich, son of Eystein Glumra.
Þeir unnu Katanes og Suðurland, Ross og Meræfi og meir en hálft Skotland.	They won Caithness and Sutherland, Ross and Moray and more than half-of Scotland.	They conquered Caithness, Sutherland, Ross, Moray, and more than half of Scotland.
Gerðist Þorsteinn þar konungur yfir áður Skotar sviku hann og féll hann þar í orustu.	Became Thorstein there king over, until Scots betrayed him, and fell he there in battle.	Thorstein became king there until the Scots betrayed him and he fell in battle.

The Saga of Erik the Red (Old Icelandic)

Old Icelandic	Literal	English
Auður var þá á Katanesi er hún spurði fall Þorsteins.	Aud was then in Caithness, when she heard-of fall Thorstein's.	Aud was then at Caithness when she learned of Thorstein's falling.
Hún lét þá gera knörr í skógi á laun en er hún var búin hélt hún út í Orkneyjar.	She had then made ship in woods of hired, and when she was ready, held she out to Orkney.	She then hired a ship to be made in the woods, and when she was ready, she set out to Orkney.
Þar gifti hún Gró dóttur Þorsteins rauðs.	There gave she Gro, daughter Thorstein the-Red's.	There she gave in marriage Gro, daughter of Thorstein the Red.
Hún var móðir Grélaðar er Þorfinnur jarl hausakljúfur átti.	She was mother-of Grelod, who Thorfin Earl Scull-Cleaver married.	She was the mother of Grelod, who was married to Earl Thorfinn the Skull-Cleaver.
Eftir það fór Auður að leita Íslands.	After that went Aud to seek Iceland.	After that Aud went to seek Iceland.
Hún hafði á skipi tuttugu karla frjálsa.	She had in ship twenty men free.	She had twenty free men on her ship.
Auður kom til Íslands og var hinn fyrsta vetur í Bjarnarhöfn með Birni bróður sínum.	Aud came to Iceland and was the first winter in Bjarnarhofn with Bjorn, brother hers.	Aud came to Iceland and spent the first winter in Bjarnarhofn with her brother Bjorn.
Síðan nam Auður öll Dalalönd milli Dögurðarár og Skraumuhlaupsár og bjó í Hvammi.	Since took Aud all Dale-land between Dogurdara and Skraumuhlaupsa and settled at Hvamm.	After that, Aud took all of the Dale lane between Dogurdara and Skraumuhlapusa and settled at Hvam.
Hún hafði bænahald í Krosshólum.	She had prayer-holdings at Krossholar.	She held prayers at Krossholar.
Þar lét hún reisa krossa því að hún var skírð og vel trúuð.	Where had she raise crosses, for that she was baptised and well religious.	There she had crosses raised, for she was baptised and a devout Christian.
Með henni komu út margir göfgir menn þeir er herteknir höfðu verið í vesturvíking og voru kallaðir ánauðgir.	With her came out many noble people, they which war-taken had been among west-raiding and were called bondsmen.	Many noble people came with her, who had been taken prisoner in viking raids and they were called bondsmen.
Einn af þeim hét Vífill.	One of them was called Vifil.	One of them was called Vifil.
Hann var ættstór maður og hafði verið hertekinn fyrir vestan haf og var kallaður ánauðigur áður Auður leysti hann.	He was high-family man and had been war-taken before western sea and was-called bondsman, before Aud released him.	He was a man of noble birth and had been taken prisoner by the western sea and was called a bondsman until Aud gave him his freedom.
Og er Auður gaf bústað skipverjum sínum þá spurði Vífill hví Auður gæfi honum öngvan bústað sem öðrum mönnum.	And when Aud gave farms crew hers, then asked Vifil, why Aud gave him no abode as other people.	When Aud gave her crew farm sites, then Vifil asked why Aud had not given him a farm as she had other people.

The Saga of Erik the Red (Old Icelandic)

Old Icelandic	Literal	English
Auður kvað eigi mundu skipta, kvað hann þar göfgan mundu þykja sem hann væri.	Aud said that not would change, called he there esteemed would-be valued, wherever he was.	Aud said that it made no difference, as he would be considered a fine man, wherever he was.
Honum gaf Auður Vífilsdal og bjó hann þar.	She gave him Vifilsdal, and settled he there.	She gave him Vifilsdal, and he settled there.
Hann átti konu.	He married a-woman.	He married a woman.
Þeirra synir voru þeir Þorgeir og Þorbjörn.	Their sons were they Thorbjorn and Thorgeir.	Their sons were Thorbjorn and Thorgeir.
Þeir voru efnilegir menn og óxu upp með föður sínum.	They were promising men and grew up with father theirs.	They were promising men and grew up with their father.

2

Þorvaldur hét maður.	Thorvald was-called a-man.	There was a man called Thorvald.
Hann var son Ásvalds Úlfssonar, Yxna-Þórissonar.	He was son Asvald's son-of-Ulf, son-of-Ox-Thorir	He was the son of Asvald, the son of Ulf, the son of Ox-Thorir.
Eiríkur rauði hét son hans.	Erik the-Red was-called son his	His son was called Erik the Red.
Þeir feðgar fóru af Jaðri til Íslands fyrir víga sakir og námu land á Hornströndum og bjuggu að Dröngum.	They father-and-son travelled from Jaeren to Iceland because-of killing conviction and took land in Hornstrandir and settled at Drangar.	Father and son travelled from Jaeran to Iceland because of a conviction for a slaying, and they took land at Hornstrandir and settled at Drangar.
Þar andaðist Þorvaldur.	There died Thorvald.	There Thorvald died.
Eiríkur fékk þá Þjóðhildar dóttur Jörundar Úlfssonar og Þorbjargar knarrarbringu er þá átti Þorbjörn hinn haukdælski.	Erik married then Thjodhild, daughter-of Jorund Ulfson and Thorbjorg Knarrarbringu, who then married Thorbjorn of Haukadal.	Erik then married Thjodhild, the daughter of Jorund Ulfson and Thorbjorn Knarrarbringu, who had since married Thorbjorn of Haukadal.
Réðst Eiríkur þá norðan og ruddi land í Haukadal og bjó á Eiríksstöðum hjá Vatnshorni.	Rode Erik then north and cleared land in Haukadal and settled at Eriksstadir near Vatnshorn.	Erik then rode north and cleared land in Haukadal and settled at Eriksstadir near Vatnshorn.
Þá felldu þrælar Eiríks skriðu á bæ Valþjófs á Valþjófsstöðum.	Then fell thralls Erik's landslide on farm Vallthjof at Vathjolfsstadr.	Then Erik's slaves caused a landslide to fall on the farm at Vallthjof at Vatnhjolfsstadr.
Eyjólfur saur frændi hans drap þrælana hjá Skeiðsbrekkum upp frá Vatnshorni.	Eyolf the-Foul, kinsman his, killed thralls beside Skeidsbrekkur up from Vatnshorn.	His kinsman Eyolf the Foul killed the slaves near Skeidsbrekkur above Vatnshorn.
Fyrir það vó Eiríkur Eyjólf saur.	For that slew Erik Eyolf the-Foul.	For that Erik killed Eyolf the Foul.

The Saga of Erik the Red (Old Icelandic)

Old Icelandic	Literal	English
Hann vó og Hólmgöngu-Hrafn að Leikskálum. Geirsteinn og Oddur á Jörva, frændur Eyjólfs, mæltu eftir hann.	He slew also Raven-the-Dueller at Leikskalar. Gerstein and Odd of Jorfi, kinsman Eyolf's, spoke after him.	He also killed Raven the Dueller at Leikskalar. Gerstein and Odd of Jorvi, Eyolf's kinsmen sought judgement for his killing.
Þá var Eiríkur ger á brott úr Haukadal. Hann nam þá Brokey og Yxney og bjó að Tröðum í Suðurey hinn fyrsta vetur. Þá léði hann Þorgesti setstokka. Síðan fór Eiríkur í Yxney og bjó á Eiríksstöðum. Þá heimti hann setstokkana og náði eigi.	Then was Erik made out from Haukadal. He took then Brokey and Oxney and settled at Tradir in Sudrey the first winter. Then lent he Thorgest seat-posts. Afterwards travelled Erik to Oxney and settled at Eriksstadir. Then claimed he seat-posts and got not.	Then Erik was outlawed from Haukadal. He took the islands Brokey and Oxney and settled at Tradir on Sudurey island that first winter. Then he lent Thorgest bedstead boards. Afterwards Erik travelled to Oxney and settled at Eriksstadir. Then he asked for the bedstead boards back, but did not get them.
Eiríkur sótti setstokkana á Breiðabólstað en Þorgestur fór eftir honum. Þeir börðust skammt frá garði að Dröngum. Þar féllu tveir synir Þorgests og nokkurir menn aðrir.	Erik took seat-posts from Breidabolstad, but Thorgest went after him. There fought short from garden at Drangar. There fell two sons Thorgest's and some men other.	Erik went to Breidabolstad and took the bedstead boards, but Thorgest went after him. They fought a short distance from the farm at Drangar. There Thorgest's two sons fell along with several other men.
Eftir það höfðu hvorirtveggju setu fjölmenna. Styr veitti Eiríki og Eyjólfur úr Svíney, Þorbjörn Vífilsson og synir Þorbrands úr Álftafirði en Þorgesti veittu synir Þórðar gellis og Þorgeir úr Hítardal og Áslákur úr Langadal og Illugi son hans.	After that had either-side sitting many-men. Styrr supported Erik and Eyolf of Sviney, Thorbjorn Vifilson and sons Thorbrand's from Alftafjord, but Thorgest supported sons Thord Gellir and Thorgeir of Hitardal, and Aslak of Langadal and Illugi, son his.	After that, both sides kept a large following of many men. Erik had the support of Styrr, Eyolf of Sviney, Thorbjorn Vifilsson, and the sons of Thorbrand of Alftafjord, while Thorgest was supported by Thord Bellower, Thorgeir of Hitardal, Aslak of Langdal, and his son Illugi.
Þeir Eiríkur urðu sekir á Þórsnessþingi.	They and Erik became outlawed at Thorsnes-Thing.	Erik and his companions became outlawed at the Thorsnes Assembly.

The Saga of Erik the Red (Old Icelandic)

Old Icelandic	Literal	English
Hann bjó skip í Eiríksvogi en Eyjólfur leyndi honum í Dímunarvogi meðan þeir Þorgestur leituðu hans um eyjarnar.	He prepared ship in Eriksvog, and Eyolf hid him in Dimunarvog, while they Thorgest sought him about islands.	He prepared a ship at Eriksvog, and Eyolf hid him in Dimunarvog while Thorgest and his men searched the islands for him.
Hann sagði þeim að hann ætlaði að leita lands þess er Gunnbjörn son Úlfs kráku sá, er hann rak vestur um haf og hann fann Gunnbjarnarsker.	He told them, that he intended to seek lands these, which Gunnbjorn, son-of Ulf Crow, saw, when he-was driven west about sea and he found Gunnbjarnarsker.	He said to them that he intended to search for the lands which Gunnbjorn son of Ulf Crow saw, when he was driven west at sea and found Gunnbjarbarsker.
Hann kveðst aftur mundu leita til vina sinna ef hann fyndi landið.	He said return would seek to friends his, if he found land.	He said that he would return to seek them out if he found land.
Þeir Þorbjörn og Styr og Eyjólfur fylgdu Eiríki út um eyjar og skildu með hinni mestu vináttu.	There Thorbjorn and Eyolf and Styrr followed Erik back around islands, and separated they with the most friendship.	Thorbjorn, Eyolf, and Styrr followed Erik through the islands, and they separated with the most friendship.
Kveðst Eiríkur þeim skyldu verða að þvílíku trausti sem hann mætti sér við koma ef þeir kynnu hans að þurfa.	Said Erik to-them should be to likewise trust, if he may them with come and circumstance they him to need.	Erik said to them that they should trust that he would help them in any way if they ever needed him.
Sigldi Eiríkur á haf undan Snæfellsjökli og kom utan að jökli þeim er Bláserkur heitir.	Sailed Erik to sea from Snaefellsjokli and came out of glacier that was Blaserkur named.	Erik sailed to sea from Snaefellsjolki and came out from a glacier that was named Blaserkur.
Hann fór þaðan suður að leita ef þar væri byggjanda.	He travelled from-there south to seek, if there was habitable.	He travelled south from there to see if there was any habitable land.
Hann var hinn fyrsta vetur í Eirkseyju, nær miðri hinni vestri byggðinni.	He was the first winter at Eriksey, near middle the western settlement.	For the first winter he was at Eriksey, near the middle of the Western Settlement.
Um vorið eftir fór hann til Eiríksfjarðar og tók sér þar bústað.	About spring after travelled he to Eriksfjord and took he there settlement.	After about spring he travelled to Eriksfjord and took settlement there.
Hann fór það sumar í hina vestri óbyggð og gaf víða örnefni.	He travelled that summer into the western settlement and gave widely place-names.	That summer he travelled into the Western Settlement and gave place names widely.
Hann var annan vetur í Eiríkshólmum við Hvarfsgnípu en hið þriðja sumar fór hann allt norður til Snæfells og inn í Hrafnsfjörð.	He was second winter at Eriksholmar off Hvarfsgnipu and the third summer went he altogether north to Snaefell and then into Hrafnsfjord.	The second winter he was at Eriksholmar near Hvarfsgnipu, and the third summer he travelled all the way north to Snaefell and into Hrafnsfjord.

The Saga of Erik the Red (Old Icelandic)

Old Icelandic	Literal	English
Þá þóttist hann kominn fyrir botn Eiríksfjarðar.	Then thought he came before the-bottom-of Eriksfjord.	There he thought he had reached the head of Eriksfjord.
Hverfur hann þá aftur og var hinn þriðja vetur í Eiríkseyju fyrir mynni Eiríksfjarðar.	Turned he then back and was in third winter at Eriksey before the-mouth-of Eriksfjord.	Then he returned to winter at Eriksey at the mouth of Eriksfjord.
Eftir um sumarið fór hann til Íslands og kom í Breiðafjörð.	But afterwards about summer travelled he to Iceland and came to Breidafjord.	Then after about summer he travelled to Iceland and came to Breidafjord.
Hann var þann vetur með Ingólfi á Hólmlátri.	He was that winter with Ingolf at Holmlatr.	That winter he was with Ingolf at Holmlatr.
Um vorið börðust þeir Þorgestur og fékk Eiríkur ósigur.	About spring fought they Thorgest, and got Erik defeat.	About spring Erik and Thorgest fought, and Erik was defeated.
Eftir það voru þeir sættir.	After that were they reconciled.	After that they were reconciled.
Það sumar fór Eiríkur að byggja landið það er hann hafði fundið og hann kallaði Grænland því að hann kvað menn það mjög mundu fýsa þangað ef landið héti vel.	That summer went Erik to settle land that, which he had found and he called Greenland, because as he said people that much would desire there, if land named well.	That summer Erik went to settle the land that he had found, which he called Greenland, because as he said, people would be attracted if the land was named well.
3	3	3
Þorgeir Vífilsson kvongaðist og fékk Arnóru dóttur Einars frá Laugarbrekku, Sigmundarsonar, Ketilssonar þistils er numið hafði Þistilsfjörð.	Thorgeir Vifilson married and got Arnora, daughter Einar's from Laugarbrekka, son-of-Sigmund, son-of-Ketil Thistle who taken had Thistilsfjord.	Thorgeir Vifilson took as his wife Arnora, daughter of Einar from Laugarbrekk, the son of Sigmund, the son of Ketil Thistle who had taken Thistilsfjord.
Önnur dóttir Einars hét Hallveig.	Second daughter Einar's was-named Hallveig.	Einar's second daughter was named Hallveig.
Hennar fékk Þorbjörn Vífilsson og tók með land á Laugarbrekku á Hellisvöllum.	She married Thorbjorn Vifilson and took with land in Laugarbrekka, at Hellisvellir.	She married Thorbjorn Vifilson and took land at Laugarbrekku in Hellisvellir.
Réðst Þorbjörn þangað byggðum og gerðist göfugmenni mikið.	Moved Thorbjorn there settlement and became noble much.	Thorbjorn moved his settlement there and became a great nobleman.
Hann var goðorðsmaður og hafði rausnarbú.	He was a-good farmer and had great-estate.	He was a good farmer and had a great estate.
Guðríður hét dóttir Þorbjarnar.	Guthrid was-called daughter Thorbjorn's.	Thorbjorn's daughter was called Gudrid.
Hún var kvenna vænst og hinn mesti skörungur í öllu athæfi sínu.	She was woman fair and the most noble in all behaviour hers.	She was a fair woman and the most noble in all her behaviour.

The Saga of Erik the Red (Old Icelandic)

Old Icelandic	Literal	English
Maður hét Ormur er bjó að Arnarstapa.	A-man was-called Orm, who settled at Arnarstapi.	There was a man called Orm who settled at Arnarstapi.
Hann átti konu þá er Halldís hét.	He had a-wife, was Halldis named.	He had a wife who was named Halldis.
Ormur var góður bóndi og vinur Þorbjarnar mikill.	Orm was a-good farmer and friend-of Thorbjorn great.	Orm was a good farmer and a great friend of Thorbjorn.
Var Guðríður þar löngum að fóstri með honum.	Was Guthrid there long to foster with him.	Gudrid was fostered there and spent long periods of time with him.
Maður hét Þorgeir er bjó að Þorgeirsfelli.	A-man was-named Thorgeir who lived at Thorgeirsfell.	There was a man named Thorgeir who lived at Thorgeirsfell.
Hann var vellauðigur að fé og hafði verið leysingi.	He was wealthy in cattle and had-been made a-freed-man.	He was rich in cattle and had been made a free man.
Hann átti son er Einar hét.	He had a-son was Einar called.	He had a son who was named Einar.
Hann var vænn maður og vel mannaður og skartsmaður mikill.	He was a-fair man and well mannered and jewelled-man much.	He was a fair man and well mannered, and much bejewelled.
Einar var í siglingu landa í milli og tókst honum það vel.	Einar was among sailing between lands, and took him that well.	Einar was sailing between lands, and he took to it well.
Var hann jafnan sinn vetur hvort á Íslandi eða í Noregi.	Was he equally the winter either to Iceland or to Norway.	In winter he was equally in either Iceland or Norway.
Nú er frá því að segja eitt haust er Einar var út hér að hann fór með varning sinn út eftir Snæfellsnesi og skyldi selja.	Now is from that to say one autumn, then that Einar was in Iceland, as he came with wares his out along Snaefellstrond and wished to-sell.	From that is there now to say that one autumn when Einar was in Iceland, he came with goods to Snaefellstrond wishing to sell.
Hann kemur til Arnarstapa.	He came to Arnarstapi.	He came to Arnarstapi.
Ormur býður honum þar að vera og það þiggur Einar því að þar var vinátta við kjörin.	Orm invited him there to be, and that accepted Einar, because that there was friendship with chosen.	Orm invited him to be there, and Einar accepted, as friendship was also chosen.
Varningurinn Einars var borinn í eitthvert útibúr.	Were carried in wares his into an out-house.	His goods were carried into an outhouse.
Einar brýtur upp varninginn og sýndi Ormi og heimamönnum og bauð Ormi slíkt af að taka sem hann vildi.	Einar divided up wares his and showed Orm and housemen and invited him of to have such that he willed.	Einar divided up his goods and showed Orm and his housemen, inviting them to have whatever they wished.

The Saga of Erik the Red (Old Icelandic)

Old Icelandic	Literal	English
Ormur þá þetta og taldi Einar vera góðan fardreng og auðnumann mikinn.	Orm then that also told Einar was good traveller-generous and fortune much.	Orm accepted and told Einar that he was a good merchant, generous, and of great fortune.
En er þeir héldu á varninginum gekk kona fyrir útibúrsdyrin.	When were they busy of wares, walked woman before outhouse-door.	While they were occupied with the goods, a woman walked in front of the outhouse door.
Einar spurði Orm hver sú hin fagra kona væri er þar gekk fyrir dyrnar "eg hefi hana eigi hér fyrr séð".	Einar asked Orm, who was that in fair woman, was there going before doorway, - "I have not her here before seen".	Einar asked Orm who that fair woman was who walked in front of the doorway: "I have not seen her here before".
Ormur segir: "Það er Guðríður fóstra mín, dóttir Þorbjarnar bónda frá Laugarbrekku".	Orm answered: "That is Guthrid, foster-child mine, daughter Thorbjorn's from Laugarbrekka".	Orm answered: "That is Gudrid, my foster child, daughter of Thorbjorn from Laugarbrekka".
Einar mælti: "Hún mun vera góður kostur.	Einar said: "She would be choice good.	Einar said: "She would be a good choice.
Eða hafa nokkurir menn til komið að biðja hennar?"	Or have some men towards come to propose her?"	Or have any men come forward to propose to her?"
Ormur svarar: "Beðið hefir hennar víst verið vinur og liggur eigi laust fyrir.	Orm answered: "Proposals have for-her made been friend and lies not less for.	Orm answered: "Proposals have been made to her, but without success.
Finnur það á að hún mun bæði vera mannvönd og faðir hennar".	Finding that of that she should choosing be husband and father hers".	She shall choose her husband, and so will her father".
"Svo fyrir það", kvað Einar, "að hún er sú kona er eg ætla mér að biðja og vildi eg að þessi mál kæmir þú fyrir mig við föður hennar og legðir á alendu að flytja því að eg skal þér fullkomna vináttu fyrir gjalda.	"So therefore that", said Einar, "That she is the woman that I intend me to propose and will I to this matter come you for me with father hers and lay all thoughts to carry because to I shall you full-come friendship for expenses.	"So be it", said Einar, "she's the woman I intend to propose to, and I would like you to seek the matter with her father Thorbjorn, and give it your thoughts, how this may be so. I will repay you with the fullest friendship, that I can say.
Má Þorbjörn bóndi á líta að okkur væru vel hentar tengdir því hann er sómamaður mikill og á staðfestu góða en lausafé hans er mér sagt að mjög sé á förum.	May Thorbjorn farmer that see, to ours would-be well suits joined, for to he is famous-man great and of established good, but liquidity his is to-me said rather to going.	Thorbjorn the farmer may see we would be well joined, as he is a man of high regard with a good farm, but it is said that his means are rather depleting".

The Saga of Erik the Red (Old Icelandic)

Old Icelandic	Literal	English
En mig skortir hvorki land né lausafé og okkur feðga og mundi Þorbirni verða að því hinn mesti styrkur ef þessi ráð tækjust".	But my shortage neither land nor liquidity and us father-and-son, and should Thorbjorn be therefore this the most strength, if this takes".	But my father and I lack neither land or means, and would therefore give the most support, if this is concluded.
Ormur svarar: "Víst þykist eg vin þinn vera en þó er eg ekki fús að bera þessi mál upp því að Þorbjörn er skapstór og þó metnaðarmaður mikill".	Orm said: "Knowing think-us I friend yours be, but though am I not with my advice willing, of to bring this up, because that Thorbjorn is temperamental and though ambitious-man much".	Orm said: "Knowing that I consider myself your friend, I am though not willing to bring up this discussion, because Thorbjorn is temperamental and a very ambitious man".
Einar kveðst ekki vilja annað en upp væri borið bónorðið.	Einar said not willing another but up would-be carried proposal.	Einar said that he would not be satisfied unless the proposal was brought up.
Ormur kvað hann ráða skyldu.	Orm said his decision shall-be.	Orm said that his decision would be so.
Einar fór suður aftur uns hann kemur heim.	Travelled Einar south back, until he came home.	Einar travelled back south until he came home.
Nokkuru síðar hafði Þorbjörn haustboð sem hann átti vanda til því að hann var stórmenni mikið.	Sometime since had Thorbjorn harvest-feast, that he had accustomed to, because to him were great-men much.	Sometime after Thorbjorn had a harvest feast, that was his custom, as he was a great man.
Kom þar Ormur frá Arnarstapa og margir aðrir vinir Þorbjarnar.	Came there Orm from Arnarstapi and many other friends Thorbjorn's.	Orm came from Arnarstapi and many of Thorbjorn's other friends.
Ormur kemur að máli við Þorbjörn og segir að Einar var þar skömmu, frá Þorgeirsfelli, og gerðist efnilegur maður.	Orm came to speak with Thorbjorn and said, that Einar was there recently, from Thorgeirsfell, and became the promising man.	Orm came to speak with Thorbjorn and said, that Einar from Thorgeirsfell had been there recently, and he had become a promising man.
Hefur Ormur nú upp bónorðið fyrir hönd Einars og sagði að það væri vel hent fyrir sumra manna sakir að hluta "má þér bóndi að því verða styrkur mikill fyrir fjárkosta sakir".	Had Orm now upped proposal for hand Einar's and said to that would-be well joined for some people's sake to part "May to-you husband to therefore be steered much for financial-cost's sake".	Orm now brought up Einar's marriage proposal and said that it would be well joined on several accounts. "It may be to you be strong support in financial terms".
Þorbjörn svarar: "Eigi varði mig slíkra orða af þér að eg mundi þrælssyni gifta dóttur mína.	Thorbjorn answered: "Not expected I such words from you, that I should give thrall's-son daughter mine.	Thorbjorn answered: "I did not expect to hear such words from you, that I should give my daughter to a slave's son.

The Saga of Erik the Red (Old Icelandic)

Old Icelandic	Literal	English
Og það finnið þér nú að fé mitt þverr er slík ráð gefið mér.	And that find you now, that wealth mine decreases, is such counsel given to-me.	As you now suggest, that my wealth is decreasing, to give such advice to me.
Og eigi skal hún fara með því ef þér þótti hún svo lítils gjaforðs verð".	And not shall she with you be longer, as you thought she such little marriage-offer deserve".	And no longer shall she be with you, as you thought she deserved such a lowly marriage offer".
Síðan fór Ormur heim og hver boðsmanna til sinna heimkynna.	Afterwards went Orm home and each other guests to their households.	Afterwards Orm went home an each of the other guests went to their homes.
Guðríður var eftir með föður sínum og var heima þann vetur.	Guthrid was remained with father hers and stayed home that winter.	Gudrid stayed behind with her father and spent that winter at home.
En að vori hafði Þorbjörn vinaboð og var veisla góð búin og kom þar margt manna og var veislan hin besta.	But in spring had Thorbjorn friend-invites, and came there many people, and was the best feast.	Then when spring came Thorbjorn invited his friends to come with many people, and there was the best feast.
Og að veislunni kvaddi Þorbjörn sér hljóðs og mælti: "Hér hefi eg búið langa ævi.	And at the-feast called Thorbjorn he be-heard and spoke: "Here have in lived long life.	During the feast, Thorbjorn asked to be heard and spoke: "Here I have lived a long life,
Hefi eg reynt góðvilja manna við mig og ástúð.	Have I experienced good-will men's to me and affection.	and I have enjoyed the good will and affection.
Kalla eg vel vor skipti farið hafa.	Call I well gone have been exchanges.	I call all our dealings well done.
En nú tekur fjárhagur minn að óhægjast fyrir lausafjár sakir en hefir kallað verið hingað til heldur virðingarráð.	But now take finances mine to maintain for liquidity's sake that have called have-been here to rather worthiness.	But now my benefit begins to be uneasy for the sake of means, though so far it has been called worthy.
Nú vil eg fyrr búi mínu bregða en sæmd minni týna, fyrr af landi fara en ætt mína svívirða.	Now will I for settlement mine foreclose than honour mine lose, for of land travel but-for lineage mine shame.	Now I wish to foreclose before I lose my honour. I intend to travel from this land, rather than shame my lineage,
Ætla eg nú að vitja um mál Eiríks rauða vinar míns er hann hafði þá er við skildum á Breiðafirði.	Intend I now to visit about matters Erik the-Red friend mine that he had then was with separated at Breidafjord.	and visit my friend Erik the Red who I was separated from at Breidafjord.
Ætla eg nú að fara til Grænlands í sumar ef svo fer sem eg vildi".	Intend I now to travel to Greenland in summer, if so goes as I wish".	I now intend to travel to Greenland I summer, if it goes as I wish".

The Saga of Erik the Red (Old Icelandic)

Old Icelandic	Literal	English
Mönnum þótti mikil tíðindi um þessa ráðagerð því að Þorbjörn hafði lengi vinsæll verið en þóttust vita að Þorbjörn mundi þetta hafa svo framt upp kveðið að hann mundi ekki stoða að letja.	People thought great this change, for that Thorbjorn was befriended man, but thought knowing, that Thorbjorn would so provide that up had declared, that not should avail to discourage.	People thought this was a great change, because Thorbjorn was a popular man, but they thought that once Thorbjorn had declared this, it would be to no avail to discourage him.
Gaf Þorbjörn mönnum gjafir og var veislu brugðið eftir þetta og fóru menn heim til heimkynna sinna.	Gave Thorbjorn people gifts and was feast brought-out after this and went people home to households theirs.	Thorbjorn gave people gifts and a feast was brought out, and afterwards everyone went to their homes.
Þorbjörn selur lendur sínar og kaupir skip er stóð uppi í Hraunhafnarósi.	Thorbjorn sold land his and bought himself ship, which up stood at Hraunhafnaros.	Thorbjorn sold his land and bought himself a ship, which stood at Hraunhafnaros.
Réðust til ferðar með honum þrír tigir manna.	Hired to travel with him three tens men.	He hired thirty men to travel with him.
Var þar Ormur frá Arnarstapa og kona hans og þeir vinir Þorbjarnar er eigi vildu við hann skilja.	Was there to travel Orm from Arnarstapi and wife his and other friends Thorbjorn's, they were not willing with him separate.	There to travel with him was Orm from Arnarstapi, and his wife, and Thorbjorn's other friends, they were not willing to separate with him.
Síðan létu þeir í haf.	Afterwards left they to sea.	Afterwards they put to sea.
Þá er þeir höfðu út látið var veður hagstætt en er þeir komu í haf tók af byri og fengu þeir mikil veður og fórst þeim ógreitt um sumarið.	Then when they had out left was weather favourable and when they came to sea taken of fair-wind and caught they much weather and went they not-without-obstacle about summer.	Then when had put to sea the weather was favourable, but when they came to sea, the fair wind disappeared, and they caught a storm and they were not without obstacles all summer.
Því næst kom sótt í lið þeirra og andaðist Ormur og Halldís kona hans og helmingur þeirra.	For next came sickness among team theirs, and died Orm and Halldis, wife his, and half team theirs.	Because next there came a sickness among their crew, and Orm died, and his wife Halldis, along with half of the crew.
Sjó tók að stæra og fengu þeir vos mikið og vesöld á marga vega og tóku þó Herjólfsnes á Grænlandi við veturnætur sjálfar.	Sea took to greatly, and endured men the most toil and misery in many ways, but took though Herjolfsnes to Greenland by winter itself.	The sea swelled, and people endured the most toil and misery in many ways, but they took land at Herjolfsnes in Greenland during the Winter Nights.
Sá maður bjó á Herjólfsnesi er Þorkell hét.	So a-man settled at Herjolfsnes was Thorkell called.	There was a man named Thorkell who lived at Herjolfsnes.
Hann var nytjumaður og hinn besti bóndi.	He was useful man the best farmer.	He was a useful man and the best farmer.

The Saga of Erik the Red (Old Icelandic)

Old Icelandic	Literal	English
Hann tók við Þorbirni og öllum skipverjum hans um veturinn.	He took with Thorbjorn and all crew his about winter.	He took with Thorbjorn and all his crew for the winter.
Þorkell veitti þeim skörulega.	Thorkell provided-for them boldly.	Thorkell provided for them generously.
Líkaði Þorbirni vel og öllum skipverjum hans.	Liked Thorbjorn well and all crew his.	He was well liked by Thorbjorn and all his crew.
4	4	4
Í þenna tíma var hallæri mikið á Grænlandi.	In that time was famine much in Greenland.	At that time there was much famine in Greenland.
Höfðu menn fengið lítið, þeir sem í veiðiferð höfðu verið, en sumir eigi aftur komnir.	Had people caught little, they which to hunting had been, and some not after returning.	People that had been hunting had caught little, and some of them had not returned.
Sú kona var þar í byggð er Þorbjörg hét.	The woman was there in settlement, was Thorbjorg called.	There was a woman in the settlement who was named Thorbjorg.
Hún var spákona og var kölluð lítilvölva.	She was prophetess and was called Little-Prophetess.	She was a prophetess, and was called Little Prophetess.
Hún hafði átt sér níu systur og voru allar spákonur og var hún ein eftir á lífi.	She had descendents hers nine sisters, and were all prophetesses, and she alone was then yet living.	Among her family were nine sisters, and all were prophetesses, and she was the only one yet living.
Það var háttur Þorbjargar á vetrum að hún fór á veislur og buðu menn henni heim, mest þeir er forvitni var á um forlög sín eða árferð.	It was way Thorbjorg's about winter, that she went to feasts, and invited they people her most homes, that curious were for to know fortune theirs or season.	It was a custom of Thorbjorg's during winter, that she went to feasts, and to homes that people had invited her to, who were curious to know their fortune for the season.
Og með því að Þorkell var þar mestur bóndi þá þótti til hans koma að vita hvenær létta mundi óárani þessu sem yfir stóð.	And with because that Thorkell was there greatest landowner, then thought to him came to know, how near relieve should scarcity this, which over stood.	And with Thorkell being the greatest landowner, it was thought that he should come to know when the scarcity that stood over them would be relieved.
Þorkell býður spákonu þangað og er henni búin góð viðtaka sem siður var til þá er við þess háttar konu skyldi taka.	Invited Thorkell prophetess home, and was she there well welcomed, as custom was to, then was with this kind woman should take.	Thorkell invited the prophetess to his home, and she was well welcomed, as was the custom, when this kind of woman was received as a guest.
Búið var henni hásæti og lagt undir hægindi.	Was she prepared a-high-seat and laid under her a-cushion.	A high seat was prepared for her, and under it a cushion.

The Saga of Erik the Red (Old Icelandic)

Old Icelandic	Literal	English
Þar skyldi í vera hænsafiðri.	There should in be hen's-feathers.	This was to be filled with hen's feathers.
En er hún kom um kveldið og sá maður er í móti henni var sendur þá var hún svo búin að hún hafði yfir sér tuglamöttul blán og var settur steinum allt í skaut ofan.	Then when she came about evening and saw a-man, who meeting her was sent, then was she such ready, for she had over her mantle blue, and was set stones all in lap of.	Then when she arrived around evening, with the man who was sent to meet her when she was ready, she had over her a blue mantle, which was set with stones in the lap.
Hún hafði á hálsi sér glertölur.	She had on neck hers glass-beads.	She had glass beads on her neck.
Hún hafði á höfði lambskinnskofra svartan og við innan kattarskinn hvítt.	She had on head lamb-skin-hood black and with in cat-skin white.	She had on her head a hood of black lamb skin, lined with white cat skin.
Staf hafði hún í hendi og var á hnappur.	And she had staff in hand, and was on a-knob	And she had in her hand a staff, which had a knob on the top.
Hann var búinn messingu og settur steinum ofan um hnappinn.	It was set with brass and set stones on about knob.	It was set with brass and had stones set about the knob.
Hún hafði um sig hnjóskulinda og var þar á skjóðupungur mikill.	She had about herself a-girdle and was there on a-skin-purse great.	She wore a girdle with a large skin purse,
Varðveitti hún þar í töfur þau er hún þurfti til fróðleiks að hafa.	Kept she there in magic hers which she needed to knowledge of have.	She kept her magic in there, which she needed to have knowledge of.
Hún hafði kálfskinnsskó loðna á fótum og í þvengi langa og sterklega, látúnshnappar miklir á endunum.	She had on feet calf-skin-shoes fur and in tied long and in pewter-buttons great on ends.	She had calf skin shoes lined with fur, with long laces with pewter knobs on the ends.
Hún hafði á höndum sér kattskinnsglófa og voru hvítir innan og loðnir.	She had on hands hers cat-skin-gloves, and were white inside and furry.	She had cat skin gloves on her hands and they were white and furry inside.
En er hún kom inn þótti öllum mönnum skylt að velja henni sæmilegar kveðjur en hún tók því eftir sem henni voru menn skapfelldir til.	Then when she came in thought all people should to will her honourable greetings which she took according after which she was people agreeable to.	When she came in, everyone was supposed to give her honourable greetings. She responded to people according to how the person appealed to her.
Tók Þorkell bóndi í hönd vísindakonunni og leiddi hana til þess sætis er henni var búið.	Took Thorkell the-Farmer in hand hers and led her to this seat, which she was prepared.	Thorkell the Farmer took her hand and led her to the seat which was prepared for her.
Þorkell bað hana þá renna þar augum yfir hjörð og hjú og híbýli.	Thorkell asked her then run there eyes over herd and hearth and so settlement.	Thorkell asked her to run her eyes over the herd, the hearth, and the settlement.
Hún var fámálug um allt.	She was silent about all.	She was silent about all of it.

The Saga of Erik the Red (Old Icelandic)

Old Icelandic	Literal	English
Borð voru upp tekin um kveldið og er frá því að segja að spákonunni var matbúið.	Tables were up taken about evening, and was from since to say, what prophetess was food-prepared.	That evening tables were set up, and afterwards it was to say, what food was prepared for the prophetess.
Henni var ger grautur af kiðjamjólk en til matar henni voru búin hjörtu úr alls konar kvikindum þeim sem þar voru til.	She was made porridge of kid's-milk and food-prepared hearts of all creatures, they that there were to.	She was made a porridge of kid's milk and hearts of all animals available there.
Hún hafði messingarspón og hníf tannskeftan, tvíhólkaðan af eiri, og var af brotinn oddurinn.	She had brass-spoon and knife walrus-tusk, two-ringed of bronze, and was broken of tip.	She had a brass spoon and a knife with a walrus tusk, two halves ringed with bronze, and the tip had been broken off.
En er borð voru upp tekin gengur Þorkell bóndi fyrir Þorbjörgu og spyr hversu henni virðist þar híbýli eða hættir manna eða hversu fljótlega hann mun þess vís verða er hann hefir spurt eftir og menn vildu vita.	Then when table was up taken, then went Thorkell farmer before Thorbjorg and asked, how she thought there about it looked or how agreeable to-her were there settlements or manner people's or how soon she could aware be this, that he had asked her and men were most curious to know.	And when the tables were taken up, then Thorkell the Farmer went before Thorbjorg and asked her what she thought of the conduct of the household, the manner of people, and how soon she would know what he had asked her, and what people were most curious to know.
Hún kveðst það ekki mundu upp bera fyrr en um morguninn þá er hún hefði sofið þar um nóttina.	She considered not would say before that about morning after, when she had after slept for night.	She said that she would not say before the following morning, when she had slept about the night.
En að áliðnum degi var henni veittur sá umbúningur sem hún skyldi til að fremja seiðinn.	Then from morning to following day was she given that clothing, which she needed to have for to perform enchantments.	Then the following morning she was given the clothing that she needed to have to perform her enchantments.
Bað hún fá sér konur þær sem kynnu fræði það er þyrfti til seiðinn að fremja og Varðlokur heita.	She asked also get the women there, who knew wisdom that, which for enchantments needed and warlock-songs called.	She asked for women who had the wisdom of the enchantments needed, which were called warlock songs.
En þær konur fundust eigi.	But those women were-found not.	But those women were not found.
Þá var að leitað um bæinn ef nokkur kynni.	They were to seek to about household, if anyone knew.	The people of the household searched for anyone who knew.

The Saga of Erik the Red (Old Icelandic)

Old Icelandic	Literal	English
Þá svarar Guðríður: "Hvorki er eg fjölkunnig né vísindakona en þó kenndi Halldís fóstra mín mér á Íslandi það fræði er hún kallaði Varðlokur".	Then said Guthrid: "Neither am I of-magic nor fore-knowing-woman, but though taught Halldis, foster mine, to-me in Iceland that poem, that she called warlock-songs".	Then Gudrid said: "I am neither of magic nor prophecy, but my foster mother, Halldis, taught me chants that she called warlock songs.
Þorbjörg svaraði: "Þá ertu fróðari en eg ætlaði".	Thorbjorg answered: "Then are-you wiser than I supposed".	Thorbjorg answered: "Then you are wiser than I supposed".
Guðríður segir: "Þetta er þess konar fræði og atferli að eg ætla í öngvum atbeina að vera því að eg er kona kristin".	Guthrid said: "That is this kind-of wisdom and ceremony that I intend to nothing assist in being because that I am woman Christian".	Gudrid said: "That is the kind of wisdom and ceremony that I intend to be no assistance to, because I am a Christian woman".
Þorbjörg svarar: "Svo mætti verða að þú yrðir mönnum að liði hér um en þú værir þá kona ekki að verri.	Thorbjorg said: "So may be, that you become people to help here about, but you would-be then woman not worse than before.	Thorbjorg said: "So it may be that you may come to help here, but you would be no worse a woman than before.
En við Þorkel met eg að fá þá hluti hér til er þarf".	But with Thorkell should I evaluate to get the things for, which have need".	But I will appreciate getting the things from Thorkell that are needed".
Þorkell herðir nú að Guðríði en hún kveðst mundu gera sem hann vildi.	Thorkell hardened now to Guthrid, but she said do would as he wished.	Thorkell now hardened towards Gudrid, and said that she should do as he wished.
Slógu þá konur hring umhverfis en Þorbjörg sat uppi á seiðhjallinum.	Formed then women a-ring around the-platform, while Thorbjorg sat on up.	The women then formed a ring around the platform, while Thorbjorg sat above.
Kvað Guðríður þá kvæðið svo fagurt og vel að engi þóttist fyrr heyrt hafa með fegri raust kveðið sá er þar var.	Said Guthrid then recited so beautiful and well, that none thought heard had with more-beautiful voice poem sung, so as there was heard.	Gudrid then recited so beautifully and so well, that no one thought they had head a poem sung with more beautiful a voice, than that which they heard.
Spákona þakkar henni kvæðið.	Prophetess thanked her poem.	The prophetess thanked her for the poem.

The Saga of Erik the Red (Old Icelandic)

Old Icelandic	Literal	English
Hún hafði margar náttúrur hingað að sótt og þótti fagurt að heyra það er kveðið var "er áður vildu frá oss snúast og oss öngva hlýðni veita.	She had many spirits here to attended and think beautiful to hear that which poem was "Who before willed from us turn and us none homage grant.	She said that the many spirits have now attended who thought it beautiful to hear, as it was so well performed: "those who before turned their backs on us and refused to grant us assistance.
En mér eru nú margir þeir hlutir auðsýnir er áður var bæði eg og aðrir duldir.	And to-me are now many those things shown, which before were I hidden, and many others.	And there are now many things shown to me which before were hidden from me and others.
En eg kann það að segja að hallæri þetta mun ekki haldast lengur en í vetur og mun batna árangur sem vorar.	And I can to-you that to say to famine this should not hold longer than to winter, and should better harvest, then spring.	And I can now say to you, that this famine should not hold longer than to winter, and there should be a better harvest in the spring.
Sóttarfar það sem lengi hefir legið mun og batna vonum bráðara.	Sickness that, which to has laid, should also better-than hope sooner.	That sickness which has happened, should hopefully be better sooner.
En þér Guðríður skal eg launa í hönd liðsinni það sem oss hefir af staðið því að þín forlög eru mér nú öll glöggsæ.	And you, Guthrid, shall I reward in hand assistance that, for us have of you stood, because that your fortunes are to-me now clear.	And you, Gudrid, I shall reward in hand for the assistance that you placed, because to me your fortunes are now clear.
Það muntu gjaforð fá hér á Grænlandi er sæmilegast er til þó að þér verði það eigi til langæðar því að vegir þínir liggja út til Íslands og mun þar koma frá þér ættbogi bæði mikill og góður og yfir þínum ættkvíslum mun skína bjartur geisli.	You shall married be here in Greenland, that which honourable is, though for you will-be that not for long, because the way yours lies out to Iceland, and shall there come from you both great descendents and good, and over your family shine bright rays.	You shall be married here in Greenland, and honourably, though you will not be married for long, because your way lies out to Iceland, and there shall come from you good descendents, and bright rays will shine over your family.
Enda far nú vel og heil, dóttir mín".	End go you now whole and well, daughter".	After all, travel you now whole and well, daughter".
Síðan gengu menn að vísindakonunni og frétti hver eftir því sem mest forvitni var á.	Afterwards went people to wise-woman, and heard then each these, were most curious was of to know.	Afterwards people went to the wise woman, and then each heard that which they were most curious to know.
Var hún og góð af frásögnum. Gekk það og lítt í tauma er hún sagði.	She was also good of account. Went that also little of reins, that she said.	She gave a good answer. Things went little from the reins of what she had said.
Þessu næst var komið eftir henni af öðrum bæ og fór hún þá þangað.	This next were come after her from another farm and went she then from-there.	Following this, someone came from another farm, and she went from there.

The Saga of Erik the Red (Old Icelandic)

Old Icelandic	Literal	English
Þá var sent eftir Þorbirni því að hann vildi eigi heima vera meðan slík heiðni var framin.	Then was sent after Thorbjorn for that she willed not home be while such heathenry was committed.	Then Thorbjorn was sent for, because she did not want to be home while such heathenry was committed.
Veðrátta batnaði skjótt þegar er vora tók sem Þorbjörg hafði sagt.	Weather bettered shortly, as Thorbjorg had said.	The weather soon bettered, as Thorbjorg had said.
Býr Þorbjörn skip sitt og fer uns hann kemur í Brattahlíð.	Prepared Thorbjorn ship his and travelled there to, that he came to Brattahlid.	Thorbjorn prepared his ship and travelled until he came to Brattahlid.
Tekur Eiríkur við honum báðum höndum og kvað það vel er hann var þar kominn.	Erik took well with him with friendliness and saying that well, that he was there coming.	Erik received him well with friendliness and said how good it was that he had come.
Var Þorbjörn með honum um veturinn og skuldalið hans.	Was Thorbjorn with him about winter and household his.	Thorbjorn was with him over the winter and his household.
Eftir um vorið gaf Eiríkur Þorbirni land á Stokkanesi og var þar ger sæmilegur bær og bjó hann þar síðan.	After about spring gave Erik Thorbjorn land in Stokkanes, and was there made honourable farm, and settled he there since.	After about spring, Erik gave Thorbjorn land in Stokkanes, and there was made an honourable farm, and he settled there since.
5	5	5
Eiríkur átti þá konu er Þjóðhildur hét og við henni tvo sonu.	Erik had then a-wife, was Thjodhild named, and with her two sons.	Erik had then a wife, who was named Thjodhild, and with her two sons.
Hét annar Þorsteinn en annar Leifur.	Was called-one Thorstein, and another Leif.	One was called Thorstein, and another Leif.
Þeir voru báðir efnilegir menn.	They were both promising men.	They were both promising men.
Var Þorsteinn heima með föður sínum og var eigi þá sá maður á Grænlandi er jafn mannvænn þótti sem hann.	Was Thorstein home with father his, and was not so a-man in Greenland, as equally-handsome thought as he.	Thorstein lived at home with his father, and there was no man in Greenland thought as equally handsome as him.
Leifur hafði siglt til Noregs.	Leif had sailed to Norway.	Leif had sailed to Norway.
Var hann þar með Ólafi konungi Tryggvasyni.	Was he there with Olaf king Tryggvason.	He was there with King Olaf Tryggvason.
En er Leifur sigldi af Grænlandi um sumarið urðu þeir sæhafa til Suðureyja.	But when Leif sailed from Greenland about summer, became they sea-scattered to Sudreyar.	But when Leif sailed from Greenland that summer, the ship was driven off course to Sudreyar.
Þaðan byrjaði þeim seint og dvöldust þar lengi um sumarið.	From-there began they late, and dwelled they there long about summer.	From there they began late, and they dwelled their a long time through the summer.

The Saga of Erik the Red (Old Icelandic)

Old Icelandic	Literal	English
Leifur lagði hug á konu þá er Þórgunna hét.	Leif laid thoughts to woman there was Thorgun called.	Leif fell in love with a woman there who was named Thorgun.
Hún var kona ættstór.	She was woman noble.	She was a noble woman.
Það sá Leifur að hún mundi kunna fleira en fátt eitt.	That saw Leif that she would-be knowing more than few alone.	Leif understood that she knew much.
En er Leifur sigldi á brott beiddist Þórgunna að fara með honum.	When was Leif prepared away, asked Thorgun to travel with him.	When Leif was preparing to leave, Thorgun asked to travel with him.
Leifur spurði hvort það væri nokkuð vilji frænda hennar.	Leif asked, if that was something wished kinsmen hers.	Leif asked if that was something her kinsmen would agree to.
Hún kveðst ekki að því fara.	She said that not consider.	She said that she did not care.
Leifur kveðst eigi kunna að gera hertekna svo stórættaða konu í ókunnu landi "en vér liðfáir".	Leif said not that know-how to make captive such noble woman in unknown land, - "as we-are few".	Leif said that he did not know how make a captive such a noble woman in an unknown land - "as we have few troops".
Þórgunna mælti: "Eigi er víst að þér þyki því betur ráðið".	Thorgun spoke: "Not is certain, that to-you seems therefore better decision".	Thorgun spoke: "I am not sure there is for you a better choice".
"Á það mun eg hætta", sagði Leifur.	"At that should I though stop", said Leif.	"I will stop at that", said Leif.
"Þá segi eg þér", sagði Þórgunna, "að eg fer eigi ein saman og mun eg vera með barni og segi eg það af þínum völdum.	"Then say I to-you", said Thorgun, "That I travel not alone together and should I be with child and say I that of your doing.	"Then I say to you", said Thorgun, "That I travel not alone, and I am with child, and I say that this is your doing.
Þess get eg og að eg muni svein fæða þá er þar kemur til.	This guess I also that I shall boy bear then is there coming to.	And I also guess that I shall give birth to a boy coming.
En þóttú viljir öngvan gaum að gefa þá mun eg upp fæða sveininn og þér senda til Grænlands þegar fara má með öðrum mönnum.	But though will-you no heed of give, then shall I up feed boy and to-you send to Greenland, when travel may with other people.	But though you will not heed him, I shall bring the boy up and send him to you in Greenland, when he may travel with other people.
En eg get að þér verði að þvílíkum nytjum sonareignin við mér sem nú verður skilnaður okkar til.	But I guess, that you will-be as for-like use son's-property as now worth parting ours to.	But I guess that he will serve you as well as you have served me with your departure.
En koma ætla eg mér til Grænlands áður en lýkur".	But come intend I myself to Greenland, before it-ends".	But I intend to come to Greenland myself, before it all ends".

The Saga of Erik the Red (Old Icelandic)

Old Icelandic	Literal	English
Hann gaf henni fingurgull og möttul grænlenskan og tannbelti.	Leif gave her finger-gold and mantle Greenland-skin and tusk-belt.	He gave her gold for her finger and a mantle of Greenland-skin and a belt with ivory.
Þessi sveinn kom til Grænlands og nefndist Þorgils.	This boy came to Greenland and named Thorgils.	The boy came to Greenland and was named Thorgils.
Leifur tók við honum að faðerni.	Leif took with him to paternity.	Leif recognised him as his son.
Og er það sumra manna sögn að þessi Þorgils kæmi til Íslands fyrir Fróðárundur um sumarið.	And was that summer people said, that this Thorgils had come to Iceland before hauntings about summer.	And that summer people said that Thorgils had come to Iceland before the hauntings in summer.
En sjá Þorgils var síðan á Grænlandi og þótti enn eigi kynjalaust um verða áður lauk.	Then seen Thorgils was since in Greenland, and thought there yet not extraordinary about him to-be, before end.	Then Thorgils was seen afterwards in Greenland, and it was thought that there was something unusual about him before it ended.
Þeir Leifur sigldu í brott úr Suðureyjum og tóku Noreg um haustið.	There Leif sailed away from Sudreyar and took-to Norway about autumn.	There Leif sailed away from Sudreyar and took to land in Norway about autumn.
Réðst Leifur til hirðar Ólafs konungs Tryggvasonar og lagði konungur á hann góða virðing og þóttist sjá að Leifur mundi vera vel menntur maður.	Rode Leif to court Olaf king Tryggvason's and laid king to him good honour and thought he-saw that Leif would be well educated man.	Leif rode to the court of King Olaf Tryggvason and had good honour towards him, and thought that he was a well educated man.
Eitt sinn kom konungur að máli við Leif og spyr hann: "Ætlar þú til Grænlands í sumar að sigla?"	Once he came king to speak to Leif and asked he: "Intend you to Greenland in summer to sail?".	One time, the king came to speak to Leif and he asked: "Do you intend to sail to Greenland in summer?".
Leifur svarar: "Það ætla eg ef sá er yðvar vilji".	"That intend I", said Leif, "If that is your will".	"That I do intend", said Leif, "If that is your will".
Konungur svarar: "Eg get að svo muni vel vera.	King answered: "I guess that so shall well be.	The king answered: "I guess that shall be well.
Skaltu fara með erindum mínum að boða kristni á Grænlandi".	Shall-you travel with errand mine to preach Christianity to Greenland".	You shall travel with my purpose of preaching Christianity to Greenland.

The Saga of Erik the Red (Old Icelandic)

Old Icelandic	Literal	English
Leifur kvað hann ráða mundu en kveðst hyggja að það erindi mundi torflutt á Grænlandi en konungur kveðst eigi þann mann sjá er betur væri til þess fallinn en hann "og muntu giftu til bera".	Leif said he decide should but said thought it that errand would difficult-be in Greenland but king said none then man seen was better would-be to this fall than he "and should luck towards carry".	Leif said that the king should decide that, but that he thought the errand would be difficult in Greenland. The king said there was no one better for the task to fall to than him, "and luck shall carry you towards".
"Það mun því að eins", kvað Leifur, "að eg njóti yðvar við".	"That should therefore by likewise", said Leif, "If I benefit yours with".	"That it should be", said Leif, "if I travel with your luck also".
Leifur lét í haf þegar hann var búinn.	Leif put to sea when he was ready.	Leif put to sea when he was ready.
Leif velkti lengi úti og hitti hann á lönd þau er hann vissi áður öngva von í.	Leif drove long about and met he to lands those that he knew before none looked to.	Leif was driven about for a long time and met lands that he knew none had looked upon.
Voru þar hveitiakrar sjálfsánir og vínviður vaxinn.	Were there wheat-acres self-sowing and vine-trees growing.	There were acres of wheat that were self-sowing, and vine trees growing.
Þar voru og þau tré er mösur hétu og höfðu þeir af öllu þessu nokkur merki, sum tré svo mikil að í hús voru lögð.	There were there trees, were maple called, and had they from this all some imprint, some trees so great, that to houses were laid.	There were trees there known as burl, and they took some specimens of all of them, and some trees were so large that houses could be laid in them.
Leifur fann menn á skipflaki og flutti heim með sér og fékk öllum vist um veturinn.	Leif found people on shipwreck and brought home with him, and got all provisions about winter.	Leif found people on a shipwreck and brought them home with him, and gave them shelter and provisions over the winter.
Sýndi hann svo mikla stórmennsku og gæsku af sér.	Showed he so much greatness and goodness of him.	He showed so much greatness and goodness of himself.
Hann kom kristni á landið og hann bjargaði mönnunum.	He came Christianity to land and he saved people.	He brought Christianity to the land and saved people.
Var hann kallaður Leifur hinn heppni.	Was he called Leif the Lucky.	He was called Leif the Lucky.
Leifur tók land í Eiríksfirði og fer heim í Brattahlíð.	Leif took land in Eriksfjord and went home afterwards to Brattahlid.	Leif took land in Eriksfjord and went home afterwards to Brattahlid.
Tóku menn vel við honum.	Took there all people well with him.	People there all received him warmly.

The Saga of Erik the Red (Old Icelandic)

Old Icelandic	Literal	English
Hann boðaði brátt kristni um landið og almennilega trú og sýndi mönnum orðsendingar Ólafs konungs Tryggvasonar og sagði hversu mörg ágæti og mikil dýrð þessum sið fylgdi.	He preached soon Christianity about land and properly faith and showed people message Olaf king Tryggvason's and said, how much excellent and great glory followed this tradition.	He soon preached the faith of Christianity throughout the land and showed people the message that King Olaf Tryggvason who said how much excellence and glory followed this tradition.
Eiríkur tók því máli seint að láta sið sinn en Þjóðhildur gekk skjótt undir og lét gera kirkju eigi allnær húsunum.	Erik took since matter late, to leave tradition his, but Thjodhild went quickly behind and had made church not all-near the-house.	Erik was reluctant to take to it and leave his tradition, but Thjodhild was quick to follow and had a church made a distance away from the house.
Var það hús kallað Þjóðhildarkirkja.	Was that house called Thjodhildkirkja.	That house was called Thjodhildakirkja.
hafði hún þar fram bænir sínar og þeir menn sem við kristni tóku en þeir voru margir.	Had she there from prayers hers and they people since with Christianity took that there were many.	She held her prayers there, and with people who had since converted to Christianity, of which there were many.
Þjóðhildur vildi ekki halda samfarar við Eirík síðan er hún tók trú en honum var það mjög í móti skapi.	Thjodhild willed not intercourse with Erik, since she took faith, but he was that much against mood.	Thjodhild did not want to have intercourse with Erik since she had taken the faith, which went very much against his mood.
Af þessu gerðist orð mikið að menn mundu leita lands þess er Leifur hafði fundið.	Then therefore made words much, to people would search lands these, that Leif had found.	Then there were many words about people searching these lands that Leif had found.
Var þar formaður Þorsteinn Eiríksson, góður maður og fróður og vinsæll.	Was there chief to Thorstein Eriksson, good man and wise and popular.	Chief among them was Thorstein Eriksson, a good man, and a wise and popular man.
Eiríkur var og til beðinn og trúðu menn því að hans gæfa mundi framast vera og forsjá.	Erik was and to asked, and believed people his gifted foremost and foresight.	Erik was also asked, and people believed he was gifted and a man of foresight.
Hann var þá fyrir en kvað eigi nei við er vinir hans fýstu hann til.	He was then before that saying not no with when friends his urged him to.	He had been saying that he would not go, but his friends urged him to.
Bjuggu þeir skip það síðan er Þorbjörn hafði út haft og voru til ráðnir tuttugu menn.	Prepared they ship that since which Thorbjorn had out had and was to appointed twenty people.	There was a ship prepared, the one which Thorbjorn had sailed out on, and twenty men were hired.
Höfðu þeir fé lítið en meir vopn og vistir.	Had they cattle little but more weapons and provisions.	They had a little cattle, but more weapons and provisions.

The Saga of Erik the Red (Old Icelandic)

Old Icelandic	Literal	English
Þann morgun er Eiríkur fór heiman tók hann kistil og var þar í gull og silfur.	That morning, was Erik riding home, took he one chest, and was there of gold and silver.	That morning, Erik was rode home, he took a chest, and therein was gold and silver.
Fal hann það fé og fór síðan leiðar sinnar.	Hid he that wealth and went afterwards way his.	He hid that and then travelled away afterwards.
Og er hann var skammt á leið kominn féll hann af baki og braut rif sín og lesti öxl sína og kvað við: "Ái, ái".	And when he was shortly on the-way coming fell he from back and broke ribs his and gripped shoulder his and said with: "Ai ái".	And when he had come a short distance, he fell back from the horse, and broke his ribs, and gripped his hand to his shoulder: "Ai! Ai!"
Af þessum atburð sendi hann konu sinni orð, að hún tæki féið á brott það er hann hafði fólgið, lét þess hafa að goldið er hann hafði féið fólgið.	Of these events said he Thjodhild, wife his, that she take treasure to away, should this have of gold, that he had wealth hidden.	He said to his wife Thjodhild what had happened, and asked her to take the treasure hidden away, and have this gold that he had hidden.
Síðan sigldu þeir út úr Eiríksfirði með gleði og þótti vænt um sitt ráð.	Since sailed they out from Eriksfjord with gladness and thought expected about their advice.	Afterwards they sailed out of Eriksfjord with much gladness. They thought expectantly about their prospects.
Þá velkti lengi úti í hafi og komu ekki á þær slóðir sem þeir vildu.	Then drove about long at sea, and came they not to those routes, which they willed.	Then they were driven about at sea for a long time, and did not come to those routes which they had wished.
Þeir komu í sýn við Ísland og svo höfðu þeir fugl af Írlandi.	They came it seemed to Iceland, and so had they birds of Ireland.	They came in sight of what seemed like Iceland they had birds of Ireland.
Reiddi þá skip þeirra um haf innan, fóru aftur um haustið og voru mæddir og mjög þrekaðir og komu við vetur sjálfan á Eiríksfjörð.	Driven then ship theirs about sea within, travelled back about autumn and were all-very worn and exhausted, came in winter itself to Eriksfjord.	Their ship was driven about the sea, and they travelled back about autumn, and all were very weary and exhausted, as winter was coming to Eriksfjord.
Þá mælti Eiríkur: "Kátari voruð þér í sumar er þér fóruð út úr firðinum en nú erum vér og eru nú þó mörg góð að".	Then said Erik: "Merrier sailed we this summer out from fjord than now are we, and are now though still many good to".	Then Erik said: "We sailed more merrily in the summer out of this fjord than we now return to it, but there is still much good".
Þorsteinn mælti: "Það er nú höfðinglegt bragð að sjá nokkuð ráð fyrir þeim mönnum sem nú eru ráðlausir og fá þeim vistir".	Thorstein answered: "That is now having-like solution to see some good proposal for those people all, which here are now disposed, and get they provisions to winter".	Thorstein answered: "Now we should propose that these people here are given provisions for the winter".

The Saga of Erik the Red (Old Icelandic)

Old Icelandic	Literal	English
Eiríkur svarar: "Skal þín orð um þetta fara".	Erik answered: "Shall your words about this go".	Erik answered: "Your words about this shall travel".
Fóru nú allir þeir er eigi höfðu áður vistir með þeim feðgum.	Went now all they, who not had other supplies, with they father-and-son.	All those who had no provisions with the father and son.
Síðan tóku þeir land og fóru heim.	Afterwards took they land and travelled home.	Afterwards they took land and travelled home.
6	6	6
Nú er frá því að segja að Þorsteinn Eiríksson vakti bónorð við Guðríði Þorbjarnardóttur.	Now is from accordingly to say that Thorstein Eriksson awoke proposal to Guthrid Thorbjornadottir.	Now following this is to say that Thorstein Eriksson brought up a marriage proposal to Gudrid Thorbjornadottir.
Var því máli vel svarað bæði af henni og svo af föður hennar og er þetta að ráðum gert að Þorsteinn gekk að eiga Guðríði og var brúðkaupið í Brattahlíð um haustið.	Was accordingly the-matter well answered both from her and so of father hers and was that the advice done that Thorstein went to marry Guthrid and was the-wedding in Brattahlid about autumn.	Accordingly the matter was well answered by both her and her father, and that which was planned was done, that Thorstein went to marry Gudrid and the wedding was in Brattahlid around autumn.
Fór sú veisla vel fram og var mjög fjölmenn.	Went seen the-feast well from, and were many-people.	The feast was well witnessed, and there were many people there.
Þorsteinn átti bú í Vestribyggð á bæ þeim er í Lýsufirði heitir.	Thorstein had a-farm in Vestribyggd in town theirs, was named it Lysufjord.	Thorstein had a farm in the Western Settlement in the worn, which was named Lysufjord.
Sá maður átti þar helming í búi er Þorsteinn hét.	But so a-man had there half a farm, was Thorstein called.	There was a man there that had a half share of a farm, who was named Thorstein.
Sigríður hét kona hans.	Sigrid was-called wife his.	His wife was named Sigrid.
Fóru þau Þorsteinn heim í Lýsufjörð og Guðríður bæði.	Went Thorstein to Lysufjord about autumn to namesake his and they Guthrid both.	They went to Lysufjord around autumn to both his namesake and Gudrid.
Var þar vel við þeim tekið.	Were there with them well taken.	They were well received by them.
Voru þau þar um veturinn.	Were they there about winter.	They were there around winter.
Það gerðist þar til tíðinda að sótt kom í bæ þeirra er lítið var af vetri.	That happened until news, that sickness came among settlement theirs, that little was from winter.	Then came the news, that sickness came among their settlement, shortly after the beginning of winter.

The Saga of Erik the Red (Old Icelandic)

Old Icelandic	Literal	English
Garði hét þar verkstjóri.	Gardi was-called there a-foreman.	There was a foreman there who was named Gardi.
Hann var óvinsæll maður.	He was not popular a-man.	He was not a popular man.
Hann tók fyrst sótt og andaðist.	He took first sickness and died.	He was the first to become ill, and he died.
Síðan var skammt að bíða að hver tók sótt að öðrum og önduðust.	Since was short to wait, that each died the others.	It was not long after that, that each of the others died.
Þá tók sótt Þorsteinn Eiríksson og Sigríður kona Þorsteins.	Then took sickness Thorstein Eriksson and Sigrid, wife Thorstein's, namesake his.	Then the sickness took Thorstein Eriksson, and his namesake's wife Sigrid.
Og eitt kveld fýsist hún að ganga til garðs þess er stóð í gegnt útidyrum.	And one evening desired Sigrid to go to outhouse, which stood about opposite the-out-door.	And one evening, Sigrid wanted to go to the outhouse, which stood opposite the farmhouse door.
Guðríður fylgdi og sóttu þær í mót dyrunum.	Guthrid followed her, and looked they towards the-out-door.	Gudrid followed her, and they looked towards the farmhouse door.
Þá kvað Sigríður: "Ó".	Then cried-out she with loud, Sigrid "Oh!".	Then Sigrid cried out loudly "Oh!".
Guðríður mælti: "Við höfum farið óhyggilega og áttu öngvan stað við að kalt veður komi á og förum inn sem skjótast".	Guthrid said: "We have unwisely gone, and have-you none stand with, that cold comes to you, and go into home then quickly".	Gudrid said: "We have acted carelessly, you should not stand in the cold, and we must go inside quickly".
Sigríður svarar: "Eigi fer eg að svo búnu.	Sigrid answered: "Not am-i going-out as so are.	Sigrid answered: "I won't go out with things as they are.
Hér er liðið allt hið dauða fyrir dyrunum og þar í sveit kenni eg Þorstein bónda þinn og kenni eg mig og er slíkt hörmung að sjá".	Here is now company that all to death before the-door and Thorstein, husband yours, and there recognise I me. And is such horrible to see".	Here are now all the companions that died standing there before the door, and Thorstein your husband, and there I recognise myself. And it is such a horrible thing to see".
Og er þetta leið af mælti hún: "Förum við nú Guðríður.	And when that passed out-of, spoke she: "Gone known now, Guthrid.	And when it had passed, she spoke: "They are gone now Gudrid".
Nú sé eg eigi liðið".	Now see I not company".	Now I don't see those companions".

The Saga of Erik the Red (Old Icelandic)

Old Icelandic	Literal	English
Var þá og verkstjórinn horfinn er henni þótti áður hafa svipu í hendi og vilja berja liðið.	Was then also the-foreman disappeared that she thought returned had whip in hand and willing to-bear-to company.	It was then that the foreman had disappeared. She thought he had returned with a whip in hand ready and willing to strike those companions.
Síðan gengu þær inn og áður morgunn kæmi var hún önduð og var ger kista að líkinu.	Afterwards went they in, and before morning came, then was she dead, and was made coffin for body.	Afterwards they went inside, and before the morning came, she was dead, and a coffin was made for her body.
Og þann sama dag ætluðu menn út að róa og leiddi Þorsteinn þá til vara og í annan lit fór hann að sjá um veiðiskap þeirra.	And then same day intended people out to row and led Thorstein they to wares and to accompany the-team went he to see about fishing there.	And then that same day people intended to row and go fishing, and they led Thorstein to where the goods were kept, and he went to see how the fishing was going.
Þá sendi Þorsteinn Eiríksson nafna sínum orð að hann kæmi til hans og sagði svo að þar var varla kyrrt og húsfreyja vildi færast á fætur og vildi undir klæðin hjá honum.	Then sent Thorstein Eriksson namesake his word, that he come to him, and said such, that there was hardly peace and housewife willed move to feet and willing under bed-clothes by him.	Then Thorstein Eriksson sent his namesake his word to come to him, and said that there was no peace at home and his housewife was trying to rise up and get into bed with him.
Og er hann kom inn var hún komin á rekkjustokkinn hjá honum.	And when he came in, was she coming up to sideboards.	And when he came in, she had reached the sideboards of the bed.
Hann tók hana höndum og lagði bolöxi fyrir brjóstið.	Then took he her hand and laid a-pole-axe for breast hers.	Then he took her hand and drove an axe into her breast.
Þorsteinn Eiríksson andaðist nær dagsetri.	Thorstein Eriksson died near day-setting.	Thorstein Eriksson died close to sunset.
Þorsteinn bað Guðríði leggjast niður og sofa en hann kveðst vaka mundu um nóttina yfir líkunum.	Thorstein farmer asked Guthrid ti-lie down and sleep, and he said awake would-be about night over the-bodies.	Thorstein the Farmer told Gudrid to lie down and sleep, and he said that he would keep watch over the bodies.
Hún gerir svo.	She did so.	She did so.

The Saga of Erik the Red (Old Icelandic)

Old Icelandic	Literal	English
Guðríður sofnar brátt og er skammt leið á nóttina reistist hann upp Þorsteinn og kveðst vilja að Guðríður væri þangað kölluð og kveðst vilja mæla við hana: "Guð vill að þessi stund sé mér gefin til leyfis og umbóta míns ráðs".	Guthrid slept soon, and that short way in night, sat Thorstein Eriksson up and spoke, saying willed, that Guthrid was there called, and saying he-willed to-speak with her: "God wills, that this time so me given to leave and offer my plans".	Gudrid soon slept, and a short way into the night, Thorstein Eriksson sat up and spoke, saying that he wished for Gudrid to be called, as he willed to speak with her. "God wills that this time has been given to me to better my prospects".
Þorsteinn gengur á fund Guðríðar og vakti hana og bað hana signa sig og biðja sér guð hjálpa "Þorsteinn Eiríksson hefur mælt við mig að hann vill finna þig.	Thorstein went to find Guthrid and woke her and asked her to sign-herself and ask herself God's help, "Thorstein Eriksson had said to me that he wills find you.	Thorstein the Farmer went to find Gudrid and woke her, asking her to sign herself with the cross, and to ask for God's help, "Thorstein Eriksson has said to me that he wishes to meet you.
Sjá þú nú ráð fyrir, hvorgis kann eg fýsa".	See you now obliged for, neither know I desire".	Are you obliged to see what you will learn from this?, for I will not advise you either way".
Hún svarar: "Vera kann að þetta sé ætlað til nokkurra hluta þeirra sem síðan eru í minni hafðir, þessi hinn undarlegi hlutur, en eg vænti að guðs gæsla mun yfir mér standa.	She answered: "Be it possible that this intends to something part there which afterwards are to mine have, this the strange lot, but I expect that God's herding shall over me stand.	She answered: "Could it possibly be that there is some purpose to this, which afterwards will have consequences for me, this strange occurrence, but I hope that God will shepherd over me".
Mun eg á hætta með guðs miskunn að mæla við hann því að eg má nú ekki forðast mein til mín.	Should I to danger with God's mercy to speak with him because that I may now not avoid harm to mine.	I will to chance, with God's mercy, to speak with him, because I may not escape any threat to myself.
Vil eg síður að hann gangi víðara.	Will I less that he go far-and-wide.	I do not wish for him to have to go further and wider.
En mig grunar að það sé að öðrum kosti".	But I suspect that it so to other choice".	And I suspect that it would be the alternative choice".

The Saga of Erik the Red (Old Icelandic)

Old Icelandic	Literal	English
Nú fór Guðríður og hitti Þorstein og sýndist henni sem hann felldi tár og mælti í eyra henni nokkur orð hljótt svo að hún ein vissi og sagði að þeir menn væru sælir er trúna héldu vel og henni fylgdi miskunn og hjálp og sagði þó að margir héldu hana illa "er það engi háttur sem hér hefir verið á Grænlandi síðan kristni var hér að setja menn niður í óvígða mold við litla yfirsöngva.	Now came Guthrid and met Thorstein and seemed to-her that he shed tears and spoke in ear hers some words quietly so that she alone knew and said that they people were happy that faith held well and he followed mercy and help and said though that many held he badly "Is that no way which here has been in Greenland after Christianity was here to set people down among unconsecrated ground with little burial-service.	Now Gudrid came and met Thorstein. It seemed to her that he had shed tears. He spoke some words in her ear quietly, so that she alone knew, and he said that those men who had kept their faith well rejoiced as it brought them mercy and salvation, but he said that some had kept their faith badly though. "It is no way to set people down among unconsecrated dust with little burial service, which people have done here in Greenland since Christianity came here.
Vil eg mig láta flytja til kirkju og aðra þá menn sem hér hafa andast en Garða vil eg láta brenna á báli sem skjótast því að hann veldur öllum afturgöngum sem hér hafa orðið í vetur.	Will I me laid carried to church and others they people, which here have died, but Gardar will I burn let to fire that quickly, because that he caused all hauntings those, which here have been in winter".	I wish that I be carried to church, along with the other people who have died here, but Gardi should be burned on a pyre straight away, because he caused all those hauntings which were here in winter".
Hann sagði henni og um sína hagi og kvað hennar forlög mikil mundu verða en hann bað hana varast að giftast grænlenskum manni.	He told her and about his state and said her fortune great would be but he asked that avoid to marry Greenlander men.	He told her about his situation and said that her fortune would be great, but warned her against marrying a Greenlander.
Bað hann og að hún legði fé þeirra til kirkju eða gefa það fátækum mönnum.	Asked he also that she lay wealth theirs to church or give that-to poor people.	He also asked that she donate their wealth to the church, and to the poor.
Og þá hneig hann aftur í öðru.	And then knee he back second his.	And then he sank back down for the second time.
Sá hafði háttur verið á Grænlandi síðan kristni kom út þangað að menn voru grafnir þar á bæjum, er menn önduðust, í óvígðri moldu.	So had the-way been in Greenland, since Christianity came there, that people were buried in farms, there which died, in unconsecrated ground.	So had been the way in Greenland, since Christianity arrived there, that people were buried in farms where they died in unconsecrated ground.

The Saga of Erik the Red (Old Icelandic)

Old Icelandic	Literal	English
Skyldi setja staur upp af brjósti en síðan er kennimenn komu til þá skyldi kippa upp staurnum og hella þar í vígðu vatni og veita þar yfirsöngva þótt það væri miklu síðar.	As-should-be set poles up on breast in the-dead, then after, a priest came to, then should-be up pulled poles and flat-stones there among ground water and supplied there burial-service, though that was much later.	A pole was set up on the breast of each corpse, then afterwards there came a priest, then the poles were pulled up, and flat stones placed on the ground, and consecrated water poured into the hole with a burial service, even though this was done much later.
Líkin voru færð til kirkju í Eiríksfjörð og veittir yfirsöngvar af kennimönnum.	Body was taken to church in Eriksfjord and supplied burial-service from priests.	The body was taken to church in Eriksfjord and priests held burial services.
Eftir það andaðist Þorbjörn. Bar þá féið allt undir Guðríði.	After that died Thorbjorn. Bore then wealth all up-to Guthrid.	After that Thorbjorn died. All of his wealth was given up to Gudrid.
Tók Eiríkur við henni og sá vel um kost hennar.	Took Erik with her and saw well about costs hers.	Erik invited her to live with him and saw that she was well provided for.
7	7	7
Maður hét Þorfinnur karlsefni, son Þórðar hesthöfða, er bjó norður í Reyninesi í Skagafirði er nú er kallað.	A-man was-called Thorfin Karlsefni, son-of-Thord Horse-Head, who lived north in Reynines in Skagafjord as now is called.	There was a man called Thorfin Karlsefni, the son of Thord Horse-Head, who lived in the north in Reynines in Skagafjord, as it is now called.
Karlsefni var ættgóður maður og auðigur að fé.	Karlsefni was family-good man and wealthy in cattle.	Karlsefni was a man of good family and was wealthy in cattle.
Þórunn hét móðir hans. Hann var í kaupferðum og þótti fardrengur góður.	Thorun was-called mother his. He was on trading-journeys and thought travelling-companion good.	His mother was called Thorun. He went on trading journeys and was thought of as a good travelling companion.
Eitt sumar býr Karlsefni skip sitt og ætlaði til Grænlands.	One summer prepared Karlsefni ship his and intended to Greenland.	One summer Karlsefni intended to go to Greenland and prepared his ship.
Réðst til ferðar með honum Snorri Þorbrandsson úr Álftafirði og voru fjórir tigir manna með þeim.	Rode to travel with him Snorri Thorbrandson from Alftafjord and was four tens men with them.	Shorri Thorbrandson rode with him from Alftafjord and there were forty men with them.

The Saga of Erik the Red (Old Icelandic)

Old Icelandic	Literal	English
Maður hét Bjarni Grímólfsson, breiðfirskur maður.	A-man was-called Bjarni Grimolfson, Breidafjord man.	There was a man called Bjarni Grimolfson, a man from Breidafjord.
Annar hét Þórhallur Gamlason, austfirskur maður.	Another was-called Thorhall Gamlason, east-fjords man.	Another was called Thorhall Gamlason, a man from the East Fjords.
Þeir bjuggu skip sitt samsumars sem Karlsefni og ætluðu til Grænlands.	There prepared ship theirs same-summer as Karlsefni and intended to Greenland.	There they prepared their ship that summer as Karlsefni intended to go to Greenland.
Þeir voru á skipi fjórir tigir manna.	They were to ship four tens men.	There were forty men on the ship.
Láta þeir í haf fram tvennum skipum þegar þeir eru búnir.	Had they to sea from two ships when they were ready.	They had the two ships put to sea as soon as they were ready.
Eigi var um það getið hversu langa útivist þeir höfðu, en frá því er að segja að bæði þessi skip komu í Eríksfjörð um haustið.	Not is about that told-of, how long out-journey they had, but from since was to say, that both these ships came to Eriksfjord about autumn.	Not much was said about how long a journey they had, but since was said that both these ships came to Eriksfjord about autumn.
Eiríkur reið til skips og aðrir landsmenn og tókst með þeim greiðleg kaupstefna.	Erik rode to ships and other landsmen and took with them promptly trading-posts.	Erik rode to the ships along with other men of the land, and they promptly took trading posts with them.
Buðu stýrimenn Eiríki að hafa slíkt af varninginum sem hann vildi.	Invited steersmen Erik to have such of wares that he willed.	The captains invited Erik to have whatever goods he wanted.
En Eiríkur sýni mikla stórmennsku af sér í móti því að hann bauð þessum skipverjunum báðum heim til sín til veturvistar í Brattahlíð.	Then Erik showed them great-man-ness of him among towards, for that he invited these two ships-ports to his home about winter to Brattahlid.	Erik then showed them great generosity, as he invited these two ships to his home for the winter at Brattahlid.
Þetta þágu kaupmenn og fóru með Eiríki.	This accepted trading-men and went with Erik.	The traders accepted this and travelled with Erik.
Síðan var fluttur heim varningur þeirra í Brattahlíð.	Then were transported home goods theirs to Brattahlid.	Later their goods were transported to Brattahlid.
Skorti þar eigi góð og stór útibúr að varðveita í.	Shortage there was-not good and great out-house of supplies to.	There was no shortage of good and large outhouses for their goods.
Líkaði kaupmönnum vel með Eiríki um veturinn.	Liked trading-men well with Erik about winter.	The traders very much enjoyed their winter with Erik.

The Saga of Erik the Red (Old Icelandic)

Old Icelandic	Literal	English
En er dró að jólum tók Eiríkur að verða óglaðari en hann átti vanda til.	But as drew to Yule, took Erik sadness much and was without-gladness that he had custom to.	But as it drew closer to Yule, Erik became sad and was without the cheerfulness that he usually had.
Eitt sinn kom Karlsefni að máli við Eirík og mælti: "Er þér þungt Eiríkur? Eg þykist finna að þú ert nokkuru fálátari en verið hefir, og þú veitir oss með mikilli rausn og erum vér skyldir að launa þér eftir því sem vér höfum föng á.	Along then came Karlsefni to speak with Erik and said: "Are you unhappy Erik I think find that you are somewhat withdrawn that been have, and you gave us with much generosity and are we obliged to repay you after because that we have possessions of.	Then along came Karlsefni to talk to Erik and said: "Are you unhappy, Erik the farmer? People seem to find that you are unhappier than usual. You have provided for us most generously, and we are obliged to repay you as best we can with everything we have.
Nú segðu hvað ógleði þinni veldur".	Now say, what sadness yours brought-about".	Now tell me, what is it that makes you sad?".
Eiríkur svarar: "Þér þiggið vel og góðmannlega.	Erik answered: "You accepted well and good-man-like.	Erik answered: "You have accepted with gratitude and respect.
Nú leikur mér það eigi í hug að á yður hallist um vor viðskipti.	Now like I that not in mind, that for you have-been inclined about what-was exchanged.	To my mind, you have not been lacking in our exchanges.
Hitt er heldur að mér þykir illt ef að er spurt að þér hafið engi jól verri haft en þessi er nú koma í hönd".	I find it rather ill if that are asked of you, have none Yule worse had than this is now coming in hand".	I find it rather bad, if you are asked, that you will have had no Yule worse than this one now approaching".
Karlsefni svarar: "Það mun ekki á þá leið.	Karlsefni answered: "That shall not so go".	Karlsefni answered: "It shall not be that way".
Vér höfum á skipum vorum malt og mjöl og korn og er yður heimilt að hafa af slíkt sem þér viljið og gerið veislu slíka sem stórmennsku ber til".	"We have in ships ours both malt and corn, have there of such that you will and make feast such great-man-ness as you like for according".	"We have malt and flour and grain aboard our ships, and you will have whatever you wish to make such a great feast according to your generosity".
Og það þiggur hann.	And that accepted he.	And he accepted this.
Var þá búið til jólaveislu og varð hún svo skörugleg að menn þóttust trautt slíka rausnarveislu séð hafa.	Were then preparations until Yule-feast and was it so honourable that people thought scarcely such generosity seen had.	There were then preparations for the Yule feast, and it was so honourable, and people thought that they had scarcely seen such generosity.

The Saga of Erik the Red (Old Icelandic)

Old Icelandic	Literal	English
Og eftir jólin vekur Karlsefni við Eirík um ráðahag við Guðríði er honum leist sem það mundi á hans forræði en honum leist kona fríð og vel kunnandi.	And after Yule awoke Karlsefni to Erik about marriage-proposal to Guthrid was he impression that it could by him power and he liked woman peaceful and well knowing.	And after Yule, Karlsefni brought up a marriage proposal to Erik about Gudrid, as he was under the impression that he had protection of her, and peaceful and knowledgeable.
Eiríkur svarar, kveðst vel mundu undir taka hans mál en kvað hana góðs gjaforð verða "er það og líklegt að hún fylgi sínum forlögum" þó að hún væri honum gefin og kvað góða frétt af honum koma.	Erik answered, saying well would up-to take his matter then said he good given was "Is that also likely to her follow her fortune" though that she would him marry and said good news of him came.	Erik answered, saying that he would support him in this matter, and said that it was a good match, and said "It is also likely that she will follow her fortune" if she did marry him, and said that there came good news of him.
Nú er vakið mál við hana og lét hún það sitt ráð sem Eiríkur vildi fyrir sjá.	Now was awoken the-matter with her and allowed she that his advice which Erik wished for seen.	Now the matter was brought up with her, and she allowed herself to be guided by Erik's advice.
Og er nú ekki að lengja um það að þessi ráð tókust og var þá veisla aukin og gert brullaup.	And was now not that long about that of this advice took and was then the-feast increased and made wedding.	It was not long after this advice was taken that the feast increased and the wedding was made.
Gleði mikið var í Brattahlíð um veturinn.	Gladness much was in Brattahlid about winter.	There was much gladness in Brattahlid over the winter.
8	8	8
Á því léku miklar umræður um veturinn í Brattahlíð að þar voru mjög töfl uppi höfð og sagnaskemmtan og margt það er til híbýlabótar mátti vera.	Then since played much discussion about winter in Brattahlid that there were many table-games up taken and short-stories and many that were to living-space that-might be.	Then there played out much discussion over the winter in Brattahlid, and there were many table games set up and short stories, and many things that might be done to improve living space.
Ætluðu þeir Karlsefni og Snorri að leita Vínlands og töluðu menn margt um það.	Intended there Karlsefni and Snorri to seek Vinland and talked people many about that.	Karlsefni and Snorri intended to seek Vinland and many people talked about it.
En því lauk svo að þeir Karlsefni og Snorri bjuggu skip sitt og ætluðu að leita Vínlands um sumarið.	Then therefore concluded so that they Karlsefni and Snorri prepared ship theirs and intended to seek Vinland about summer.	Then it was settled that Karlsefni and Snorri prepared their ship and intended to seek Vinland during the summer.

The Saga of Erik the Red (Old Icelandic)

Old Icelandic	Literal	English
Til þeirrar ferðar réðust þeir Bjarni og Þórhallur með skip sitt og það föruneyti er þeim hafði fylgt.	To their travel appointed they Bjarni and Thorhall with ship theirs and that companions, that they had followed.	For their voyage, they hired Bjarni and Thorhall with their own ship, and their companions who followed them.
Maður hét Þorvarður.	A-man was-called Thorvard.	There was a man called Thorvard.
Hann átti Freydísi, dóttur Eiríks rauða laungetna.	He married Freydis, daughter Erik the-Red's, illegitimate.	He married Freydis, the illegitimate daughter of Erik the Red.
Hann fór með þeim og Þorvaldur son Eiríks og Þórhallur er var kallaður veiðimaður.	He went also with them and Thorvald, son Erik's, and Thorhall, who called was hunter.	He also travelled with them, along with Thorvald, Erik's son, and Thorhall, who was called the hunter.
Hann hafði lengi verið í veiðiförum með Eiríki um sumrum og hafði hann margar varðveislur.	He had long been to hunting with Erik around summer and had he much guarded.	He had long been hunting with Erik during the summer, and he had many times watched over him.
Þórhallur var mikill vexti, svartur og þurslegur.	Thorhall was large grown, dark and giant.	Thorhall was large grown, dark and giant.
Hann var heldur við aldur, ódæll í skapi, hljóðlyndur, fámálugur hversdaglega, undirförull og þó atmælasamur og fýstist jafnan hins verra.	He was held with age, unruly in mood, quiet, few-words always, scheming and though measured and desired equally the worst.	He was rather with age, unruly in mood, a man of few words, always scheming, usually desired to make trouble.
Hann hafði lítt við trú blandast síðan hún kom á Grænland.	He had little with faith mixed since it came to Greenland.	He had mixed little with the faith since it came to Greenland.
Þórhallur var lítt vinsældum horfinn en þó hafði Eiríkur lengi tal af honum haldið.	Thorhall was little-with popularity disappeared but though had Erik long talked of him staying.	Thorhall was not very popular with those around him, but Erik had long been in his confidence.
Hann var á skipi með þeim Þorvaldi því að honum var víða kunnigt í óbyggðum.	He was in ship with them Thorvald because that he was widely known to unsettled-land.	He was in the ship with Thorvald because he knew widely the unsettled land.
Þeir höfðu það skip er Þorbjörn hafði út þangað og réðust til ferðar með þeim Karlsefni og voru þar flestir grænlenskir menn á.	They had the ship that Thorbjorn had back there and appointed to travel with them Karlsefni and were there mostly Greenlander men on.	They had the ship that Thorbjorn had brought back there and Karlsefni hired people to travel with them, and they were mostly men from Greenland.
Á skipum þeirra voru fjórir tigir manna annars hundraðs.	On the-ship there were four tens men also hundred.	There were a hundred and forty men on their ships.
Sigldu þeir undan síðan til Vestribyggðar og til Bjarneyja.	Sailed they away since to Vestribyggd and to Bjarney.	They sailed away afterwards to the Western Settlement and to Bjarney.

The Saga of Erik the Red (Old Icelandic)

Old Icelandic	Literal	English
Sigldu þeir þaðan undan Bjarneyjum norðan veður.	Sailed they from-there away-from Bjarney north winds.	They sailed away from Bjarney with the north winds.
Voru þeir úti tvö dægur.	Were they out two days.	They were out for two days.
Þá fundu þeir land og reru fyrir á bátum og könnuðu landið og fundu þar hellur margar og svo stórar að tveir menn máttu vel spyrnast í iljar.	Then found they land and rowed for in the-boat and explored land and found there slabs many and so large that two people may well touch of feet.	Then they found land and rowed towards in the boat, and explored the land, and found there many slabs, and they were so large that two people could lie across it touching feet.
Melrakkar voru þar margir.	Melrakka were there many.	There were many melrakka.
Þeir gáfu nafn landinu og kölluð Helluland.	They gave name to-the-land and called Helluland.	They gave a name to the land and called it Helluland.
Þá sigldu þeir norðan veður tvö dægur og var þá land fyrir þeim og var á skógur mikill og dýr mörg.	Then sailed they north winds two days and were then land for they and was of forest great and wild-animals many.	Then they sailed with a northerly wind for two days, and they were before land, and it was much forested and with many wild animals.
Ey lá í landsuður undan landinu og fundu þeir þar bjarndýr og kölluðu Bjarney en landið kölluðu þeir Markland.	An-island lay to south-east from land and found they there bear and called Bjarney and land called they Markland.	An island lay to the south east of the lane, and they found a bear there, and called it Bjarney, and called the land Markland.
Þar er skógurinn.	There were forests.	There were forests.
Þá er liðin voru tvö dægur sjá þeir land og þeir sigldu undir landið.	Then the teams were two days saw they land and they sailed near the-land.	Then the crew were sailing for two days when they saw land and sailed close by it.
Þar var nes er þeir komu að.	There was headland that they came to.	There was a headland which they came to.
Þeir beittu með landinu og létu landið á stjórnborða.	They applied with the-land and let land to starboard.	They kept the land to their starboard.
Þar var öræfi og strandir langar og sandar.	There was wilderness and beaches long and sands.	There was wilderness and long beaches and sands.
Fara þeir á bátum til lands og fundu þar á nesinu kjöl af skipi og köllu þar Kjalarnes.	Went they in the-boat to land and found there on the-headland a-keel from a-ship and called they Kjalarnes.	They went in the boat to land and found there on the headland a keel from a ship, and they called there Kjalarnes.
Þeir gáfu og nafn ströndunum og köllu Furðustrandir því að langt var með að sigla.	They called and beaches Furdustrandir, because by long was along to sail.	The called the beaches Furdustrandir because they were long to sail by.
Þá gerðist vogskorið landið og héldu þeir skipunum að vogunum.	Then became creek-indented land and held they ship to inlets.	Then the land became indented with creeks, and they kept their ship in an inlet.

The Saga of Erik the Red (Old Icelandic)

Old Icelandic	Literal	English
Það var þá er Leifur var með Ólafi konungi Tryggvasyni og hann bað hann boða kristni á Grænlandi og þá gaf konungur honum tvo menn skoska.	That was then that Leif was with Olaf king Tryggvason and he asked him to-preach Christianity in Greenland and then gave king to-him two men Scottish.	When Leif was with King Olaf Tryggvason and he had asked him to preach Christianity in Greenland, the king then gave him two Scottish people.
Hét karlmaðurinn Haki en konan Hekja.	Called servants Haki, and woman Hekja.	The servants were called Haki, and a woman Hekja.
Konungur bað Leif taka til þessara manna ef hann þyrfti skjótleiks við því að þau voru dýrum skjótari.	The-king bid Leif take to these people if he needed speed with because that these were wild-animals faster-than.	The king offered Leif to take these people if he needed someone with speed, because they were faster than wild animals.
Þessa menn fengu þeir Leifur og Eiríkur til fylgdar við Karlsefni.	These people gathered they Leif and Erik to follow with Karlsefni.	Leif and Erik sent these people to follow with Karlsefni.
En er þeir höfðu siglt fyrir Furðustrandir þá létu þeir hina skosku menn á land og báðu þau hlaupa í suðurátt og leita landskosta og koma aftur áður þrjú dægur væru liðin.	Then when they had sailed for Furdustrandir, they let they the Scottish people to land and asked them run south of land to seek land-benefits and coming back, before three days would-be passed.	Then when they had sailed along Furdustrandir, the put the Scottish people on land and asked them to run southwards and explore the land and come back before three days were passed.
Þau voru svo búin að þau höfðu það klæði er þau kölluð kjafal.	They were so ready that they had the clothes that they called kjafal.	They were so prepared that they had the clothing that they called a kjafal.
Það var svo gert að hötturinn var á upp og opið að hliðum og engar ermar á og hneppt í milli fóta.	That was so made that hoods were for up and opened at sides and no sleeves of and fastened in between feet.	It was made with a hood at the top, with openings at the sides, and no sleeves, fastened between the feet.
Hélt þar saman hnappur og nesla en ber voru annars staðar.	Held they together fastening and nettle but bare were other places.	It was held together with a button and a loop, they were bare in other places.
Þeir köstuðu akkerum og lágu þar þessa stund.	They cast anchor and lay there this while.	They cast anchor and lay there awhile.
Og er þrír dagar voru liðnir hljópu þau af landi ofan og hafði annað þeirra í hendi vínber en annað hveiti sjálfsáið.	And when three days were passed ran they from land over and had one of-them in hand grapes and another wheat self-sowing.	And when three days were passed, they ran over from the land, and one of them had in hand grapes, and another self-sowing wheat.
Sagði Karlsefni að þau þóttust fundið hafa landskosti góða.	Said Karlsefni that they thought found had land-benefits good.	Karlsefni said that they thought they had found good benefit from the land.

The Saga of Erik the Red (Old Icelandic)

Old Icelandic	Literal	English
Tóku þeir þau á skip sitt og fóru leiðar sinnar þar til er varð fjarðskorið.	Took they these on ship theirs and travelled route theirs that towards then became fjords-carving.	They took these on their ship and travelled on their way until the land became a carved fjord.
Þeir lögðu skipunum inn á fjörðinn.	They put ship in to fjord.	They put the ship into the fjord.
Þar var ey ein út fyrir og voru þar straumar miklir og um eyna.	There was an-island alone out before and was there a-stream great and about island.	There was an island laying before it, and there were great streams surrounding the island.
Þeir kölluð hana Straumsey.	They called it Straumsey.	They called it Straumsey.
Fugl var þar svo margur að trautt mátti fæti niður koma í milli eggjanna.	Wild-birds were there so many that scarcely may feet down come in between eggs.	There were so many wild birds there that the could scarcely put down their feet between them.
Þeir héldu inn með firðinum og kölluðu hann Straumsfjörð og báru farminn af skipunum og bjuggust þar um.	They held in with fjord and called it Straumsfjord and carried cargo of ship and prepared there about.	They kept in the fjord and called it Straumsfjord, and carried their cargo out of the ship and settled thereabouts.
Þeir höfðu með sér alls konar fé og leituðu sér þar landsnytja.	They had with them all kinds cattle and sought they there land-benefits.	They had with them all kinds of livestock, and they sought the land's resources.
Fjöll voru þar og fagurt var þar um að litast.	Mountains were there and beautiful were they about to look.	The mountains there were beautiful to look upon.
Þeir gáðu einskis nema að kanna landið.	They looked only taken to exploring land.	They looked only to exploring the land.
Þar voru grös mikil.	There was grass great.	There was tall grass there.
Þar voru þeir um veturinn og gerðist vetur mikill en ekki fyrir unnið og gerðist illt til matarins og tókust af veiðarnar.	They were there about winter and happened winter much but nothing before working and becoming ill for food and taking of hunting.	They were there about winter, and the winter was harsh, and they had done nothing in preparation for it, and they became ill for want of food, and took they to hunting and fishing.
Þá fóru þeir út í eyna og væntu að þar mundi gefa nokkuð af veiðum eða rekum.	Then went they out to the-island and expected that there could give some of fishing or foraging.	They went out to the island and hoped to be given something of fishing or foraging.
Þar var þó lítið til matfanga en fé þeirra varð þar vel.	There was though little to hunt but cattle theirs was there well.	There was though little caught from hunting, but their livestock were well.
Síðan hétu þeir á guð að hann sendi þeim nokkuð til matfanga og var eigi svo brátt við látið sem þeim var annt til.	Afterwards pledged they to God that he send them something to hunt and was not so soon with left which they were wishing for.	Afterwards they prayed to God for him to send them something to hunt, but was not so soon anything left that they were wishing for.

The Saga of Erik the Red (Old Icelandic)

Old Icelandic	Literal	English
Þórhallur hvarf á brott og gengu menn að leita hans.	Thorhall disappeared to away and went people to seek him.	Thorhall disappeared away and people went to find him.
Stóð það yfir þrjú dægur í samt.	Was this over three days the same.	It was the same way for three days.
Á hinu fjórða dægri fundu þeir Karlsefni og Bjarni hann Þórhall á hamargnípu einni.	On the fourth day found they Karlsefni and Bjarni him Thorhall on cliff-top alone.	On the fourth day Karlsefni and Bjarni found Thorhall on a clip top alone.
Hann horfði í loft upp og gapti hann, bæði augum og munni og nösum, og kóraði sér og klípti sig og þuldi nokkuð.	He looked to sky up and agape he, both eyes and mouth and nose, and scratched himself and pinched himself and reciting something.	He was looking up to the sky, eyes, mouth, and nose agape, and scratched and pinched himself and he was reciting something.
Þeir spurðu hví hann væri þar kominn.	They asked why he was there come.	They asked why he had come there.
Hann kvað það öngu skipta.	He said that nothing of-exchange.	He said that it was nothing of any concern.
Bað hann þá ekki það undrast, kveðst svo lengst lifað hafa að þeir þurftu eigi ráð fyrir honum að gera.	Asked he then not that wonder, saying so long lived had that you need not advise for to-him to do.	He asked them not to wonder about it, saying that as long as he had lived, he had not needed their advice.
Þeir báðu hann fara heim með sér.	They asked him travel home with them.	They asked him to travel home with them.
Hann gerði svo.	He did so.	He did so.
Litlu síðar kom þar hvalur og drifu menn til og skáru hann en þó kenndu menn eigi hvað hval það var.	Little afterwards came there whale and drove men to and cut it and though knew people not what whale it was.	Shortly afterwards there came a whale, and men flocked to carve it up, though they did not know what kind of whale it was.
Karlsefni kunni mikla skyn á hvalnum og kenndi hann þó eigi.	Karlsefni knew much understanding of whales and knew he though not.	Karlsefni knew much about whales, though he did not know.
Þenna hval suðu matsveinar og átu af og varð þó öllum illt af.	This whale boiled ship's-cook and ate they and were though all ill from.	The ship's cook boiled the whale and they ate, and everyone was ill from it.
Þá gengur Þórhallur að og mælti: "Var eigi svo að hinn rauðskeggjaði varð drjúgari enn Kristur yðvar? Þetta hafði eg nú fyrir skáldskap minn er eg orti um Þór fulltrúann.	Then went Thorhall to and spoke: "Was not so that the Red-bearded was ample but Christ yours this have I now for poetry mine that I wrote about Thor patron.	Thorhall then spoke: "Ampler was the Red-Beard now than your Christ. I had this now for my poem, which I wrote about Thor, my guardian.
Sjaldan hefir hann mér brugðist".	Seldom has he me broken".	Seldom has he broken me".

The Saga of Erik the Red (Old Icelandic)

Old Icelandic	Literal	English
Og er menn vissu þetta vildu öngvir nýta og köstuðu fyrir björg ofan og sneru sínu máli til guðs miskunnar.	And when people knew this willed none take-advantage and cast before rocks over and turned their matter to God's mercy.	And when people knew this, they carried the whale to cast to sea, and threw themselves on God's mercy.
Gaf þeim þá út að róa og skorti þá eigi birgðir.	Gave they then back to row and shortage then not supplies.	They were then given back to rowing, and the found no shortage of supplies.
Um vorið fara þeir inn í Straumsfjörð og höfðu föng af hvorutveggja landinu, veiðar af meginlandinu, eggver og útróðra af sjónum.	About spring went they in to Straumsfjord and had provisions of either-way land, hunting of mainland, egg-gathering and fishing from sea.	About spring they went into Straumsfjord and had supplies from both shores, hunting on the mainland, gathering eggs and fishing from the sea.
9	9	9
Nú ræða þeir um ferð sína og hafa tilskipan.	Now discussed they about journey theirs and had decided.	Now they discussed about their journey and planned.
Vill Þórhallur veiðimaður fara norður um Furðustrandir og fyrir Kjalarnes og leita svo Vínlands en Karlsefni vill fara suður fyrir land og fyrir austan og þykir land því meira sem suður er meir og þykir honum það ráðlegra að kanna hvorttveggja.	Willed Thorhall the-Hunter go north about Furdustrandir and for Kjalarnes and seek so Vinland but Karlsefni willed to-travel south for land and for eastwards and thinking land for more which south was more and thought he that advisable to explore each-way.	Thorhall the Hunter wished to go north along Furdustrandir and Kjalarnes to seek Vinland, but Karlsefni wished to travel south along the land and east, thinking that the further south they went, the more the could explore either way.
Nú býst Þórhallur út undir eynni og urðu eigi meir í ferð með honum en níu menn.	Now prepared Thorhall out under island and became not more to travel with him but nine people.	Now Thorhall prepared his ship close to the island and there were not more than nine people to travel with him.
En með Karlsefni fór annað liðið þeirra.	And with Karlsefni went second group theirs.	And the second group went with Karlsefni.
Og einn dag er Þórhallur bar vatn á skip sitt þá drakk hann og kvað vísu þessa:	And one day was Thorhall carrying water to ship theirs then drank he and said verse this:	And one day when Thorhall was carrying water to their ship, he drank from it and said this verse:
Hafa kváðu mig meiðar málmþings, er kom eg hingað,	Shores sang me hurt metal-assemblied, when coming here,	The shores sang me hurt Metal assembled, when I came here,
mér samir láð fyr lýðum	To-me same invited for people	I have the same advice for the people
lasta, drykk hinn basta.	Load, drink the best.	Loaded, drink the best.
Bílds hattar verðr byttu	Axe hoods become replaced	Axe hoods will be replaced

The Saga of Erik the Red (Old Icelandic)

Old Icelandic	Literal	English
beiði-Týr að reiða.	Bids-Tyr to ruling.	Asking for Tyr's ruling.
Heldr er svo að eg krýp að keldu,	Rather is so that I creep to the well,	It is rather that I creep to the well,
komat vín á grön mína.	Come wine to green mine.	Bring green wine to me.
Láta þeir út síðan og fylgir Karlsefni þeim undir eyna.	Put they out afterwards and followed Karlsefni they under the-island.	They put out to sea afterwards and Karlsefni followed the as far as the island.
Áður þeir drógu seglið upp kvað Þórhallur vísu:	Before they drew sails up said Thorhall verse:	Before they drew up the sails, Thorhall said this verse:
Förum aftr þar er órir	Travel-we back, there where others	We travel back to where the others
eru sandhimins landar,	are, sand-heaven's, land,	Are, the heavens of the sands, land,
látum kenni-Val kanna	let-us know-choose explore	Let us knowing choose to explore
knarrar skeið hin breiðu.	Ship sheathed-sword in wide,	Ship of swords in the wide,
Meðan bilstyggir byggja	while space settle	Among the space settle.
bellendr og hval vella	partakers and whale boil	Participants and boil the whale
Laufa veðrs, þeir er leyfa	leaf weathered, they have	Leaf weathered, they have
lönd, á Furðuströndum.	land, to Furdustrandir.	Land, in Furdustrandir.
Síðan skildu þeir og sigldu norður fyrir Furðustrandir og Kjalarnes og vildu beita þar fyrir vestan.	Then sailed they north along Furdustrandir and Kjalarnes and willed applied west for.	Then they sailed north along Furdustrandir and Kjalarnes, and wished to head for the west.
Kom þá veður á móti þeim og rak þá upp við Írland og voru þar mjög þjáðir og barðir.	Came then weather to meet them and drove then up to Ireland and were there very enslaved and beaten.	Then the west wind came towards them, and they were driven up to Ireland, and there they were beaten and enslaved.
Þá lét Þórhallur líf sitt.	Then laid Thorhall life his.	There Thorhall lost his life.
10	10	10
Karlsefni fór suður fyrir land og Snorri og Bjarni og annað lið þeirra.	Karlsefni came south along land and Snorri and Bjarni and another team theirs.	Now it is said of Karlsefni, that he went south along the land, with Snorri and Bjarni and the rest of their company.
Þeir fóru lengi og til þess er þeir komu að á þeirri er féll af landi ofan og í vatn og svo til sjóvar.	They travelled along and all there until, then they came to river one, which fell from land off and into lake single to sea.	They travelled along the land until they came to a river which fell from the land into a lake, and into the sea.
Eyrar voru þar miklar fyrir árósinum og mátti eigi komast inn í ána nema að háflæðum.	Islands were there great, and may not come in to river out of high-tide.	There were large islands there, and they could not come into the river outside of high tide.

The Saga of Erik the Red (Old Icelandic)

Old Icelandic	Literal	English
Sigldu þeir Karlsefni þá til áróssins og kölluðu í Hópi landið.	Sailed they Karlsefni then to river-mouth and called it Hop land.	There Karlsefni sailed them to the river mouth, and called the land Hop.
Þar fundu þeir sjálfsána hveitiakra þar sem lægðir voru en vínviður allt þar sem holta kenndi.	There found they of land self-sowing wheat-acres, there where low-ground was, and vines all there, which hills knew.	There they found acres of self-sowing wheat, where the low ground was, and vines growing on the hills.
Hver lækur var þar fullur af fiskum.	Every stream was there full of fish.	Every stream there was full of fish.
Þeir gerðu þar grafir sem landið mættist og flóðið gekk efst, og er út féll voru helgir fiskar í gröfunum.	They made trenches, there which may land and tide went highest, and then when back fell sea, were flat fish in trenches.	They made trenches in the land where the tide reached its highest, and then when the sea fell back, there were flat fish in the trenches.
Þar var mikill fjöldi dýra á skógi með öllu móti.	There were great many animals in forest with all met.	There were a great many wild animals of all kinds in the forest.
Þeir voru þar hálfan mánuð og skemmtu sér og urðu við ekki varir.	They were there half month and entertained themselves and became with nothing aware.	They were there half a month and entertained themselves and were not aware of anything unusual.
Fé sitt höfðu þeir með sér.	Cattle theirs had they with them.	They had their livestock with them.
Og einn morgunn snemma er þeir lituðust um sáu þeir níu húðkeipa og var veift trjánum af skipunum og lét því líkast í sem í hálmþústum og fer sólarsinnis.	And one morning early, when they looked about, saw they great many skin-boats, and were waving poles from boats, and had accordingly like as to straw-staves, and were waved sun-wise-motion.	And early one morning, when they looked about, they saw a great many hide-boats, and there were poles waving from the boats, which made a sound like a straw man, and they were waved in a sun-wise motion.
Þá mælti Karlsefni: "Hvað mun þetta tákna?"	Then spoke Karlsefni: "What could this have to betoken?"	Then spoke Karlsefni: "What could this mean?"
Snorri svarar honum: "Vera kann að þetta sé friðartákn og tökum skjöld hvítan og berum í mót".	Snorri Thorbrandson answered he: "Be-it can, that this so peace-mark, and take shield white and bear it towards".	Snorri Thorbrandson answered: "Maybe it can be a peace sign, and we should take a white shield and show it to them".
Og svo gerðu þeir.	And so did they.	And so they did.
Þá reru hinir í mót og undruðust þá og gengu þeir á land.	Then rowed they to meet and astonished they, as present were, and went to land up.	Then they rowed to meet them, and they were astonished as they came up on land to meet them.

The Saga of Erik the Red (Old Icelandic)

Old Icelandic	Literal	English
Þeir voru smáir menn og illilegir og illt höfðu þeir hár á höfði.	They were small men and ill-looking and disorderly heads their hair on heads.	They were small men, and looked threatening, with tangled hair on their heads.
Eygðir voru þeir mjög og breiðir í kinnunum og dvöldust þeir um stund og undruðust, reru síðan í brott og suður fyrir nesið.	Eyes were theirs large and broad in cheeks and dwelled they about awhile and marvelled, rowed then to away and south before headland.	They had large eyes and broad cheeks. They stayed around awhile and marvelled at those who were present, and then they rowed away and headed south around the headland.
Þeir höfðu gert byggðir sínar upp frá vatninu og voru sumir skálarnir nær vatninu en sumir firr.	They had made booths theirs up from lake and were some cabins near lake but some further.	They made their booths up from the lake, and there were some cabins near the lake, but some further inland.
Nú voru þeir þar þann vetur.	Now were they therefore then winter.	They were there for the winter.
Þar kom alls engi snjár og allur fénaður gekk þar úti sjálfala.	There came no snow, and all going cattle they themselves from.	There was no snow there, and all the livestock could fend for themselves outside.

11

En er vora tók geta þeir að líta einn morgun snemma að fjöldi húðkeipa reri sunnan fyrir nesið, svo margir sem kolum væri sáð og var þó veift á hverju skipi trjánum.	Then when spring took could they the company one morning early that many skin-boats rowing south before the-headland, so many as-if coal were sown and were though waving on each ship poles.	Then when spring came, early one morning they saw many hide boats rowing up from the south around the headland, so many that it looked like coal had been thrown across the water. They were also waving poles from each ship.
Þeir brugðu þá skjöldum upp og tóku kaupstefnu sín á millum og vildi það fólk helst kaupa rautt klæði.	They brought then shields up and took trading-posts theirs in between and willed that people preferably buy red cloth.	They brought up their shields and set up their trading posts between them and the people wanted to buy red cloth.
Þeir vildu og kaupa sverð og spjót en það bönnuðu þeir Karlsefni og Snorri.	They willed also purchase swords and spears but that banned they Karlsefni and Snorri.	They also wanted to purchase swords and spears, but Karlsefni and Snorri banned this.
Þeir höfðu ófölvan belg fyrir klæðið og tóku spannarlangt klæði fyrir belg og bundu um höfuð sér og fór svo um stund.	They had dark pelts and clothes and took spanning-long clothing for pelts and bound about heads theirs and went so about awhile.	They had dark pelts and clothes, and they took spans of cloth in exchange for pelts and tier the cloth around their heads, and so the trading went on in this way for a while.

The Saga of Erik the Red (Old Icelandic)

Old Icelandic	Literal	English
En er minnka tók klæðið þá skáru þeir í sundur svo að eigi var breiðara en þvers fingrar breitt.	But as decreased took cloth then cut they to apart so that not was broader than across finger broad.	But as the amount of cloth decreased, they cut it so that it was not as broad, and only a finger width.
Gáfu þeir Skrælingjar jafnmikið fyrir eða meira.	Gave they Skraelings equal for or more.	The Skraelings exchanged for the same price or more.
Það bar til að griðungur hljóp úr skógi er þeir Karlsefni áttu og gall hátt við.	That bore towards that a-bull ran out-of woods which they Karlsefni owned and bellowed loudly with.	Then a bull which Karlsefni owned ran out of the woods towards them, bellowing loudly.
Þeir fælast við Skrælingjar og hlaupa út á keipana og reru suður fyrir land.	This frightened to Skraelings and ran out of trading and rowed south for land.	This frightened the Skraelings and they ran away from the trading posts and rowed away south around the headland.
Varð þá ekki vart við þá þrjár vikur í samt.	Were they not noticed by them three weeks at together.	They did not notice them again for another three weeks.
En er sjá stund var liðin sjá þeir sunnan fara mikinn fjölda skipa Skrælingja svo sem straumur stæði.	And when seen awhile was company, saw there travelling south great many Skraelings, so as stream steady.	Then after a while their company saw travelling from the south, a great many Skraelings, like a steady stream.
Var þá veift trjánum öllum rangsælis og ýla allir Skrælingjar hátt upp.	Were they waving poles all anti-sun-wise and howling all Skraelings loudly up.	They were all waving their poles anti-sunwise now, and all were howling very loudly.
Þá tóku þeir rauða skjöldu og báru í mót.	Then took they red shields and bore to meet.	Then Karlsefni's company took their red shields and carried them up to meet them.
Gengu þeir þá saman og börðust.	Went they then together and fought.	Then they went together to battle.
Varð þar skothríð hörð.	Were there launching hard.	They were launching hard.
Þeir höfðu og valslöngur Skrælingjar.	They had also war-slings Skraelings.	The Skraelings also had catapults.
Það sjá þeir Karlsefni og Snorri að þeir færðu upp á stöngum Skrælingjarnir knött mikinn og blán að lit og fló upp á land yfir liðið og lét illilega við þar er niður kom.	That saw they Karlsefni and Snorri that they went up to poles Skraelings balls great and blue that colour and flew up to land over team and lay badly with there that down came.	Karlsefni and Snorri saw that the Skraelings raised up poles, with large round objects on them, blue in colour, and they flew to the land where the company were, and the landed terribly wherever they fell.

The Saga of Erik the Red (Old Icelandic)

Old Icelandic	Literal	English
Við þetta sló ótta miklum yfir Karlsefni og á lið hans svo að þá fýsti einskis annars en halda undan og upp með ánni því að þeim þótti lið Skrælingja drífa að sér öllum megin og létta eigi fyrr en þeir koma til hamra nokkurra.	With that struck fear much over Karlsefni and to team his so that then desired nothing else than hold away and up along the-river because that they thought the-company-of Skrælings drove at them all ways and let not before that they came to crags some.	This struck great fear into Karlsefni and his men, so much so that they wanted nothing else but to flee up the river, since the Skraelings seemed to be attacking from all angles, and not stop until they reached a cliff.
Veittu þeir þar viðtöku harða.	Gave they there resistance hard.	They have a stiff resistance.
Freydís kom út og sá er þeir héldu undan.	Freydis came out and saw that they held ahead.	Freydis came out and saw that Karlsefni's company were fleeing,
Hún kallaði: "Hví rennið þér undan slíkum auvirðismönnum, svo gildir menn er mér þætti líklegt að þér mættuð drepa þá svo sem búfé? Og ef eg hefði vopn þætti mér sem eg mundi betur berjast en einnhver yðvar".	She called: "Why run you away such un-worthy-men, so thick men that to-me seems likely that you may kill them such as livestock and if I had weapon seems to-me that I would better fight than any-of you".	She called out: "Why are you running away from such unworthy opponents? such men that you are, who look to me like you could kill them as easily as livestock, and if I had a weapon I would fight them better than any of you".
Þeir gáfu öngvan gaum hvað sem hún sagði.	They gave no heed to-that which she said.	They paid no attention to what she said.
Freydís vildi fylgja þeim og varð hún heldur sein því að hún var eigi heil.	Freydis willed to-follow them and became she behind late because that she was not well.	Freydis wanted to follow them, and fell behind, because she was with child.
Gekk hún þá eftir þeim í skóginn en Skrælingjar sækja að henni.	Went she though after them into woods, but Skraelings sought towards her.	She went after them into the forest, but the Skraelings reached her.
Hún fann fyrir sér mann dauðan, Þorbrand Snorrason, og stóð hellusteinn í höfði honum.	She found ahead their man dead, Thorbrand Snorrason, and stood a-slab-stone in head his.	She found in front of her one of their men who had died. It was Thorbrand Snorrason, and a stone slab was buried in his head.
Sverðið lá hjá honum og hún tók það upp og býst að verja sig með.	Sword lay by him and she took that up and prepared to protect herself with.	A sword lay unsheathed next to him. She took that sword and prepared to protect herself.
Þá koma Skrælingjar að henni.	Then came the-Skraelings to her.	Then the Skraelings came to her.
Hún tekur brjóstið upp úr serkinum og slettir á sverðið.	She pulled then out breast from clothes and slapped on open sword.	She pulled out one of her breasts from her clothes, and slapped the sword against it.

The Saga of Erik the Red (Old Icelandic)

Old Icelandic	Literal	English
Þeir fælast við og hlaupa undan og á skip sín og héldu á brottu.	With that feared Skraelings and ran away to ships theirs and rowed to away.	With that the Skraelings became afraid and they ran away to their ships and rowed away.
Þeir Karlsefni finna hana og lofa happ hennar.	There Karlsefni found her and praised zeal hers.	Here Karlsefni found her and praised her bravery.
Tveir menn féllu af Karlsefni en fjórir af Skrælingjum en þó urðu þeir Karlsefni ofurliði bornir.	Two men fell of Karlsefni but many of Skraelings but though became they Karlsefni outnumbered borne.	Two men from Karlsefni's company fell, and many of the Skraelings, but Karlsefni and his men were outnumbered.
Fara þeir nú til búða sinna og íhuga hvað fjölmenni það var er að þeim sótti á landinu.	Went they now to settlement theirs and thought what many that were that which they encountered on land.	They now went to their settlement and thought about what they had encountered on the land.
Sýnist þeim nú að það eina mun liðið hafa verið er á skipunum kom an annað liðið mun hafa verið þversýningar.	Seemed they now that the one could company at-sea have-been where the ships came but other company could have been illusions.	It seemed now that there could have been one team at sea where the ships came, but other people could have been illusions.
Þeir Skrælingjar fundu og mann dauðan og lá öx hjá honum.	There Skraelings found also a-man dead and lay an-axe by him.	The Skraelings also found a man dead, and an axe laying near to him.
Einn þeirra tók upp öxina og höggur með tré og þá hver að öðrum og þótti þeim vera gersemi og bíta vel.	One there took up the-axe and hewed with tree and then each to other and thought they it-was treasure and bit well.	One of them there took up the axe and hewed at a tree, and then each of them took turns trying it, and they thought it was a treasure that cut so well.
Síðan tók einn og hjó í stein og brotnaði öxin.	Then took one and struck at stone and broke the-axe.	Then one of them took up the axe and struck at stone with it, and the axe broke,
Þótti honum þá öngu nýt er eigi stóð við grjótinu og kastaði niður.	Thought he then no use that not withstood with stones and cast down.	and then they thought it was of no use, as it did not withstand stone, and they threw it down.
Þeir þóttust nú sjá þótt þar væru landskostir góðir að þar mundi jafnan ófriður og ótti á liggja af þeim er fyrir bjuggu.	There thought now looked thought there were land-benefits good that there could-be equal without-peace and fear to lay of them as before inhabitants.	There Karlsefni's company thought that although there were many benefits in that land, they would always be without peace, fearing attack by the inhabitants.

The Saga of Erik the Red (Old Icelandic)

Old Icelandic	Literal	English
Síðan bjuggust þeir á brottu og ætluðu til síns lands og sigldu norður fyrir landið og fundu fimm Skrælingja í skinnhjúpum, sofnaða, nær sjó.	Afterwards prepared they to leave and intended towards they land and sailed north along the land and found five Skraelings in skin-sacks, sleeping, near sea.	Afterwards they prepared to leave and intended to sail north around the land, and they found five Skraelings in skin sacks sleeping near the sea.
Þeir höfðu með sér stokka og í dýramerg, dreyra blandinn.	They had with them stock of in animal-marrow, blood mixed.	
Þóttust þeir Karlsefni það skilja að þessir menn myndu hafa verið gervir brott af landinu.	Thought they Karlsefni that separated which these people would have been made away from land.	Karlsefni's company thought that they must have been outlaws.
Þeir drápu þá.	They killed then.	They then killed them.
Síðan fundu þeir Karlsefni nes eitt og á fjölda dýra.	Afterwards found they Karlsefni headland one and of many animals.	Afterwards Karlsefni's company found a headland that had many wild animals.
Var nesið að sjá sem mykiskán væri af því að dýrin lágu þar um næturnar.	Was headland to see which muck-encrusted was of therefore were wild-animals laying there about night.	The headland looked like it was covered with dung, as the deer gathered there at night to sleep.
Nú koma þeir Karlsefni aftur í Straumsfjörð og voru þar fyrir alls gnóttir þess er þeir þurftu að hafa.	Now came they Karlsefni back to Straumfjord and were there before all abundance this as they needed to have.	Now Karlsefni's company came back to Straumfjord, where they found all in abundance, everything that they needed.
Það er sumra manna sögn að þau Bjarni og Guðríður hafi þar eftir verið og tíu tigir manna með þeim og hafi eigi farið lengra, en þeir Karlsefni og Snorri hafi suður farið og fjórir tigir manna með þeim og hafi eigi lengur verið í Hópi en vart tvo mánuði og hafi sama sumar aftur komið.	It was some men said that those Bjarni and Guthrid had there after been and ten tens men with them and have not travelled further, but there Karlsefni and Snorri had south travelled and four ten men with them and have no longer been in tidal-pool but hardly two months and had the-same summer returned come.	Some say that Bjarni and Gudrid had remained behind with a hundred men and had not travelled further, and that it was Karlsefni and Snorri who went further south with forty men, stayed at Hop for not longer than two months, and returned that same summer.
Karlsefni fór þá einu skipi að leita Þórhalls veiðimanns en annað liðið var eftir og fóru þeir norður fyrir Kjalarnes og ber þá fyrir vestan fram og var landið á bakborða þeim.	Karlsefni travelled then one ship to seek Thorhall the-Hunter but another team were remained and travelled they north for Kjalarnes and bore then for west from and was the-land to larboard-side theirs.	Karlsefni then travelled with one ship to find Thorhall the Hunter, while the other tem stayed behind, and they travelled north around Kjalarnes, and they then bore west, and the land was to their port side.

The Saga of Erik the Red (Old Icelandic)

Old Icelandic	Literal	English
Þar voru þá eyðimerkur einar allt að sjá fyrir þeim og nær hvergi rjóður í.	There was then deserted-forest only all to see before them and near neither clearing among.	There was then nothing to see except deserted forest before them, with no clearing among them.
Og er þeir höfðu lengi farið fellur á af landi ofan úr austri og í vestur.	And were they had long travelled, falls to out-of land above out east and to west.	And after they had travelled for a long time, they reached a river flowing from east to west.
Þeir lögðu inn í árósinn og lágu við hinn syðra bakkann.	They laid in to river-mouth and laid to in southern bank.	They sailed into the mouth of the river and lay to near the south bank.
12	12	12
Það var einn morgun er þeir Karlsefni sáu fyrir ofan rjóðrið flekk nokkurn sem glitraði við þeim og æptu þeir á það.	It was one morning, that they Karlsefni saw before above clearing speck certain, that glittered by them, and shouted they at that.	It was one morning that Karlsefni's company saw a clearing before them, and a speck of light that glittered before them, and they shouted at it.
Það hrærðist og var það einfætingur og skaust ofan á þann árbakkann sem þeir lágu við.	It stirred, and was it a-one-footer and launched down towards the river-bank, where they lay by.	It stirred, and it was a one legged creature, and it launched down towards the river bank there the ship was laid.
Þorvaldur Eiríksson rauða sat við stýri.	Thorvald son-of-Erik the-Red sat by steering.	Thorvald, son of Erik the Red, sat by the helm.
Þá mælti Þorvaldur: "Gott land höfum vér fengið".	Then spoke Thorvald: "Good land have we found".	Then Thorvald spoke: "Good land we have found here".
Þá hleypur einfætingurinn á brott og norður aftur og skaut áður í smáþarma á Þorvald.	Then ran one-footer to away and north back and shot back to small-intestine of Thorvald.	Then the one legged creature ran away back to the north and shot an arrow into Thorvald's intestine.
Hann dró út örina.	He dragged out the-arrow.	He dragged out the arrow.
Þá mælti Þorvaldur: "Feitt er um ístruna".	Then spoke Thorvald: "Bold is around the-belly".	Then Thorvald spoke: "Bold it is around the belly".
Þeir hljópu eftir einfætingi og sáu hann stundum og þótti sem hann leitaði undan.	They ran after one-footer and saw him sometimes and thought that he sought ahead.	They ran after the one legged creature and thought that they saw it ahead.
Hljóp hann út á vog einn.	Ran he out to inlet one.	He ran into an inlet.
Þá hurfu þeir aftur.	Then disappeared they returned.	Then he disappeared and they returned.
Þá kvað einn maður kviðling þenna:	Then said one man verse this:	Then one man said this verse:

The Saga of Erik the Red (Old Icelandic)

Old Icelandic	Literal	English
Eltu seggir, *allsatt var það,* *einn einfæting* *ofan til strandar* *en kynlegr maðr* *kostaði rásar* *hart of stopir,* *heyrðu, Karlsefni.*	"Pursued said, true was that, a one-footer down to shore, but uncanny man exerted rushed rough about stopped. Hear, Karlsefni".	"Pursued it was said true it was a one-footer down to the shore, but the uncanny man rushed away hard of stopping. Hear us, Karlsefni".
Þeir fóru þá í brott og norður aftur og þóttust sjá Einfætingaland.	They went then to away and north returning and thought saw One-Footer-Land.	Then they went away and headed back north and thought they saw One Footer Land.
Vildu þeir þá eigi lengur hætta liði sínu.	Willed they then not danger team theirs further.	They did not wish to put themselves in any further danger.
Þeir ætluðu öll ein fjöll, þau er í Hópi voru og þessi er nú fundu þeir, og það stæðist mjög svo á og væri jafnlangt úr Straumsfirði beggja vegna.	They supposed all same mountains, these, were among Hop was, and this, was now found they, and that place much so that also was equal-long from Straumfjord both ways.	They supposed that the mountains they saw were the same as the ones at Hop, and so that place was equally distant from Straumfjord.
Fóru þeir aftur og voru í Straumsfirði hinn þriðja vetur.	Went they again and were in Straumfjord the third winter.	They went back and spent the third winter in Straumfjord.
Gengu menn þá mjög sleitum.	Went men then much fighting.	Then there was much fighting among the men.
Sóttu þeir er kvonlausir voru í hendur þeim er kvongaðir voru.	Sought they which unmarried were in hand that who married were.	Some of them who were not married sought the women who were married.
Þar kom til hið fyrsta haust Snorri son Karlsefnis og var hann þá þrívetur er þeir fóru á brott.	There came to the first autumn Snorri son Karlsefni's and was he then three-winters when they went out away.	Karlsefni's son Snorri was born there the first autumn, and he was three winters old when they left.
Höfðu þeir sunnanveður og hittu Markland og fundu Skrælingja fimm.	Had they southern-winds and met Markland and found Skraelings five.	They were taken by a southerly wind and reached Markland, and found there five Skraelings.
Var einn skeggjaður og tvær konur, börn tvö.	Was one bearded and two women, children two.	One of them was bearded, two were women, and two were children.
Tóku þeir Karlsefni til sveinanna en hitt komst undan og sukku í jörð niður.	Took they Karlsefni young-men, and others went away, and sank they Skraelings among land down.	Karlsefni's company took the two boys, and the others went away, and then the Skraelings disappeared into the earth.

The Saga of Erik the Red (Old Icelandic)

Old Icelandic	Literal	English
En sveinana höfðu þeir með sér og kenndu þeim mál og voru skírðir.	Then young-men had they with them and taught them language and were baptised.	They kept the young men with them and taught them their language, and they were baptised.
Þeir nefndu móður sína Vethildi og föður Óvægi.	They named mother theirs Vethild and father Ovaegi.	Their mother was named Vethildi and their father Ovaegi.
Þeir sögðu að konungar stjórnuðu Skrælingjalandi.	They said that kings greatly-ruled-over Skraelings.	They said that there were great kings who ruled over the Skraelings,
Hét annar þeirra Avaldamon en annar hét Valdidida.	Called one theirs Avaldamon and another called Avaldidida.	one of them was called Avaldamon, and the other Valdidida.
Þeir kváðu þar engi hús og lágu menn í hellum eða holum.	They said there no houses and laid people in caves or holes.	They said that there were no houses there and people laid in caves or holes.
Þeir sögðu land þar öðrumegin gagnvart sínu landi og gengu menn þar í hvítum klæðum og æptu hátt og báru stangir og fóru með flíkur.	They said land there other-side going-from their land and went people there to white clothes and called-out loudly and bore poles and went with banners.	They said there was another land on the other side across from their land, and there people wore white clothes, and shouted loudly and carried poles fixed with banners.
Það ætla menn Hvítramannaland.	That supposed people White-man-land.	They supposed that this was White Man Land.
Nú komu þeir til Grænlands og eru með Eiríki rauða um veturinn.	Now came they to Greenland and were with Erik the-Red about winter.	Now they came to Greenland and were with Erik the Red by about winter.
13	13	13
Þá Bjarna Grímólfsson bar í Grænlandshaf og komu í maðksjá.	Then Bjarni Grimolfson carried to Greenland-Sea and came into ship-worms.	Then Bjarni Grimolfson was carried to the Greenland Sea and the ship was beset with ship worms.
Fundu þeir eigi fyrr en skipið gerist maðksmogið undir þeim.	Found they not before that ship was worm-eaten under them.	They found that the ship was eaten by worms underneath them.
Þá töluðu þeir um hvert ráð þeir skyldu taka.	Then talked they about what advice they should take.	Then they talked about what they should decision they should take.
Þeir höfðu eftirbát þann er bræddur var seltjöru.	They had boat then which spread was seal-fat.	They had a boat which had been spread with seal far.
Það segja menn að skelmaðkurinn smjúgi eigi það tré er seltjörunni er brætt.	That said people that shell-worms pierce not the beams that seal-fat are spread.	So people said that shell worms would not pierce the beams where seal fat was spread.

The Saga of Erik the Red (Old Icelandic)

Old Icelandic	Literal	English
Var það flestra manna sögn og tillaga að skipa mönnum bátinn svo sem hann tæki upp.	Was that most people said and suggested to ships people boat so which he take up.	The majority of people said that they should fit as many people on the boat as they could.
En er það var reynt þá tók báturinn eigi meir upp en helming manna.	But was that was tried then took boat not more up than half the people.	But as they tried to board the boat, not more than half the people could fit on it.
Bjarni mælti þá að menn skyldu fara í bátinn og skyldi það fara að hlutföllum en eigi að mannvirðingum.	Bjarni said then that people should go to boat and should it go to lot-taking but not to rank.	Bjarni then said that people should go on to the boat according to drawing lots, not deciding it by rank.
En hver þeirra manna vildi fara í bátinn sem þar voru, þá mátti hann eigi við öllum taka.	Although each-of them men willed to-go among the-boat as they were, then may it not with all take.	Although each of the men wanted to go on to the boat, it would not take them all.
Fyrir því tóku þeir þetta ráð að hluta menn í bátinn og af kaupskipinu.	For therefore took they this advice that lots people to boat and of merchant-ship.	They therefore took this advice to draw lots to see who would board the boat from the merchant vessel.
Hlutaðist þar svo til að Bjarni hlaut að fara í bátinn og nær helmingur manna með honum.	Lots there so until that Bjarni lot to travel in the-boat and near half the-people with him.	The lots were drawn, and so it was Bjarni's lot to travel in the boat with nearly half the people with him.
Þá gengu þeir af skipinu og í bátinn er til þess höfðu hlotist.	Then went they out-of ship and to boat that to this had lots.	They went out of the ship and into the boat according to the lots they had drawn.
Þá er menn voru komnir í bátinn mælti einn ungur maður íslenskur sá er verið hafði förunautur Bjarna: "Ætlar þú Bjarna að skiljast hér við mig?"	Then spoke man was came to boat spoke one younger man Icelander so that been had crew Bjarni: "Intend you Bjarni to separate here with me?"	Then an Icelander who was in the ship spoke, who Bjarni had followed from Iceland: "Do you intend to separate with me now Bjarni?".
Bjarni svarar: "Svo verður nú að vera".	Bjarni answered: "So becomes now to be".	Bjarni answered: "So it has now come to be".
Hann segir: "Svo með því að þú hést mér eigi því þá er eg fór með þér frá Íslandi frá búi föður míns".	He said: "So with therefore that you promised to-me not for then that I went with you from Iceland from farm father mine".	He said: "So it goes not with what you promised me then, when I left my father's farm to follow you".
Bjarni segir: "Eigi sé eg hér þó annað ráð til eða hvað leggur þú hér til ráðs?"	Bjarni said: "Not see I here though other advice to but what have you here to advise?"	Bjarni said: "I do not see that here, but what other choice do we have?"

The Saga of Erik the Red (Old Icelandic)

Old Icelandic	Literal	English
Hann segir: "Sé eg ráðið til að við skiptumst í rúmunum og farir þú hingað en eg mun þangað".	He said: "Say I advise to that with exchange of our-places and travel you here while I should there".	He said: "I say that we change places and you travel here while I should be there".
Bjarni svarar: "Svo skal vera og það sé eg að þú vinnur gjarna til lífs og þykir mikið fyrir að deyja".	Bjarni answered: "So shall be and that see I that you friend gladly to life and think much for to die".	Bjarni answered: "So it shall be, and I see that you my friend are glad in life, and think it too much to die".
Skiptust þeir þá í rúmunum. Gekk þessi maður í bátinn en Bjarni upp í skipið og er það sögn manna að Bjarni létist þar í maðkahafinu og þeir menn sem í skipinu voru með honum.	Exchanged they then of places. Went this man to boat while Bjarni up to-the-ship and was it said-of people that Bjarni perished there in the-worm-sea and they people which among the-ship were with him.	They then exchanged places. This man went on to the boat while Bjarni went up to the ship, and it was said by people that Bjarni perished there in the worm sea, and so did the people who were on the ship with him.
En báturinn og þeir er þar voru á fóru leiðar sinnar til þess er þeir tóku land og sögðu þessa sögu síðan.	But the-boat and they who there were in went route theirs until this that they took land and said this saga since.	Then the boat and they who were on board went on their way until they reached land and told this story since.
14	14	14
Annað sumar eftir fór Karlsefni til Íslands og Guðríður með honum og fór hann heim til bús síns í Reynines.	Next summer after went Karlsefni to Iceland and Guthrid with him and went he home to house his in Reynines.	The next summer Karlsefni went to Iceland with Gudrid and they went home to his house in Reynines.
Móður hans þótti sem hann hefði lítt til kostar tekið og var hún eigi heima þar hinn fyrsta vetur.	Mother his thought that he had little for choice taken and was she not home there the first winter.	His mother thought he had made a bad choice, and she did not stay with them for the first winter.
En er hún reyndi að Guðríður var skörungur mikill fór hún heim.	But when she experienced that Guthrid was noble much went she home.	But when she experienced that Gudrid was very noble, she went home.
Og voru samfarar þeirra góðar.	And was interaction theirs good.	And their relationship was good.
Dóttir Snorra Karlsefnissonar var Hallfríður móðir Þorláks byskups Runólfssonar.	Daughter-of Snorri Karlsefnison was Hallfrid, Mother Thorlak's the-Bishop son-of-Runolf.	Snorri Karlsefnison's daughter was Hallfrid, mother to Thorlak the Bishop, son of Runolf.
Þau áttu son er Þorbjörn hét.	They had a-son, was Thorbjorn named.	They had a son who was named Thorbjorn.

The Saga of Erik the Red (Old Icelandic)

Old Icelandic	Literal	English
Hans dóttir hét Þórunn, móðir Bjarnar byskups.	His daughter was-called Thorun, mother Bjarn's the-Bishop.	His daughter was named Thorun, the mother of Bishop Bjarn.
Þorgeir hét sonur Snorra Karlsefnissonar, faðir Yngveldar, móður Brands byskups hins fyrra.	Thorgeir was-called son-of Snorri Karlsefnison, father-to Yngvild, mother-of Brand Bishop the first.	Snorri Karlsefnison's son was named Thorgeir, he was the father of Yngvild, the mother of the first Bishop Brand.
Og lýkur þar þessi sögu.	And ends here this saga.	And here ends this saga.

Word List *(Norse to English)*

OI = Old Icelandic   ON = Old Norse

Norse	English
A, a	
að	as OI, at OI, by OI, for OI, in OI, it OI, of OI, possible OI, that OI, the OI, to OI, towards OI, were OI, what OI, which OI
aðra	others ON, others OI
aðrar	other ON
aðrir	other ON, other OI, others ON, others OI
af	for OI, from ON, from ON, from OI, of ON, of ON, of OI, off ON, on ON, on OI, out OI, out-of ON, out-of OI, they OI
aftr	back ON, back OI, return ON, returned ON, returning ON
aftrgöngum	hauntings ON
aftur	after OI, again OI, back OI, return OI, returned OI, returning OI
afturgöngum	hauntings OI
akkerum	anchor OI
aldur	age OI
alendu	thoughts OI
algrá	grey ON
allan	all ON, all ON
allar	all ON, all OI
allfjölmennt	many-people ON
allglöggsæ	clear ON
allir	all ON, all ON, all OI
allmjök	all-very ON
allnær	all-near ON, near OI
alls	all ON, all ON, all OI
allsatt	true ON, true OI
allt	all ON, all ON, all OI, altogether ON, altogether OI
allur	all OI
allvænt	expected ON
almennilega	properly OI
almenniliga	properly ON
an	but OI
andaðist	died ON, died ON, died OI
andast	died OI
andazt	died ON
andsælis	anti-sun-wise ON
annað	another OI, another OI, next OI, one OI, other OI, other OI, second OI
annan	accompany OI, others ON, second ON, second OI
annar	another OI, another OI, one OI
annarr	another ON, called-one ON, other ON
annars	also OI, else ON, else OI, other ON, other OI, to-another ON
annat	another ON, another ON, next ON, one ON, other ON
annt	wishing OI
ari	Ari (name) ON
arnarstapa	Arnarstapa (place) ON, Arnarstapa (place) OI, Arnarstapi (place) ON, Arnarstapi (place) OI
arnóru	Arnora (name) ON, Arnora (name) OI
at	a ON, as ON, at ON, but ON, by ON, for ON, from ON, in ON, it ON, man ON, of ON, that ON, the ON, therefore ON, to ON, towards ON, were ON, which ON
atbeina	assist OI, assistance ON
atburð	events ON, events OI
atferli	ceremony ON, ceremony OI

102

Word List (Norse to English)

Norse	English
athæfi	behaviour ON, behaviour OI
atmælasamur	measured OI
auðar	Aud (name) ON, Aud (name) OI
auðigr	wealthy ON
auðigur	wealthy OI
auðnumann	fortune ON, fortune OI
auðr	Aud (name) ON
auðsýnir	shown ON, shown OI
auður	Aud (name) OI
augum	eyes ON, eyes OI
aukin	increased ON, increased OI
austan	eastwards OI
austfirskur	East-Fjords (place) OI
austfirzkr	east-fjords ON
austmanns	The-Easterner (name) OI, the-easternman ON
austri	east ON, east OI
auvirðismönnum	un-worthy-men ON, un-worthy-men OI
avaldamon	Avaldamon (name) ON, Avaldamon (name) OI
avaldidida	Valdidida (name) ON
axlarliðnum	shoulder ON

Á, á

Norse	English
á	about OI, all OI, a-river OI, at ON, at OI, be ON, by OI, for ON, for OI, from ON, from OI, in ON, in OI, of ON, of OI, on ON, on OI, out OI, river ON, that ON, that OI, the OI, then ON, then OI, to ON, to OI, towards ON, towards OI, with OI, yet ON, yet OI
áðr	after ON, before ON, returned ON, until ON
áður	back OI, before OI, returned OI, until OI
ágæti	excellent ON, excellent OI
ágæts	an-excellent OI, excellent ON
ái	ai OI, ái OI
álftafirði	Alftafjord (place) ON, Alftafjord (place) ON, Alftafjord (place) OI
áliðnum	following ON, following OI
álna	cubits ON
ána	river ON, river OI
ánauðgir	bondsmen ON, bondsmen OI
ánauðigr	bondsman ON
ánauðigur	bondsman OI
ánni	river ON, the-river OI
árangr	harvest ON
árangur	harvest OI
árbakkann	river-bank ON, river-bank OI
árferð	season ON, season OI
árósinn	river-mouth ON, river-mouth OI
árósinum	river-mouth OI
áróssins	river-mouth OI
áslákr	Aslak (name) ON
áslákssonar	Son-of-Aslak (name) ON
áslákur	Aslak (name) OI
ástúð	affection ON, affection OI
ásvalds	Asvald (name) OI, Asvald's (name) ON
átt	descendents ON, descendents OI, have ON
átti	had ON, had OI, married ON, married OI
áttu	had ON, had OI, have-you ON, have-you OI, owned ON, owned OI
átu	ate ON, ate OI

Æ, æ

Norse	English
æðr	eider-birds ON
æpðu	shouted ON
æptu	called-out OI, shouted OI

103

Word List (Norse to English)

Norse	English
ætla	intend ON, intend OI, supposed ON, supposed OI
ætlað	intends OI
ætlaði	intended ON, intended OI, supposed OI
ætlan	supposing ON
ætlar	intend ON, intend OI, intended ON
ætlat	purpose ON
ætluðu	intended ON, intended OI, supposed ON, supposed OI
ætt	ancestry ON, descendents ON, lineage ON, lineage OI
ættbogi	descendents OI
ættgóður	family-good OI
ættkvíslum	family OI
ættstór	high-family OI, noble ON, noble OI
ættstórr	high-family ON
ævi	life ON, life OI

B, b

Norse	English
bað	asked ON, asked OI
báða	both ON
báðir	both ON, both OI
báðu	asked ON, asked OI
báðum	both OI
bæ	dwelling ON, dwelling OI, estate ON, estate OI, farm ON, farm OI, town ON, town OI
bæði	both ON, both OI, choosing OI
bæinn	dwellings ON, dwellings OI
bæjum	farms ON, farms OI
bænahald	prayer-holdings ON, prayer-holdings OI
bænir	prayers ON, prayers OI
bær	farm ON, farm OI
bakborða	larboard-side ON, larboard-side OI
baki	back ON, back OI
bakkann	bank ON, bank OI
báli	fire ON, fire OI
bar	bore ON, bore OI, carried OI, carrying ON, carrying OI, was-carried ON
barðir	beaten ON, beaten OI
barni	child ON, child OI
báru	bore ON, bore OI, carried ON, carried OI
basta	best OI
bát	boat ON
báti	boat ON
bátinn	boat ON, boat OI, the-boat ON, the-boat OI
batna	better ON, better OI, better-than ON, better-than OI
batnaði	bettered ON, bettered OI
bátrinn	boat ON
bátum	the-boat OI
báturinn	boat OI, the-boat OI
bauð	invited ON, invited OI
bazta	best ON
beðið	proposals OI
beðinn	asked ON, asked OI
beðit	proposals ON
beggja	both ON, both OI
beiddist	asked ON, asked OI
beiði-týr	bids-tyr ON, Bids-Tyr (name) OI
beita	applied ON, bid OI
beittu	applied OI
belg	pelts ON, pelts OI
bellendr	partakers ON, partakers OI
ber	bare ON, bare OI, bore OI, carried OI
bera	bear OI, bring OI, carry ON, carry OI
berim	bring ON
berja	to-bear ON, to-bear-to OI
berjast	fight ON, fight OI
berr	bore ON
bert	uncovered ON
beru	open ON

Word List (Norse to English)

Norse	English	Norse	English
berum	bear ON, bear OI	björn	bear ON
besta	best OI	bjóst	prepared ON
besti	best OI	bjuggu	dwelt ON, dwelt OI, inhabitants ON, inhabitants OI, prepared ON, prepared OI
betr	better ON		
betur	better OI		
bezta	best ON		
bezti	best ON		
bíða	wait ON, wait OI	bjuggust	prepared ON, prepared OI, settled ON
biðja	ask ON, ask OI, propose ON, propose OI		
		blán	blue ON, blue OI
biðr	asked ON	blandast	mixed OI
biðuðu	settled ON	blandinn	mixed ON, mixed OI
bílds	blood-letting ON, blood-letting OI	bláserkr	Blaserkur (place) ON
		bláserkur	Blaserkur (place) OI
bilstyggir	space OI	blíðu	friendliness ON
bilstyggvir	space ON	boða	preach ON, preach OI, to-preach OI
birgðir	supplies OI		
birni	Bjorn (name) ON, Bjorn (name) OI	boðaði	preached ON, preached OI
bíta	bit ON, bit OI	boðit	bid ON
bjargaði	saved OI	boðsmanna	guests ON, guests OI
bjarna	Bjarni (name) ON, Bjarni (name) OI	bolöxi	a-pole-axe ON, a-pole-axe OI
bjarnar	Bjarn (name) ON, Bjarn (name) OI, Bjarn's (name) ON	bónda	farmer OI, husband OI
		bóndi	farmer ON, farmer OI, husband ON, husband OI, landowner ON, landowner OI, the-farmer ON, The-Farmer (name) OI
bjarnarhöfn	Bjarnarhofn (place) ON, Bjarnarhofn (place) OI		
bjarnarsonar	Son-of-Bjorn (name) ON, Son-Of-Bjorn (name) OI		
		bóndum	farms ON
		bönnuðu	banned ON, banned OI
bjarndýr	bear OI	bónorð	proposal ON, proposal OI
bjarney	Bjarney (place) ON, Bjarney (place) OI		
		bónorðið	proposal OI
bjarneyja	Bjarney (place) OI	bónorðit	proposal ON
bjarneyjar	Bjarney (place) ON	borð	table ON, table OI, tables ON, tables OI
bjarneyjum	Bjarney (place) OI		
bjarni	Bjarni (name) ON, Bjarni (name) OI	börðust	battled ON, fought ON, fought OI
bjartari	bright ON	borgarfirði	Borgafjord (place) ON
bjartur	bright OI	borið	carried OI
bjó	dwelt ON, dwelt OI, lived ON, lived OI, prepared ON, prepared OI, settled ON	borinn	carried ON, carried OI
		borit	carried ON
		börn	children ON, children OI
björg	rocks OI	bornir	borne ON, borne OI

Word List (Norse to English)

Norse	English	Norse	English
botn	the-bottom-of ON, the-bottom-of OI	brúðkaupið	the-wedding OI
brá	drew ON	brugðið	brought-out OI
bráðara	sooner ON, sooner OI	brugðist	broken OI
bræddr	spread ON	brugðit	brought-out ON
bræddur	spread OI	brugðizt	broken ON
brætt	spread OI	brugðu	brought ON, brought OI
bragð	solution ON, solution OI	brullaup	wedding ON, wedding OI
brands	Brand (name) OI, Brand's (name) ON	bryti	steward ON
brátt	soon ON, soon OI	brýtur	divided OI
brattahlíð	Brattahlid (place) ON, Brattahlid (place) OI	bú	a-farm ON, farm OI
brattahlíð]	Brattahlid (place) ON	búða	settlement ON, settlement OI
braut	away ON, broke OI, divided ON	búðir	booths ON
bregða	foreclose ON, foreclose OI	buðu	invited ON, invited OI
breiðabólstað	Breidabolstad (place) ON, Breidabolstad (place) OI	búfé	livestock ON, livestock OI
breiðafirði	Breidafjord (place) ON, Breidafjord (place) OI	búi	dwelling OI, farm ON, farm OI
breiðafjörð	Breidafjord (place) ON, Breidafjord (place) OI	búið	dwelt OI, preparations OI, prepared OI
breiðara	broad ON, broader OI	búin	prepared OI, ready ON, ready OI
breiðfirskur	Breidafjord (place) OI	búinn	prepared ON, prepared-with OI, ready OI
breiðfirzkr	Breidafjord (place) ON		
breiðir	broad ON, broad OI	búinu	dwelling ON
breiðu	wide ON, wide OI	búit	dwelt ON, preparations ON, prepared ON
breitt	broad OI	bundu	bound ON, bound OI
brenna	burn ON, let OI	búnir	ready ON, ready OI
brjóst	breast ON	bunu	Buna (name) ON, Buna (name) OI
brjósti	breast ON, breast OI		
brjóstið	breast OI, the-breast OI	búnu	are ON, are OI
brjóstit	breast ON	bús	house OI
bróður	brother ON, brother OI	bústað	abode ON, abode OI, dwelling ON, dwelling OI, dwellings OI
brokey	Brokey (place) ON, Brokey (place) OI	bústaði	dwellings ON
brotinn	broken ON, broken OI	býðr	invited ON
brotna	broke ON	býður	invited OI
brotnaði	broke ON, broke OI	byggð	settlement ON, settlement OI
brott	away ON, away OI, out ON, out OI	byggðinni	settlement OI
		byggðir	booths OI
brottu	away OI, leave ON, leave OI	byggðu	settled ON
		byggðum	settlement ON, settlement OI
brúðkaup	wedding ON	byggja	settle ON, settle OI

106

Word List (Norse to English)

Norse	English
byggjanda	habitable ON, habitable OI
byggva	settle ON
býr	prepared ON, prepared OI
byrðusmjörs	Byrdusmjors (name) ON
byri	fair-wind ON, fair-wind OI
byrjaði	began ON, began OI
byskups	bishop ON, Bishop (name) OI, Bishop'S (name) OI, the-bishop ON
býst	prepared ON, prepared OI
byttu	buckets ON, buckets OI

D, d

Norse	English
dægr	days ON
dægri	day OI
dægur	days OI
dag	day ON, day OI
dagar	days OI
dagsetri	day-setting ON, day-setting OI
dalalönd	dale-land ON, Dale-Land (place) OI
dauða	dead OI, death ON, the-dead ON
dauðan	dead ON, dead OI
degi	day ON, day OI
deyja	die OI
dímunarvági	Dimunarvog (place) ON
dímunarvogi	Dimunarvog (place) OI
djúpúðgu	the-deep-minded ON, The-Deep-Minded (name) OI
dó	died ON
dögurðarár	Dogurdara (place) ON, Dogurdara (place) OI
dóttir	daughter ON, daughter OI, daughter-of ON, daughter-of OI
dóttur	daughter ON, daughter OI, daughter-of ON, daughter-of OI

Norse	English
drakk	drank ON, drank OI
drap	killed ON, killed OI
drápu	killed ON, killed OI
drengiliga	bravely ON
drengskap	honour ON
drepa	kill ON, kill OI
dreyra	blood ON, blood OI
drífa	drove ON, drove OI
drifu	drove OI
drjúgari	ample ON, ample OI
drjúgum	greatly ON
dró	dragged ON, dragged OI, drew ON, drew OI, pulled ON
drógu	drew OI
dröngum	Drangar (place) ON, Drangar (place) OI
drukkit	drink ON
drykk	drink ON, drink OI
duldið	hidden ON
duldir	hidden OI
durunum	the-door ON
dvöldust	dwelled OI
dvölðust	dwelled ON
dyflinnar	Dublin (place) ON
dyflinnarskíri	Dublinshire (place) ON, Dublinshire (place) OI
dyflinni	Dublin (place) ON, Dublin (place) OI
dýr	wild-animals ON, wild-animals OI
dýra	animals ON, animals OI
dýramerg	animal-marrow ON, animal-marrow OI
dýraveiðr	animal-hunting ON
dýrð	glory ON, glory OI
dýrin	wild-animals ON, wild-animals OI
dyrnar	doorway OI
dyrrin	doorway ON
dýrum	wild-animals ON, wild-animals OI
dyrunum	out-door OI, the-door OI

E, e

Word List (Norse to English)

Norse	English	Norse	English
		einn	a ON, a OI, one ON, one OI
eða	or ON, or OI	einnhver	any-of OI
ef	if ON, if OI	einnhverr	any-of ON
efni	prospects ON	einni	alone ON, alone OI, one ON
efnilegir	promising OI		
efnilegur	promising OI	eins	likewise ON, likewise OI
efniligir	promising ON		
efniligsti	promising ON	einskis	nothing ON, nothing OI, only OI
efst	highest OI		
eftir	after ON, after OI, afterwards ON, afterwards OI, along ON, along OI, remained ON, remained OI	einu	one ON, one OI
		eiri	bronze ON, bronze OI
		eirík	Erik (name) ON, Erik (name) OI
		eiríki	Erik (name) ON, Erik (name) OI
eftirbát	boat OI	eiríkr	Erik (name) ON
eg	i OI, in OI	eiríks	Erik (name) ON, Erik (name) OI, Erik's (name) ON, Erik'S (name) OI
eggjaði	urged ON		
eggjanna	eggs OI		
eggjum	eggs ON		
eggver	egg-gathering OI, eggs ON		
		eiríksey	Eriksey (place) ON
eiga	marry ON, marry OI	eiríkseyju	Eriksey (place) OI
eigi	no ON, no OI, none ON, none OI, not ON, not OI, was-not ON, was-not OI	eiríksfirði	Eriksfjord (place) ON, Eriksfjord (place) OI
		eiríksfjarðar	Eriksfjord (place) ON, Eriksfjord (place) OI
		eiríksfjörð	Eriksfjord (place) ON, Eriksfjord (place) OI
ein	alone ON, alone OI, along OI, an ON, same ON, same OI	eiríkshólmum	Eriksholmar (place) ON, Eriksholmar (place) OI
eina	one ON, one OI, only ON	eiríksson	Eriksson (name) ON, Eriksson (name) OI, Son-of-Erik (name) ON, Son-Of-Erik (name) OI
einar	Einar (name) ON, Einar (name) OI, only ON, only OI		
einarr	Einar (name) ON		
einars	einar's ON, Einar's (name) ON, Einar'S (name) OI	eiríksstöðum	Eriksstadir (place) ON, Eriksstadir (place) ON, Eriksstadir (place) OI
einfæting	one-footer ON, one-footer OI	eiríksvági	Eriksvog (place) ON
einfætingaland	One-Footer-Land (place) ON, One-Footer-Land (place) OI	eiríksvogi	Eriksvog (place) OI
		eiríkur	Erik (name) OI
einfætingi	one-footer OI	eitt	alone OI, along ON, along OI, an ON, once ON, once OI, one ON, one OI, single ON
einfætingr	a-one-footer ON, one-footer ON, the-one-footer ON		
		eitthvert	some OI
einfætingur	a-one-footer OI	ek	i ON
einfætingurinn	one-footer OI		

Word List (Norse to English)

Norse	English
ekki	not ON, not OI, nothing ON, nothing OI
eltu	pursued ON, pursued OI
em	am ON
en	and ON, and OI, before ON, but ON, but OI, but-for ON, but-for OI, than ON, than OI, that ON, that OI, then ON, then OI, when ON, when OI, which OI, while ON, while OI
enda	end ON, end OI
endunum	ends ON, ends OI
enga	any ON, none ON
engan	no ON, none ON
engar	no ON, no OI
engi	no ON, no OI, none ON, none OI, no-one ON, not ON
engin	no ON
enginn	no ON
engu	none ON, nothing ON
engum	no ON
enn	but OI, still ON, yet ON, yet OI
er	a ON, am OI, am-i ON, are ON, are OI, as ON, as OI, for ON, is ON, is OI, spoke OI, that ON, that OI, the OI, then ON, then OI, to ON, to OI, was ON, was OI, were ON, were OI, when ON, when OI, where ON, where OI, which ON, which OI, who ON, who OI, who-was ON
erendi	errand ON
erendum	errand ON
eríksfjörð	Eriksfjord (place) ON, Eriksfjord (place) OI
erindi	errand OI
erindum	errand OI
ermar	sleeves ON, sleeves OI
ert	are ON, are OI
ertu	are-you ON, are-you OI
eru	are ON, are OI, were ON, were OI
eruð	are ON
erum	are ON, are OI
es	where ON, which ON
ey	an-island OI, island ON
eyðimerkr	deserted-forest ON
eyðimerkur	deserted-forest OI
eygðir	eyed ON, eyes OI
eyjar	islands OI
eyjarnar	islands ON, islands OI
eyjólf	Eyolf (name) ON, Eyolf (name) OI
eyjólfr	Eyolf (name) ON
eyjólfs	Eyolf's (name) ON, Eyolf'S (name) OI
eyjólfur	Eyolf (name) OI
eyna	island OI, the-island OI
eynni	island ON, island OI
eyra	ear ON, ear OI
eyrar	islands ON, Islands (place) OI
eysteins	Eystein (name) ON, Eystein (name) OI
eystri	eastern ON
eyvindar	Eyvind (name) ON, Eyvind (name) OI

F, f

Norse	English
fá	be ON, be OI, get ON, get OI
faðerni	paternity ON, paternity OI
faðir	father ON, father OI, father-of ON, father-to OI
fæð	sadness ON
fæða	bear OI, feed ON, feed OI
fæðist	born ON
fælast	frightened ON, frightened OI
fær	go ON
færast	move ON, move OI
færð	taken ON, taken OI
færðu	went ON, went OI
fært	going-out ON

Word List (Norse to English)

Norse	English
fæti	feet OI
fætr	feet ON
fættast	carry ON
fætur	feet OI
fagnat	welcomed ON
fagra	fair ON, fair OI
fagrt	beautiful ON
fagurt	beautiful OI
fal	hid ON, hid OI
fálátari	withdrawn OI
fall	fall ON, fall OI
fallinn	fall ON, fall OI
fámálug	silent ON, silent OI
fámálugur	few-words OI
fang	provisions ON
fann	found ON, found OI
far	go ON, go OI
fara	go ON, go OI, to-go OI, to-travel OI, travel ON, travel OI, travelling ON, travelling OI, went OI
fardreng	traveller-generous ON, traveller-generous OI
fardrengr	travelling-companion ON
fardrengur	travelling-companion OI
farið	gone OI, travelled OI
farir	travel OI
farit	gone ON, travelled ON
farm	from ON
farminn	cargo OI
fátæku	poor ON
fátækum	poor ON, poor OI
fátt	few OI
fé	cattle ON, cattle OI, wealth ON, wealth OI
feðga	father-and-son ON, father-and-son OI
feðgar	father-and-son ON, father-and-son OI
feðgum	father-and-son ON, father-and-son OI
fegri	more-beautiful ON, more-beautiful OI
féið	treasure OI, wealth OI
féit	treasure ON, wealth ON
feitt	bold ON, bold OI
fekk	got ON, married ON
fékk	got OI, married OI
fell	fell ON
féll	fell OI
felldi	shed ON, shed OI
felldu	fell ON, fell OI
fellr	falls ON
fellu	fell ON
féllu	fell OI
fellur	falls OI
fénað	cattle ON
fénaður	cattle OI
fengið	caught OI, found OI
fengit	caught ON, found ON
fengu	caught ON, caught OI, gathered OI, got OI
fer	goes OI, going OI, travel OI, travelled OI, went OI
ferð	journey OI, travel ON, travel OI
ferðar	travel ON, travel OI
ferr	goes ON, journeyed ON, travelled ON
festar	fixed ON
festi	joined ON
fimm	five ON, five OI
fimmtán	fifteen ON
fingrar	finger ON, finger OI
fingrgull	finger-gold ON
fingurgull	finger-gold OI
finna	find ON, find OI, found ON, found OI
finnið	find ON, find OI
finnst	finding ON
finnur	finding OI
firðinum	fjord ON, fjord OI
firr	further ON, further OI
fiskar	fish ON, fish OI
fiski	fishing ON
fiskum	fish ON, fish OI
fjarðskorið	fjords-carving OI
fjárhagur	finances OI
fjárkosta	financial-cost's ON, financial-cost's OI
fjölda	many OI
fjölða	many ON

110

Word List (Norse to English)

Norse	English
fjöldi	many OI
fjölði	many ON
fjölkunnig	full-knowing ON, full-knowing OI
fjöll	mountains ON, mountains OI
fjölmenn	many-people OI
fjölmenna	many-men ON, many-men OI
fjölmenni	many ON, many OI
fjóra	forty ON
fjörð	fjord ON
fjórða	fourth OI
fjörðinn	fjord OI
fjórir	four ON, four OI, many OI
fjörsins	live ON
fjórtán	fourteen ON
flatnefs	Flat-Nose (name) ON, Flat-Nose (name) OI
fleira	more OI
fleiri	more ON
flekk	a-speck OI, speck ON
flestir	mostly OI
flestra	most ON, most OI
fleygðu	flew ON
flíkr	banners ON
flíkur	banners OI
fljótlega	soon OI
fljótliga	soon ON
fló	flew OI
flóðið	tide OI
flóðit	tide ON
flutt	performed ON
flutti	brought ON, brought OI
fluttr	transferred ON
fluttur	transferred OI
flýja	fleeing ON
flytist	flows ON
flytja	carried ON, carried OI, carry OI
föður	father ON, father OI, father's ON
fólgið	hidden OI
fólgit	hidden ON
fólk	people ON, people OI
fólki	folk ON
fólkit	people ON
föng	possessions ON, possessions OI, provisions OI, supplies ON
fór	came ON, came OI, journeyed OI, returned OI, travelled ON, travelled OI, travelling OI, went ON, went OI
forðast	avoid ON, avoid OI
forlög	fortune ON, fortune OI, fortunes ON, fortunes OI
forlögum	fortune ON, fortune OI
formaðr	chief ON
formaður	chief OI
forræði	power ON, power OI
forsjá	foresight ON, foresight OI
fórst	went ON, went OI
fóru	travelled ON, travelled OI, went ON, went OI
fóruð	travelled OI
förum	go ON, go OI, going ON, going OI, gone ON, gone OI, travel-we ON, travel-we OI
förunautur	ship's-company OI
föruneyti	companions ON, companions OI
forvitni	curiosity OI, curious ON, curious ON, curious OI
fóstra	foster ON, foster OI, foster-child ON, foster-child OI
fóstri	foster ON, foster OI
fóta	feet ON, feet OI
fótum	feet ON, feet OI
frá	from ON, from OI, time ON, time OI
fræði	knowledge OI, wisdom ON, wisdom OI
frænda	kinsmen ON, kinsmen OI
frændi	kinsman ON, kinsman OI
frændur	kinsman OI
fram	from ON, from ON, from OI

Word List (Norse to English)

Norse	English	Norse	English
framast	foremost ON, foremost OI	fúss	willing ON
framgengt	from-going ON	fylgdar	follow OI
framið	committed ON	fylgdi	followed OI
framin	committed OI	fylgði	followed ON
framt	provide OI	fylgdu	followed OI
frásögnum	account ON, account OI	fylgðu	followed ON
fremi	provide ON	fylgi	follow OI
fremja	perform ON, perform OI	fylgir	followed OI
frétt	news ON, news OI	fylgja	follow ON, to-follow OI
frétti	heard ON, heard OI	fylgt	followed ON, followed OI
freydís	Freydis (name) ON, Freydis (name) OI	fyndi	found ON, found OI
freydísi	Freydis (name) ON, Freydis (name) OI	fyr	for ON, for OI
		fyrir	ahead ON, ahead OI, along ON, along OI, and OI, because-of ON, because-of OI, before ON, before OI, for ON, for OI, present ON, therefore OI, to ON
frið	peaceful OI		
friðarmark	peace-mark ON		
friðartákn	peace-mark OI		
friðgerðar	Fridgerdar (name) ON		
frjálsa	free ON, free OI		
fróðari	wiser OI	fyrr	before ON, before OI, for ON, for OI
fróðárundr	hauntings ON		
fróðárundur	hauntings OI	fyrra	first ON, first OI
fróðleiks	knowledge ON, knowledge OI	fyrst	first ON, first OI
		fyrsta	first ON, first OI
fróðr	wise ON	fýsa	desire ON, desire OI
fróður	wise OI	fýsist	desired OI
fugl	birds ON, birds OI, wild-birds OI	fýsti	desired ON, desired OI
		fýstist	desired ON, desired OI
fullkomna	full-come ON, full-come OI	fýstu	urged OI

G, g

Norse	English
fullr	full ON
fulltrúann	patron ON, patron OI
fullur	full OI
fund	find ON, find OI
fundið	found OI
fundit	found ON
fundu	found ON, found OI
fundust	found OI, met ON, were-found ON
furðustrandir	Furdustrandir (place) ON, Furdustrandir (place) OI
furðuströndum	Furdustrandir (place) ON, Furdustrandir (place) OI
fús	willing OI

Norse	English
gáðu	heeded ON, looked OI
gæfa	gift OI
gæfi	gave ON, gave OI
gæfu	gifted ON
gæsku	goodness OI
gæsla	herding OI
gæzla	herding ON
gaf	gave ON, gave OI
gáfu	gave ON, gave OI
gagnvart	going-from ON, going-from OI
gakk	go ON
gall	bellowed OI

112

Word List (Norse to English)

Norse	English
gamlason	Gamlason (name) ON, Gamlason (name) OI
ganga	go ON, go OI, walk ON
gangi	go ON, go OI
gapði	gaping ON
gapti	agape OI
garða	Gardar (place) OI
garðar	Gardar (place) ON
garðarr	Gardi (name) ON
garði	garden ON, garden OI, Gardi (name) OI
garðs	garden OI
gaum	heed ON, heed OI
geðjaðir	agreeable ON
gefa	give ON, give OI
gefið	given ON, given OI
gefin	given ON, given OI, marry OI
gefit	given ON
gegnt	opposite ON, opposite OI
geirsteinn	Gerstein (name) ON, Gerstein (name) OI
geislar	rays ON
geisli	rays OI
gekk	going ON, going OI, walked ON, walked OI, went ON, went OI
gellis	Gellir (name) ON, Gellir (name) OI, Gellis (name) ON
gellr	bellowed ON
gengr	went ON
gengu	went ON, went OI
gengur	went OI
ger	made ON, made OI
gera	do ON, do OI, made ON, made OI, make ON, make OI
gerði	did ON, did OI
gerðist	became ON, became OI, became-a ON, becoming OI, happened ON, happened OI, made ON
gerðu	did ON, did OI, made ON, made OI
gerið	make ON, make OI
gerir	did ON, did OI
gerist	was OI
gerr	made ON
gersemi	treasure OI
gersimi	treasure ON
gert	done OI, made ON, made OI, was-done ON
gervir	made ON, made OI
get	can ON, do ON, guess ON, guess OI
geta	can ON, could OI
getið	told-of OI
getit	told-of ON
gifta	give ON, give OI
giftast	marry ON, marry OI
gifti	gave ON, gave OI
giftu	luck ON, luck OI
gildir	thick ON, thick OI
gjafar	gifts ON
gjafir	gifts OI
gjaforð	given OI, married ON, married OI
gjaforðs	marriage-offer ON, marriage-offer OI
gjalda	expenses ON, expenses OI
gjarna	gladly OI
gleði	gladness ON, gladness OI
glertölur	glass-beads ON, glass-beads OI
glitraði	glittered ON, glittered OI
glöggsæ	clear OI
glumru	Glumra (name) ON, Glumra (name) OI
gnóttir	abundance ON, abundance OI
góð	good ON, good OI
góða	good ON, good OI
góðan	good ON, good OI
góðar	good ON, good OI
góðir	good ON, good OI
góðmannlega	good-man-like OI
góðmannliga	good-man-like ON
goðorðsmaður	good-words-man OI
góðr	a-good ON, good ON
góðra	good ON

Word List (Norse to English)

Norse	English
góðs	good OI
góðu	good ON
góður	a-good OI, good OI
góðvilja	good-will ON, good-will OI
göfgan	esteemed ON, esteemed OI
göfgir	noble ON, noble OI
göfugmenni	noble ON, noble OI
goldið	gold OI
goldit	gold ON
gott	good ON, good OI
grænland	Greenland (place) ON, Greenland (place) OI
grænlandi	Greenland (place) ON, Greenland (place) OI
grænlands	Greenland (place) ON, Greenland (place) OI
grænlandshaf	Greenland-Sea (place) OI
grænlenskan	Greenland-Skin (place) OI
grænlenskir	Greenlander (place) OI
grænlenskum	Greenlander (place) OI
grænlenzkan	greenland-skin ON
grænlenzkum	Greenlander (place) ON
grafar	trenches ON
grafir	trenches OI
grafnir	buried ON, buried OI
grautr	porridge ON
grautur	porridge OI
greiðleg	smoothly OI
greiðlig	smoothly ON
grélaðar	Grelod (name) ON, Grelod (name) OI
griðungr	bull ON
griðungur	a-bull OI
grímólfsson	Grimolfson (name) ON, Grimolfson (name) OI
grjótinu	stones OI
grjótit	stones ON
gró	Gro (name) ON, Groa (name) OI
gröfunum	trenches ON, trenches OI
grön	green ON, green OI
grös	grass OI
grunar	suspect ON, suspect OI
guð	god ON, God (name) OI, God's (name) ON, God'S (name) OI
guðríðar	Guthrid (name) ON, Guthrid (name) OI
guðríði	Guthrid (name) ON, Guthrid (name) OI
guðríðr	Guthrid (name) ON
guðríður	Guthrid (name) OI
guðröðarsonar	Son-of-Gudrod (name) ON, Son-Of-Gudrod (name) OI
guðs	god ON, God's (name) ON, God'S (name) OI
gull	gold ON, gold OI
gunnbjarnarsker	Gunnbjarnarsker (place) ON, Gunnbjarnarsker (place) OI
gunnbjörn	Gunnbjorn (name) ON, Gunnbjorn (name) OI

H, h

Norse	English
hægendi	a-cushion ON
hægindi	pillows OI
hænsafiðri	hen's-feathers ON, hen's-feathers OI
hætta	danger ON, danger OI, leave ON, leave OI
hættir	manner ON, mannered OI
haf	sea ON, sea OI
hafa	at-sea ON, at-sea OI, had ON, had OI, have ON, have OI, have-been OI, having ON
hafði	had ON, had OI, had-been ON, had-been OI, have OI
hafðir	have ON, have OI
hafi	had ON, had OI, have ON, have OI, sea ON, sea OI
hafið	have ON, have OI
háflæðum	high-tide ON, high-tide OI

Word List (Norse to English)

Norse	English
haft	had ON, had OI
hafvillur	open-sea ON
hagi	state ON, state OI
hagr	benefits ON
hagstætt	favourable OI
haki	Haki (name) ON, Haki (name) OI
halda	have OI, hold OI, holding ON
haldast	hold ON, hold OI
haldið	staying OI
hálfan	half ON, half OI
hálfdanarsonar	Son-of-Halfdan (name) ON, Son-Of-Halfdan (name) OI
hálfr	half-of ON
hálft	half-of ON, half-of OI
hallæri	famine ON, famine OI
hallat	inclined ON
halldís	Halldis (name) ON, Halldis (name) OI
hallfríðr	Hallfrid (name) ON
hallfríður	Hallfrid (name) OI
hallist	will-be OI
hallveig	Hallveig (name) ON, Hallveig (name) OI
hálmbúst	straw-staves ON
hálmbústum	straw-staves OI
hálsi	neck ON, neck OI
hamargnípu	cliff-top ON, cliff-top OI
hamra	crags ON, crags OI
hana	he OI, her ON, her OI, it ON, it OI, she ON, that OI
hann	[she] ON, he ON, he OI, he-was ON, him ON, him OI, himself ON, it ON, it OI, she OI
hans	him ON, him OI, his ON, his OI, to-him ON
happ	zeal ON, zeal OI
happfróð	lucky-wise ON
hár	hair ON, hair OI
harða	hard ON, hard OI
hart	rough ON, rough OI
hásæti	a-high-seat ON, a-high-seat OI
háseta	men ON
hátt	loud ON, loudly ON, loudly OI
hattar	customs ON, customs OI
háttar	kind ON, kind OI
háttr	the-way ON, way ON
háttur	the-way OI, way OI
haukadal	Haukadal (place) ON, Haukadal (place) OI
haukdælski	Haukadal (place) ON, Haukadal (place) OI
hausakljúfr	Scull-Cleaver (name) ON
hausakljúfur	Scull-Cleaver (name) OI
haust	autumn ON, autumn OI
haustboð	harvest-feast ON, harvest-feast OI
haustið	autumn OI
haustit	autumn ON
hefða	had ON
hefði	had ON, had OI
hefi	have ON, have OI
hefir	had ON, had OI, has ON, has OI, have ON, have OI
hefr	had ON
hefur	had OI
heiðni	heathenry OI
heil	well ON, well OI, whole ON, whole OI
heim	home ON, home OI, homes ON
heima	home ON, home OI, homes ON
heimamönnum	housemen ON, housemen OI
heiman	home ON, home OI
heimilis	households ON
heimilt	may OI
heimkynna	households OI
heimti	claimed ON, claimed OI
heita	called ON, named OI
heitir	called ON, named ON, named OI
heitit	called ON
hekja	Hekja (name) ON, Hekja (name) OI
heldi	held ON

Word List (Norse to English)

Norse	English	Norse	English
heldr	behold ON, held ON, Heldr'S (name) OI, rather ON	herjaði	harried ON, harried OI
heldr's	Heldr's (name) ON	herjólfsnes	Herjolfsnes (place) ON, Herjolfsnes (place) OI
heldu	busy ON, held ON	herjólfsnesi	Herjolfsnes (place) ON, Herjolfsnes (place) OI
héldu	busy OI, held OI		
heldur	behind OI, behold OI, held OI, rather OI	herkonungr	warrior-king ON
helga	Helga (name) ON, Helgi (name) OI	herkonungur	a-warrior-king OI
helgasonar	Helgason (name) OI, Son-of-Helga (name) ON	hertekinn	war-taken ON, war-taken OI
		hertekna	captive ON, captive OI
helgir	flat ON, flat OI	herteknir	war-taken ON, war-taken OI
hella	flat-stones ON, flat-stones OI	hést	promised OI
hellisvöllum	Hellisvellir (place) ON, Hellisvellir (place) OI	hesthöfða	Horse-Head (name) OI
helluland	Helluland (place) ON, Helluland (place) OI	hesthöfði	Horse-Head (name) ON
hellum	caves ON, caves OI	hét	called ON, named OI, was ON, was-called ON, was-named ON, was-named OI
hellur	slabs ON, slabs OI		
hellusteinn	a-slab-stone OI, slab-stone ON		
helming	half ON, half OI	héti	named ON, named OI
helmingr	half ON	hétu	called ON, named OI, pledged OI
helmingur	half OI		
helst	preferably OI	heyr	hear ON
helt	held ON	heyra	hear ON, hear OI
hélt	held OI	heyrðu	hear OI, heard ON
helzt	preferably ON, rather ON	heyrt	heard ON, heard OI
		hézt	promised ON
hendi	hand ON, hand OI	híbýlabótar	living-space OI
hendr	hand ON	híbýli	dwelling ON, dwelling OI, dwellings ON, dwellings OI
hendur	hand OI		
hennar	for-her ON, for-her OI, her ON, her OI, hers ON, hers OI, she ON, she OI	hið	the OI
		hímu	aunt ON
		hin	in OI, that OI, the OI
		hina	the OI
henni	he OI, her ON, her OI, hers ON, hers OI, him ON, she ON, she OI, to-her ON, to-her OI	hindrvitni	hindered-knowledge ON
		hingað	here OI
		hingat	here ON
hent	joined ON, joined OI	hinir	others ON, others OI
hentar	suits ON, suits OI	hinn	in OI, of OI, the OI
heppni	lucky ON, lucky OI	hinni	the OI
hér	here ON, here OI, she ON	hins	the OI
		hinu	the OI
herðir	hardened ON, hardened OI	hinum	the OI

Word List (Norse to English)

Norse	English
hirða	consider ON
hirðar	court ON, court OI
hítardal	Hitardal (place) ON, Hitardal (place) OI
hitt	encounter ON, encounter OI, other ON, they OI
hitti	met ON, met OI
hittir	met ON
hittu	met ON, met OI
hjá	beside ON, beside OI, by ON, by OI, heard ON, near ON, near OI
hjallinn	the-platform ON
hjálp	help ON, help OI
hjálpa	help OI
hjálpar	help ON
hjó	struck ON, struck OI
hjörð	hearth ON, herd OI
hjörtu	hearts ON, hearts OI
hjú	hearth OI, herd ON
hlaupa	ran ON, ran OI, run ON, run OI
hlaut	lot ON, lot OI
hleypr	ran ON
hleypur	ran OI
hliðum	sides OI
hliðunum	sides ON
hljóðlyndr	quiet ON
hljóðlyndur	quiet OI
hljóðs	be-heard ON, be-heard OI
hljóp	ran ON, ran OI
hljópu	ran ON, ran OI
hljótt	quietly ON, quietly OI
hlotist	lots OI
hlupu	running ON
hluta	lot ON, lots OI, part OI, Part's (name) ON
hlutaðir	lots ON
hlutaðist	lots OI
hlutföllum	lot-taking OI
hluti	things ON, things OI
hlutir	things ON, things OI
hlutr	lot ON
hlutuðu	lots ON
hlutur	lot OI
hlýðni	homage ON, homage OI
hnappinn	knob OI
hnappur	a-knob OI, fastening OI
hné	knee ON
hneig	knee OI
hneppt	fastened OI
hníf	knife ON, knife OI
hnjóskulinda	a-girdle ON, a-girdle OI
höfð	taken OI
höfða	Hofda (place) ON
höfðaströnd	Hofdastrond (place) ON
höfði	head ON, head OI, heads ON, heads OI
höfðinglegt	having-like OI
höfðingligt	having-like ON
höfðu	had ON, had OI, heads OI
höfuð	heads ON, heads OI
höfum	have ON, have OI
hófust	began ON
höggr	hewed ON
höggur	hewed OI
hólmgöngu-hrafn	Raven-the-Dueller (name) ON, Raven-The-Dueller (name) OI
hólmlátri	Holmlatr (place) ON, Holmlatr (place) OI
holta	hills ON, hills OI
holum	holes ON, holes OI
hon	it ON, she ON
hönd	hand ON, hand OI
höndina	hand ON
höndum	hand ON, hand OI, hands ON, hands OI
honum	he ON, he OI, her OI, him ON, him OI, his ON, his OI, to-him OI
hópi	Hop (place) ON, Hop (place) OI, tidal-pool ON, tidal-pool OI
hópit	group ON
hörð	hard ON, hard OI
horfði	looked OI, looking ON
horfðu	looked ON
horfinn	disappeared ON, disappeared OI
hörmung	horrible ON, horrible OI

Word List (Norse to English)

Norse	English
hornströndum	Hornstrandir (place) ON, Hornstrandir (place) OI
höttr	hood ON
hötturinn	hoods OI
hrærðist	stirred ON, stirred OI
hrafnsfjörð	Hrafnsfjord (place) ON, Hrafnsfjord (place) OI
hraunhafnarósi	Hraunhafnaros (place) ON, Hraunhafnaros (place) OI
hríð	awhile ON
hring	a-ring ON, a-ring OI
hróaldssonar	Roaldsson (name) ON
hryggs	the-sad ON
húðkeipa	skin-boats ON, skin-boats OI
hug	mind ON, mind OI, thoughts ON, thoughts OI
hún	her OI, it OI, she OI
hundrað	hundred ON
hundraðs	hundred OI
hurfu	disappeared ON, disappeared OI
hús	house ON, house OI, houses ON, houses OI
húsfreyja	housewife ON, housewife OI
húsunum	the-house ON, the-house OI
hvað	to-that OI, what ON, what OI
hval	whale ON, whale OI
hvala	whale ON
hvalinn	whale ON
hvalnum	whales OI
hvalr	a-whale ON
hvalur	whale OI
hvammi	Hvamm (place) ON, Hvamm (place) OI
hvarf	disappeared ON, disappeared OI
hvarfsgnípu	Hvarfsgnipu (place) ON, Hvarfsgnipu (place) OI
hvárirtveggju	either-side ON
hvárki	neither ON
hvárkis	neither ON
hvárt	either ON, if ON
hvat	what ON
hvé	how ON
hveiti	wheat OI
hveitiakra	wheat-acres ON, wheat-acres OI
hveitiakrar	wheat-acres ON, wheat-acres OI
hveitiax	wheat ON
hvenær	when OI
hver	each OI, each-of OI, every OI, who ON, who OI
hverfr	turned ON
hverfur	turned OI
hvergi	neither ON, neither OI
hverju	each ON, each OI
hverr	each ON, every ON
hversdaglega	always OI
hversu	how ON, how OI
hvert	what OI
hví	why ON, why OI
hvít	white ON
hvítan	white ON, white OI
hvítbeins	White-Leg (name) ON, White-Leg (name) OI
hvíti	the-White (name) ON, The-White (name) OI
hvítir	white ON, white OI
hvítramannaland	White-Man-Land (place) ON, White-Man-Land (place) OI
hvítt	white OI
hvítum	white ON, white OI
hvorgis	neither OI
hvorirtveggju	either-side OI
hvorki	neither OI
hvort	either OI, whether OI
hvorttveggja	each-way OI
hvorutveggja	either-way OI
hyggja	thought ON, thought OI

I, i

Norse	English
iljar	feet OI

Word List (Norse to English)

Norse	English	Norse	English
illa	a-bad ON, badly ON, badly OI	ísland	Iceland (place) ON, Iceland (place) OI
illilega	badly OI	íslandi	Iceland (place) ON, Iceland (place) OI
illilegir	ill-looking OI	íslands	Iceland (place) ON, Iceland (place) OI
illiliga	badly ON	íslenskur	Icelander (place) OI
illiligir	ill-looking ON	íslenzkr	Icelander (place) ON
illorðr	difficult-of-words ON	ístruna	belly-fat ON, the belly OI
illt	disorderly ON, disorderly OI, ill ON, ill OI		
illugi	Illugi (name) ON, Illugi (name) OI		
in	in ON, the ON	**J, j**	
ina	the ON	jaðri	Jaeren (place) ON, Jaeren (place) OI
ingjalds	Ingjald's (name) ON, Ingjald'S (name) OI	jafn	equal OI
ingólfi	Ingolf (name) ON, Ingolf (name) OI	jafna	equal ON
inn	in ON, in OI, inside OI, of ON, the ON, then ON, then OI	jafnan	equal ON, equal OI, equally ON, equally OI, ever ON
innan	in ON, in OI, inside ON, inside OI, within ON, within OI	jafnlangt	equal-long ON, equal-long OI
		jafnmannvænn	equally-handsome ON
inni	of-the ON, the ON	jafnmikið	equal OI
ins	the ON	jafnmikit	equal ON
inum	in ON, the ON	jarl	Earl (name) ON, Earl (name) OI
it	the ON, to ON	jarli	Earl (name) ON, Earl (name) OI
		járnsíðu	Ironside (name) ON
Í, í		jökli	glacier ON, glacier OI
í	a ON, a OI, about ON, about OI, among ON, among OI, at ON, at OI, in ON, in OI, into ON, into OI, it ON, it OI, of ON, of OI, on ON, on OI, the OI, this ON, to ON, to OI	jól	Yule (name) ON, Yule (name) OI
		jólaveislu	Yule-Feast (name) OI
		jólaveizlu	yule-feast ON
		jólin	Yule (name) ON, Yule (name) OI
		jólum	Yule (name) ON, Yule (name) OI
íhuga	thought ON, thought OI	jörð	land ON, the-earth OI
írakonungs	Ireland-King (name) ON	jörundar	Jorund (name) ON, Jorund (name) OI
írland	Ireland (place) ON, Ireland (place) OI	jörva	Jorfi (name) ON, Jorfi (place) OI
írlandi	Ireland (place) ON, Ireland (place) OI		
írlandshaf	the-Irish-Sea (place) ON	**K, k**	

Word List (Norse to English)

Norse	English
kæmi	came ON, came OI, come ON, come OI
kæmir	come OI
kaf	submerge ON
kálfskinnsskó	calf-skin-shoes OI
kálfskinnsskúa	calf-skin-shoes ON
kalla	call ON, call OI
kallað	called OI
kallaði	called ON, called OI
kallaðir	called ON, called OI
kallaðr	called ON
kallaður	called OI
kallast	considered ON
kallat	called ON
kalt	cold ON, cold OI
kann	can ON, can OI, can-it ON, it OI, know ON, know OI, known ON
kanna	explore ON, explore OI, exploring OI
karla	men ON, men OI
karlmaðrinn	menservants ON
karlmaðurinn	servants OI
karlsefni	Karlsefni (name) ON, Karlsefni (name) OI
karlsefnis	Karlsefni's (name) ON, Karlsefni'S (name) OI
karlsefnissonar	Karlsefnison (name) ON, Karlsefnison (name) OI, Son-of-Karlsefni (name) ON
kastaði	cast OI
katanes	Caithness (place) ON, Caithness (place) OI
katanesi	Caithness (place) ON, Caithness (place) OI
kátari	merrier ON, merrier OI
kattarskinn	cat-skin ON, cat-skin OI
kattskinnsglófa	cat-skin-gloves ON, cat-skin-gloves OI
kaupa	buy OI, purchase ON, purchase OI
kaupferðum	trading-journeys ON, trading-journeys OI
kaupir	bought ON, bought OI
kaupmenn	trading-men ON, trading-men OI
kaupmönnum	trading-men ON, trading-men OI
kaupskipinu	merchant-ship OI
kaupstefna	trading-posts ON, trading-posts OI
kaupstefnu	trading-posts ON, trading-posts OI
keipana	trading ON, trading OI
keldu	wellspring ON, wellspring OI
kemr	came ON
kemur	came OI, coming OI
kenndi	knew ON, knew OI, taught ON, taught OI
kenndu	knew OI, taught ON, taught OI
kenni	recognise ON, recognise OI
kennimenn	priest ON, priests OI
kennimönnum	priests ON, priests OI
kenni-val	know-choose ON, know-choose OI
ketils	Ketil (name) OI, Ketil's (name) ON
ketilssonar	Son-of-Ketil (name) ON, Son-Of-Ketil (name) OI
kiðjamjólk	kid's-milk ON, kid's-milk OI
kinnum	cheeks ON
kinnunum	cheeks OI
kippa	pulled ON, pulled OI
kirkju	church ON, church OI, the-church ON
kista	coffin ON, coffin OI
kistil	chest ON, chest OI
kjafal	kjafal ON, kjafal OI
kjalarnes	Kjalarnes (place) ON, Kjalarnes (place) OI
kjarvals	Kjarval (name) ON
kjöl	a-keel OI, keel ON
kjörin	chosen OI
klæði	cloth OI, clothes ON, clothes OI, clothing OI
klæðið	cloth OI, clothes OI
klæðin	bed-clothes ON, bed-clothes OI
klæðum	clothes ON, clothes OI
klæðunum	clothes ON

Word List (Norse to English)

Norse	English
klípti	pinched OI
klóraði	scratched OI
knappi	fastening ON
knappinn	knob ON
knappr	a-knob ON
knarrar	merchant-ship ON, ship OI
knarrarbringu	Knarrarbringu (name) ON, Knarrarbringu (name) OI
kneppt	fastened ON
knörr	ship ON, ship OI
knött	balls ON, balls OI
köllu	called OI
kölluð	called ON, called OI
kölluðu	called ON, called OI
kolum	coal ON, coal OI
kom	came ON, came OI, come OI
koma	came ON, came OI, come ON, come OI, coming ON, coming OI
komast	come ON, come OI
komat	come ON, come OI
komi	come OI, comes ON
komið	come ON, come OI
komin	coming ON, coming OI
kominn	came ON, came OI, come ON, come OI, coming ON, coming OI
komit	come ON
komk	come ON
komnir	came ON, came OI, coming ON, returning OI
komst	came OI
komu	came OI
kómu	came ON
kómust	arrived ON, went ON
kona	as-a-woman ON, wife ON, wife OI, woman ON, woman OI
konan	the-woman OI, woman ON
konar	kind-of OI, kinds ON, kinds OI
könnuðu	explore ON, explored OI
konu	a-wife ON, a-wife OI, a-woman ON, a-woman OI, wife ON, wife OI, woman ON, woman OI
konum	woman ON
konungar	kings ON, kings OI
konungi	king ON, king OI
konungr	king ON, King (name) ON, the-king ON
konungs	king ON, king OI, the-King (name) ON, The-King (name) OI
konungur	king OI, King (name) OI, The-King (name) OI
konur	women ON, women OI
körin	chosen ON
korn	corn ON, corn OI
kost	costs OI, provided ON
kostaði	exerted ON, exerted OI
kostar	choice ON, choice OI
kosti	benefits OI
kostr	choice ON
köstuðu	cast ON, cast OI
kostum	benefit ON
kostur	choice OI
krafði	called ON
kráku	Crow (name) ON, Crow (name) OI
kristin	Christian (name) ON, Christian (name) OI
kristinn	Christian (name) ON
kristni	Christianity (name) ON, Christianity (name) OI
kristr	Christ (name) ON
kristur	Christ (name) OI
krossa	crosses ON, crosses OI
krosshólum	Krossholar (place) ON, Krossholar (place) OI
krýp	creep OI
krýpk	creep ON
kunna	know-how ON, know-how OI, knowing OI
kunnandi	knowing OI
kunni	knew OI
kunnigt	known ON, known OI

Word List (Norse to English)

Norse	English
kvað	called ON, cried-out ON, cried-out OI, said ON, said OI, saying ON, saying OI
kvaddi	called OI
kváðu	said ON, said OI
kvæði	poem ON
kvæðið	poem OI
kvæðit	poem ON, recited ON
kvæntir	married ON
kvángaðist	married ON
kveðið	declaring OI, poem OI, sung OI
kveðit	declared ON, sung ON
kveðjur	greetings ON, greetings OI
kveðst	said ON, said OI, saying ON, saying OI
kveld	evening ON, evening OI
kveldið	evening OI
kveldit	evening ON
kvenna	woman ON, woman OI
kvenskörungr	noble ON
kviðling	verse ON, verse OI
kvikindum	creatures OI
kvongaðir	married OI
kvongaðist	married OI
kvonlausir	unmarried OI
kykvendum	creatures ON
kynjalaust	extraordinary ON, extraordinary OI
kynkvíslum	family ON
kynlegr	wonderful OI
kynligr	wonderful ON
kynni	circumstance ON, knew ON, knew OI
kynnu	circumstance OI, knew OI
kyrrt	peace ON, peace OI

L, l

Norse	English
lá	lay ON, lay OI, laying ON
láð	invited ON, invited OI
lægðir	low-ground ON, low-ground OI
lækr	stream ON
lækur	stream OI
lætr	let ON
lagði	laid ON, laid OI
lags	position ON, position OI
lagt	laid ON, laid OI
lágu	laid ON, laid OI, lay ON, lay OI, laying ON, laying OI
lambskinnskofra	lamb-skin-hood ON, lamb-skin-hood OI
land	land ON, land OI
landa	lands ON, lands OI
landar	land ON, land OI
landi	land ON, land OI
landið	land OI, the-land OI
landinu	land ON, land OI, the-land OI, to-the-land OI
landit	land ON, the-land ON
landkosta	land-benefits ON
lands	land ON, land OI, lands ON, lands OI
landsins	lands ON
landskosta	land-benefits ON, land-benefits OI
landskosti	land-benefits OI
landskostir	land-benefits ON, land-benefits OI
landsleg	landscape ON
landsmenn	landsmen ON, landsmen OI
landsnytja	land-benefits OI
landsuðr	south-east ON
landsuðrs	south-east ON
landsuður	south-east OI
langa	long ON, long ON, long OI
langadal	Langadal (place) ON, Langadal (place) OI
langæðar	long ON, long OI
langar	long ON, long OI
langt	long ON, long OI
lasta	blamed ON, blamed OI
láta	burn OI, laid ON, leave ON, leave OI, let ON, let OI
látið	left OI
látin	dead ON

Word List (Norse to English)

Norse	English
látizt	died ON
látum	let-us ON, let-us OI
látúnshnappar	brass-buttons OI
laufa	leaf ON, leaf OI
laugarbrekku	Laugarbrekka (place) ON, Laugarbrekka (place) OI
lauk	end ON, end OI, ended ON, ended OI
laun	hired ON, hired OI
launa	loan ON, loan OI, repay ON, repay OI
laungetna	illegitimate ON, illegitimate OI
lausafé	liquidity ON, liquidity OI
lausafjár	liquidity's ON, liquidity's OI
laust	less ON, less OI
léði	lent ON, lent OI
legði	lay OI, leave ON
legðir	lay ON, lay OI
leggjast	to-lie ON, to-lie OI
leggur	have OI
legið	laid OI
legit	laid ON
leið	during OI, lay OI, passed ON, passed OI, the-way OI, way ON
leiðar	route ON, route OI, way ON, way OI
leiddi	led ON, led OI
leif	Leif (name) ON, Leif (name) OI
leifi	Leif (name) ON
leifr	Leif (name) ON
leifur	Leif (name) OI
leikr	like ON
leikskálum	Leikskalar (place) ON, Leikskalar (place) OI
leikur	like OI
leist	impression OI, liked OI
leita	search ON, search OI, seek ON, seek OI
leitað	seek OI
leitaði	sought OI
leitaðir	seek ON
leitat	seek ON
leituðu	sought ON, sought OI
leizt	looked-like ON
léku	played OI
lendur	land OI
lengi	along ON, along OI, long ON, long OI
lengja	long OI
lengr	longer ON
lengra	further ON, further OI
lengst	long OI
lengur	longer OI
lesti	gripped ON, gripped OI
lét	allowed OI, laid OI, lay ON, lay OI, let ON, let OI, lost ON
létist	perished OI
letja	discourage ON, discourage OI
létta	let ON, let OI, relieve ON, relieve OI
létu	left ON, left OI, let ON, let OI
leyfa	allow ON, allow OI
leyfis	leave ON, leave OI
leyndi	concealed ON, concealed OI
leysingi	a-freed-man ON, a-freed-man OI
leysti	released ON, released OI
lézt	died ON, should ON
lið	company ON, team ON, team OI, the-company-of OI
liðfáir	few ON, few OI
liði	help ON, help OI, team ON, team OI
liðið	company OI, team OI
liðin	a-company OI, company ON, passed ON, passed OI, teams OI
liðit	company ON, team ON, the-company ON
liðnir	passed OI
liðs	team ON
liðsinni	assistance ON, assistance OI
líf	life ON, life OI
lifað	lived OI

Word List (Norse to English)

Norse	English
lífi	living ON, living OI
lífs	life OI
liggja	lay ON, lay OI, lies ON, lies OI, lying ON, the-alternative ON
liggr	lies ON
liggur	lies OI
lík	body ON
líkaði	liked ON, liked OI
líkar	like ON
líkast	like ON, like OI
líkin	body OI
líkinu	body ON, body OI, the-bodies ON
líklegt	likely OI
líkunum	the-bodies OI
lit	around ON, colour OI, the-team ON, the-team OI
líta	company OI, look OI
litast	look OI
lítast	looked ON
lítið	little OI
lítils	little ON, little OI
lítilvölva	Little-Prophetess (name) ON, Little-Prophetess (name) OI
lítit	little ON
litla	little ON, little OI
litlu	a-little ON, little ON, Little (name) OI
lítt	little ON, little OI, little-with OI
lituðust	looked ON, looked OI
loðbrókar	Lothbrok (name) ON
loðna	fur ON, hair OI
loðnir	furry ON, furry OI
lofa	praised ON, praised OI
loft	sky ON, sky OI
lög	law ON
lögð	laid ON, laid OI
lögðu	laid ON, laid OI
lönd	land ON, land OI, lands ON, lands OI
löngum	long ON, long OI
lýðum	people ON, people OI
lýkr	ends ON, it-ends ON
lýkur	ends OI
lýsufirði	Lysufjord (place) ON, Lysufjord (place) OI
lýsufjörð	Lysufjord (place) ON, Lysufjord (place) OI

M, m

Norse	English
má	may ON, may OI
maðkahafinu	The-Worm-Sea (place) OI
maðksjá	ship-worms OI
maðksjó	ship-worms ON
maðksjónum	the-worm-sea ON
maðksmogið	worm-eaten OI
maðr	a-man ON, man ON, man OI
maður	a-man OI, man OI
mæddir	wearied OI
mæla	speak ON, speak OI, to-speak OI
mælt	said ON, said OI
mælti	said ON, said OI, spoke ON, spoke OI
mæltu	spoke ON, spoke OI
mætti	may ON, may OI
mættið	may ON
mættist	may ON, may OI
mættuð	may OI
magra	Lean (name) ON, Lean (name) OI
mál	language ON, language OI, matter OI, matters OI, the-matter OI
mála	matter ON
máli	matter ON, matter OI, speak ON, speak OI, the-matter ON, the-matter OI
malmþings	metal-assemblies ON
málmþings	metal-assemblies OI
malt	malt ON, malt OI
mann	a-man OI, man ON, man OI, men ON

Word List (Norse to English)

Norse	English	Norse	English
manna	men ON, men OI, men's OI, Men's (name) ON, people ON, people OI, people's ON, people's ON, people's OI, the people OI, the-men ON, the-people OI	megum	may ON
		meiðar	hurt ON, hurt OI
		mein	harm ON, harm OI
		meir	more ON, more OI
		meira	more ON, more OI
		melrakka	melrakka ON
		melrakkar	melrakka OI
mannaðr	attended ON	menn	man OI, men ON, men OI, people ON, people OI
mannaður	attended OI		
manni	men OI	mennina	men ON
manns	man ON, man OI	menntr	well-educated ON
mannvænn	handsome OI	menntur	educated OI
mannvirðingu	rank ON	mér	i ON, i OI, me ON, me OI, more OI, myself ON, myself OI, to-me ON, to-me OI
mannvirðingum	rank OI		
mannvönd	husband ON, husband OI		
mánuð	month ON, month OI	meræfi	Moray (place) ON, Moray (place) OI
mánuði	months ON, months OI		
marga	many ON, many OI	merki	imprint ON, imprint OI
margar	as-much-as ON, many ON, many OI	messingarspón	brass-spoon ON, brass-spoon OI
margir	many ON, many OI	messingu	brass ON, brass OI
margkunnig	many-knowing ON	mest	most ON, most OI
margt	many ON, many OI	mesta	most ON
margur	many OI	mesti	most ON, most OI
markland	Markland (place) ON, Markland (place) OI	mestr	greatest ON
		mestu	most ON, most OI
matar	food ON, food OI	mestur	greatest OI
matarins	food OI	met	evaluate OI
matbúið	food-prepared OI	meta	evaluate ON
matbúin	food-prepared ON	metnaðarmaðr	ambitious-man ON
matbúit	food-prepared ON	metnaðarmaður	ambitious-man OI
matfanga	hunt OI	miðri	middle OI, the-middle ON
matsveinar	ship's-cook ON, ship's-cook OI		
		mig	i OI, me OI, my OI
mátti	may ON, may OI, that-might OI	mik	i ON, me ON, my ON
		mikið	much OI
máttu	may OI	mikil	great ON, great OI, much OI
með	along ON, along OI, well ON, with ON, with OI		
		mikill	great ON, great OI, large OI, much ON, much OI
meðal	between ON		
meðan	while ON, while OI	mikilli	much ON, much OI
mega	be-able ON	mikinn	a-great OI, as-big ON, great ON, great OI, much ON, much OI
megin	most ON, side ON, ways ON, ways OI		
meginlandinu	mainland OI	mikit	much ON

125

Word List (Norse to English)

Norse	English	Norse	English
mikla	great ON, much ON, much OI	*mót*	meet ON, meet OI, towards OI
miklar	great ON, great OI, much ON, much OI	*móti*	against ON, against OI, meet ON, meet OI, meeting ON, met ON, met OI, towards ON, towards OI
miklir	great ON, great OI		
miklu	much ON, much OI		
miklum	much ON, much OI		
milli	between ON, between OI	*móts*	meet ON
		möttul	mantle OI
millum	between OI	*mun*	could ON, could OI, shall ON, shall OI, should ON, should OI, will ON, would ON, would OI
mín	mine ON, mine OI		
mína	mine OI		
minn	mine ON, mine OI		
minni	mind ON, mine OI		
minnka	decreased OI	*mundi*	could OI, could-be OI, should OI, would ON, would OI, would-be OI
míns	mine OI, my ON, my OI		
mínu	mine OI	*mundu*	should OI, would ON, would OI, would-be ON, would-be OI
mínum	mine ON, mine OI		
miskunn	mercy ON, mercy OI		
miskunnar	mercy OI	*muni*	shall ON, shall OI, should ON
mitt	mine ON, mine OI, my ON		
		munni	mouth ON, mouth OI
mjög	large OI, many OI, much OI, very OI	*munt*	shall ON
mjök	much ON, very ON	*muntu*	shall OI, should ON, should OI
mjöl	meal OI	*mykiskán*	muck-encrusted ON, muck-encrusted OI
móðir	mother ON, mother OI, mother-of ON, mother-of OI, mother-to OI		
		mynda	should ON
		myndi	should ON, would ON
móður	mother ON, mother OI, mother-of ON, mother-of OI	*myndu*	would OI
		mynni	the-mouth-of ON, the-mouth-of OI
mold	dust ON, ground OI	*myrgin*	morning ON
moldu	ground ON, ground OI		
mönnum	men ON, men OI, people ON, people OI		

N, n

Norse	English
mönnunum	people OI
mörg	many ON, many OI
morgin	morning ON	*náðahúss*	outhouse ON
morgininn	morning ON	*náði*	got ON, got OI
morginn	morning ON	*nær*	near ON, near OI, nearly ON
mörgu	many ON	*næst*	next ON, next OI
morgun	morning OI	*nætrnar*	night ON
morguninn	morning OI	*næturnar*	night OI
morgunn	morning OI	*nafn*	name ON, name OI, named OI
mösur	maple OI		
mösurr	maple ON	*nafna*	namesake ON, namesake OI

126

Word List (Norse to English)

Norse	English
nam	took ON, took OI
námu	took ON, took OI
náttúrur	spirits ON, spirits OI
né	nor ON, nor OI
nefndist	named ON, named OI
nefndu	named ON, named OI
nei	no ON, no OI
nema	taken OI, taking OI
nes	headland ON, headland OI
nesi	headland ON
nesið	headland OI, the-headland OI
nesinu	headland ON, the-headland OI
nesit	headland ON
nesla	nettle OI
nezlu	nettle ON
niðr	down ON
niður	down OI
níu	nine ON, nine OI
njóta	enjoy ON
njóti	benefit OI
nokkuð	some OI, something OI
nokkur	anyone OI, some OI
nökkur	some ON
nokkurir	some OI
nökkurir	some ON
nokkurn	certain OI
nökkurn	certain ON, some ON
nökkurr	anyone ON
nokkurra	some OI, something OI
nökkurra	some ON, something ON
nokkuru	sometime OI, somewhat OI
nökkuru	sometime ON
nökkut	some ON, something ON
norðan	north ON, north OI
norðr	north ON
norður	north OI
noreg	Norway (place) OI
nóreg	Norway (place) ON
noregi	Norway (place) OI
nóregi	Norway (place) ON
noregs	Norway (place) OI
nóregs	Norway (place) ON
nösum	nose ON, nose OI
nóttina	night ON, night OI
nú	now ON, now OI
numið	taken OI
numit	taken ON
nýt	benefit ON, use ON, use OI
nýta	take-advantage OI
nytjum	use ON, use OI
nytjumaður	useful OI

O, o

Norse	English
oddr	Odd (name) ON
oddrinn	tip ON
oddur	Odd (name) OI
oddurinn	tip OI
of	about ON, about OI
ofan	above ON, above OI, down ON, down OI, of ON, of OI, off ON, off OI, on ON, on OI, over OI
ofast	highest ON
ofrliði	outnumbered ON
ofurliði	outnumbered OI
og	also OI, and ON, and OI, but OI, man OI, of OI
ok	also ON, and ON, of ON
okkar	ours OI
okkarr	ours ON
okkr	ours ON, us ON
okkur	our OI, us OI
opið	opened OI
opit	opened ON
orð	word ON, word OI, words ON, words OI
orða	words ON, words OI
orðið	become OI
orðsending	message ON
orðsendingar	message OI
orðum	words ON
orkneyjar	Orkney (place) ON, Orkney (place) OI
orm	Orm (name) ON, Orm (name) OI

127

Word List (Norse to English)

Norse	English
ormi	Orm (name) ON, Orm (name) OI
ormr	Orm (name) ON
ormur	Orm (name) OI
orrostu	battle ON
orta	wrote ON
orti	wrote OI
orustu	battle OI
oss	us ON, us OI

Ó, ó

Norse	English
ó	oh OI
óárani	scarcity ON, scarcity OI
óbyggð	settlement ON, settlement OI
óbyggðum	unsettled-land ON, unsettled-land OI
ódæll	unruly OI
ófölvan	dark ON, dark OI
ófriðr	without-peace ON
ófriður	without-peace OI
óglaðari	un-glad ON, without-gladness ON, without-gladness OI
ógleði	sadness ON, sadness OI
ógreitt	not-without-obstacle ON, not-without-obstacle OI
óhægjast	maintain ON, maintain OI
óhyggilega	unwisely OI
ókunnu	unknown ON, unknown OI
ókvæntir	unmarried ON
ólafi	Olaf (name) OI
óláfi	Olaf (name) ON
óláfr	Olaf (name) ON
ólafs	Olaf (name) OI
óláfs	Olaf (name) ON
ólafssonar	Son-Of-Olaf (name) OI
óláfssonar	Son-of-Olaf (name) ON
óleifur	Olaf (name) OI
ór	from ON, of ON, out ON
órir	others ON, others OI
óró	uneasiness ON
ósigr	defeat ON
ósigur	defeat OI
ósinn	inlet ON
ótta	fear ON, fear OI
óttast	feared ON
ótti	fear ON, fear OI
óvægi	Ovaegi (name) ON, Ovaegi (name) OI
óvarliga	unwisely ON
óvígða	un-consecrated ON, un-consecrated OI
óvígðri	unconsecrated ON, unconsecrated OI
óvinsæll	not-popular OI
óxu	grew ON, grew OI

Ö, ö

Norse	English
öðru	other ON, other OI, otherwise ON
öðrum	another ON, another OI, other ON, other OI, others ON, others OI
öðrumegin	other-side OI
öll	all ON, all OI
öllu	all ON, all OI
öllum	all ON, all OI
önduð	dead OI
önduðust	died ON, died OI
öngu	no OI, nothing OI
öngva	any OI, none OI
öngvan	no OI, none OI
öngvir	none OI
öngvum	nothing OI
önnur	second ON, second OI
ör	arrow ON
öræfi	wilderness OI
örina	arrow ON, the-arrow OI
örnefni	place-names ON, place-names OI
öx	an-axe OI, axe ON
öxin	axe ON, the-axe OI
öxina	axe ON, the-axe OI
öxl	shoulder OI

Word List (Norse to English)

Norse	English
öxna-þórissonar	Son-of-Ox-Thorir (name) ON
öxney	Oxney (place) ON

R, r

Norse	English
ráð	advice ON, advice OI, advise OI, counsel ON, counsel OI, obliged ON, obliged OI, proposal ON, proposal OI
ráða	advise ON, advise OI, decide ON, decide OI
ráðabreytni	important ON
ráðagerð	important OI
ráðahag	marriage-proposal OI
ráði	advice ON, advised ON
ráðið	advice OI, advise OI
ráðit	advice ON
ráðlausir	disposed OI
ráðlegra	advisable OI
ráðnir	appointed ON, appointed OI
ráðs	advise OI, plans ON, plans OI
ráðstafalausir	disposed ON
ráðum	advice OI
ræða	discussed OI
ragnarssonar	Son-of-Ragnar (name) ON
rak	driven ON, driven OI, drove OI
rangsælis	anti-sun-wise OI
rásar	rushed ON, rushed OI
rauða	red OI, Red (name) ON, the-Red (name) ON, The-Red (name) OI, the-Red's (name) ON, The-Red'S (name) OI
rauðan	Red (name) ON
rauði	Red (name) ON, the-Red (name) ON, The-Red (name) OI
rauðr	the-Red (name) ON
rauðs	The-Red'S (name) OI, the-Red's (name) ON
rauðskeggjaði	Redbeard (name) ON, red-bearded OI
rauður	The-Red (name) OI
rausn	generosity ON, generosity OI, generous ON
rausnarbú	great-estate OI
rausnarráð	great-estate ON
rausnarveislu	generosity OI
raust	voice OI
rautt	red ON, red OI
réðst	appointed ON, appointed OI, moved ON, moved OI, rode ON, rode OI
réðust	appointed ON, appointed OI
reið	riding ON, rode ON, rode OI
reiða	advice ON, advice OI
reiddi	driven OI
reisa	raise ON, raised OI
reistist	rose OI
rekkjustokkinn	sideboards ON, sideboards OI
rekum	foraging OI
renna	run ON, run OI
rennið	run ON, run OI
reri	rowing ON, rowing OI
reru	rowed ON, rowed OI
reyndi	experienced ON, experienced OI
reynines	Reynines (place) ON, Reynines (place) OI
reyninesi	Reynines (place) OI
reynt	experienced ON, experienced OI, tried OI
rif	ribs OI
rifin	rib ON
ríka	rich OI, Rich (name) ON
rjóðr	clearing ON
rjóðrið	clearing OI
rjóðrit	clearing ON
rjóður	clearing OI
rjúpu	Rjupa (name) ON
róa	row ON, row OI

Word List (Norse to English)

Norse	English
rödd	voice ON
ross	Ross (place) ON, Ross (place) OI
ruddi	cleared ON, cleared OI
rúmunum	our-places OI, places OI
runólfssonar	Runolfsson (name) OI, Son-of-Runolf (name) ON

S, s

Norse	English
sá	saw ON, saw OI, so ON, so OI, that ON, that OI
sáð	sown OI
sæhafa	sea-scattered ON, sea-scattered OI
sækja	seek ON, sought ON, sought OI
sælir	happy ON, happy OI
sæmd	honour OI
sæmðinni	honour ON
sæmilegar	honourable OI
sæmilegast	honourable OI
sæmilegur	honourable OI
sæmiligar	honourable ON
sæmiligast	honourable ON
sæmiligr	honourable ON
sæmiligsta	honourable ON
sætis	seat ON, seat OI
sættir	reconciled ON, reconciled OI
sagði	said ON, said OI, told ON, told ON, told OI
sagðir	said ON
sagnaskemmtan	short-stories OI
sagt	said ON, said OI
sáit	seen ON
sakar	conviction ON, sake ON
sakir	conviction OI, sake OI
sama	same ON, same OI, the-same ON, the-same OI
saman	together ON, together OI
samfarar	interaction ON, interaction OI, intercourse OI
samir	same ON, same OI
samræði	intercourse ON
samsumars	same-summer OI
samt	same OI, together ON, together OI
sandar	sands OI, sandy ON
sandhimins	sand-heaven's ON, sand-heaven's OI
sár	wounds ON
sári	wound ON
sat	sat ON, sat OI
satt	true ON
sáu	saw OI
sauðarvömb	sheep's-stomach ON
saur	the-Foul (name) ON, The-Foul (name) OI
saurr	the-Foul (name) ON
sé	say OI, see ON, see OI, so ON, so OI, this OI, which ON
séð	seen OI
segðu	say ON, say OI
seggir	said ON, said OI
segi	say ON, say OI
segir	answered OI, said ON, said OI
segja	said ON, said OI, say ON, say OI
segl	sails ON
seglið	sails OI
seiðhjallinum	spell-platform OI
seiðinn	enchantments ON, enchantments OI
seiðsins	enchantments ON
sein	late OI
seinni	behind ON
seint	late ON, late OI
sekir	outlawed ON, outlawed OI
selja	to-sell ON, to-sell OI
selr	sold ON
seltjöru	seal-fat ON, seal-fat OI
seltjörunni	seal-fat OI
selur	sold OI

Word List (Norse to English)

Norse	English
sem	as ON, as OI, as-if OI, if OI, since ON, since OI, so ON, that ON, that OI, then ON, then OI, where ON, where OI, wherever ON, wherever OI, which ON, which OI, while OI, who ON, who OI
senda	send ON, send OI
sendi	send OI, sent ON, sent OI
sendr	sent ON
sendur	sent OI
sent	sent ON, sent OI
sér	he ON, he OI, her ON, her OI, hers ON, hers OI, herself ON, herself OI, him ON, him OI, himself ON, himself OI, the ON, the OI, their ON, their OI, theirs ON, theirs OI, them ON, them OI, themselves ON, themselves OI, they OI
serkinum	shirt OI
sét	seen ON
setja	set ON, set OI
setstokka	seat-posts ON, seat-posts OI
setstokkana	seat-posts ON, seat-posts OI
settist	sat ON
settr	set ON
settur	set OI
setu	sitting ON, sitting OI
sið	tradition ON, tradition OI
síðan	after ON, after OI, afterwards ON, afterwards OI, since ON, since OI, then ON, then OI
síðar	afterwards ON, afterwards OI, later ON, later OI, since ON, since OI
síðast	last ON
siðr	custom ON
síðr	less ON
síðunni	his ON
siður	custom OI
síður	less OI
sig	herself OI, himself OI, sign-herself OI
sigla	sail ON, sail OI
sigldi	sailed ON, sailed OI
sigldu	sailed ON, sailed OI
sigldum	sailed ON
siglingu	sailing OI
siglingum	sailing ON
siglt	sailed ON, sailed OI
sigmundarsonar	Son-of-Sigmund (name) ON, Son-Of-Sigmund (name) OI
signa	to OI, to-sign ON
sigríðr	Sigrid (name) ON
sigríður	Sigrid (name) OI
sigurði	Sigurd (name) ON, Sigurd (name) OI
sik	herself ON
sildu	sailed ON
silfr	silver ON
silfur	silver OI
silgdu	sailed ON
sín	hers ON, his ON, his OI, theirs ON, theirs OI
sína	his ON, his OI, theirs ON, theirs OI
sínar	hers ON, hers OI, his OI, theirs ON, theirs OI
sinn	he ON, he OI, his ON, his OI, the ON, the OI, then ON, then OI
sinna	his ON, his OI, their OI, theirs ON, theirs OI
sinnar	his ON, his OI, theirs ON, theirs OI
sinni	his ON, his OI
sins	their ON
síns	his ON, his OI, their ON, they ON, they OI
sínu	her ON, hers ON, hers OI, their ON, their OI, theirs ON, theirs OI, they ON

Word List (Norse to English)

Norse	English
sínum	her ON, her OI, hers ON, hers OI, his ON, his OI, theirs ON, theirs OI
sitt	his ON, his OI, their ON, their OI, theirs ON, theirs OI
sjá	he-saw OI, looked ON, looked OI, saw ON, saw OI, see ON, see OI, seen ON, seen OI, they-saw OI
sjaldan	seldom ON, seldom OI
sjálfala	themselves ON, themselves OI
sjálfan	itself ON, itself OI
sjálfar	itself OI
sjálfsáið	self-sowing OI
sjálfsáit	self-sowing ON
sjálfsána	self-sowing ON, self-sowing OI
sjálfsánir	self-sowing ON, self-sowing OI
sjó	sea ON, sea OI, the-sea OI
sjómaðkr	sea-worms ON
sjónhverfingar	illusions ON
sjónum	sea ON, sea OI
sjórinn	sea ON
sjóvar	sea ON, sea OI
skagafirði	Skagafjord (place) OI
skal	shall ON, shall OI
skálarnir	cabins ON, cabins OI
skáldskap	poetry ON, poetry OI
skaltu	shall-you ON, shall-you OI
skammt	short ON, short OI, shortly OI
skapfelld	agreeable ON
skapfelldir	agreeable OI
skapi	mood ON, mood OI
skapstór	temperamental OI
skapstórr	temperamental ON
skartsmaðr	jewelled-man ON
skartsmaður	jewelled-man OI
skáru	cut ON, cut OI
skaust	launched OI
skaut	lap ON, lap OI, shot ON, shot OI
skauzt	launched ON
skeggjaðr	bearded ON
skeggjaður	bearded OI
skeið	sheathed-sword ON, sheathed-sword OI
skeiðsbrekkum	Skeidsbrekkur (place) ON, Skeidsbrekkur (place) OI
skelmaðkurinn	shell-worms OI
skemmtu	entertained OI
skemmtuðu	entertained ON
skilði	understood ON
skildu	left OI, separated OI
skildum	separated OI
skilðum	separated ON
skilðust	separated ON
skilja	separate ON, separate OI, separated ON, separated OI
skiljast	separate ON, separate OI
skilnaðr	parting ON
skilnaður	parting OI
skína	shine ON, shine OI
skinn	skins ON
skinnavöru	skin-wares ON
skinnhjúpum	skin-sacks ON, skin-sacks OI
skip	ship ON, ship OI, ships ON, ships OI, then ON
skipa	ships ON, ships OI
skipflaki	shipwreck ON, shipwreck OI
skipi	a-ship OI, ship ON, ship OI, ships ON, the-ship ON
skipið	ship OI, the-ship OI
skipinu	ship ON, ship OI, the-ship ON, the-ship OI
skipit	ship ON
skips	ships ON, ships OI
skipshöfnum	ships-ports ON
skipta	change ON, change OI, of-exchange OI
skipti	exchanged ON, exchanges ON, exchanges OI
skiptumst	exchange OI

Word List (Norse to English)

Norse	English
skiptust	exchanged OI
skipum	ship ON, ships ON, ships OI, the-ship OI
skipunum	boats ON, boats OI, ship ON, ship OI, ships ON, ships OI
skipverjum	ship's-company ON, ship's-company OI
skipverjunum	ships-ports OI
skírð	baptised ON, baptised OI
skírðir	baptised ON, baptised OI
skjóðupungr	skin-purse ON
skjóðupungur	a-skin-purse OI
skjöld	shield ON, shield OI, shields ON
skjöldu	shields OI
skjöldum	shields ON, shields OI
skjótari	faster-than ON, faster-than OI
skjótast	quickly ON, quickly OI
skjótleiks	speed OI
skjótt	quickly ON, quickly OI, shortly ON, shortly OI
skógi	forest OI, woods ON, woods OI
skóginn	the-woods OI, woods ON
skóginum	forest ON
skógur	forest OI
skógurinn	forests OI
skógvaxit	forest-grown ON
skömmu	recently ON, recently OI
skorti	shortage ON, shortage OI
skortir	shortage ON, shortage OI
sköruleg	honourable OI
skörulega	boldly OI
sköruliga	boldly ON
skörungr	noble ON
skörungur	noble OI
skoska	Scottish (place) OI
skosku	Scottish (place) OI
skotar	Scots (name) ON, Scots (place) OI
skothríð	launching ON, launching OI
skotland	Scotland (place) ON, Scotland (place) OI
skozka	Scottish (place) ON
skozku	Scottish (place) ON
skrælinga	Skraelings (name) ON
skrælingar	Skraelings (name) ON
skrælingaskipa	Skraelings (name) ON
skrælingja	Skraelings (name) OI
skrælingjalandi	Skraelings (place) OI
skrælingjar	Skraelings (name) OI, The-Skraelings (name) OI
skrælingjarnir	Skraelings (name) OI
skrælingjum	Skraelings (name) OI
skrælingum	Skraelings (name) ON
skraumuhlaupsár	Skraumuhlaupsa (place) ON, Skraumuhlaupsa (place) OI
skriðu	landslide ON, landslide OI
skrúð	cloth ON
skrúðit	cloth ON
skuldalið	indebted ON, indebted-to OI
skutu	launched ON
skylda	should ON
skyldi	as-should-be ON, as-should-be OI, should ON, should OI, should-be ON, should-be OI, wished OI
skyldir	obliged ON, obliged OI
skyldu	should ON, should OI, would ON, would OI
skylt	should ON, should OI
skyn	understanding OI
sleitum	slighting OI
slettir	slapped ON, slapped OI
slík	such ON, such OI
slíka	such OI
slíkra	such ON, such OI
slikt	such ON
slíkt	such ON, such OI
slíku	such ON
slíkum	such OI
sló	struck ON, struck OI

Word List (Norse to English)

Norse	English
slóðir	routes ON, routes OI
slógu	struck ON, struck OI
smáir	small OI
smáþarma	small-intestine ON, small-intestine OI
smátt	small ON
smjúgi	pierce OI
snæfells	Snaefell (place) ON, Snaefell (place) OI
snæfellsjökli	Snaefellsjokli (place) ON, Snaefellsjokli (place) OI
snæfellsnesi	Snaefellstrond (place) OI
snæfellströnd	Snaefellstrond (place) ON
snemma	early ON, early OI
sneru	turned OI
snjár	snow OI
snjór	snow ON
snorra	Snorri (name) ON, Snorri (name) OI, Snorri'S (name) OI
snorrason	Snorrason (name) ON, Snorrason (name) OI
snorri	Snorri (name) ON, Snorri (name) OI
snúast	turn OI
sofa	sleep ON, sleep OI
sofið	slept OI
sofit	slept ON
sofnaða	sleeping ON, sleeping OI
sofnar	slept OI
sögðu	said ON, said OI, told ON
sögn	said ON, said OI, said-of OI
sögu	saga ON, saga OI
sökk	sank ON
sólarsinnis	sun-wise-motion ON, sun-wise-motion OI
sómamaðr	famous-man ON
sómamaður	famous-man OI
son	a-son ON, a-son OI, son OI, Son-Of (name) OI
sonareignin	son's-property ON, son's-property OI
sonr	of ON, son ON, Son-of (name) ON
sonu	sons ON, sons OI
sonur	Son-Of (name) OI
sótt	attended ON, attended OI, sickness ON, sickness OI
sóttarfar	sickness ON, sickness OI
sótti	encountered ON, encountered OI, took ON, took OI
sóttu	looked OI, sought OI
spákona	prophetess ON, prophetess OI, Prophetess (name) OI
spákonan	prophetess ON
spákonu	prophetess OI
spákonunni	prophetess ON, prophetess OI
spákonur	prophetesses ON, prophetesses OI
spannarlangt	long-spanning ON, spanning-long OI
spjót	spears ON, spears OI
spurði	asked ON, asked OI, heard-of ON, heard-of OI
spurðist	heard ON
spurðu	asked ON, asked OI
spurt	asked ON, asked OI
spyr	asked OI
spyrnast	touch OI
spyrr	asked ON
stað	place ON, stand ON, stand OI
staðar	place ON, places ON, places OI
staðfestu	established ON, established OI
staðið	stood OI
staðit	stood ON
stæði	steady ON, steady OI
stæðist	place ON, place OI
stæra	greatly ON, greatly OI
staf	staff ON, staff OI
standa	stand ON, stand OI
stangir	poles ON, poles OI
staur	poles ON, poles OI

134

Word List (Norse to English)

Norse	English	Norse	English
staurinum	poles ON	stund	awhile ON, awhile OI, time ON, time OI, while ON, while OI
staurnum	poles OI		
stein	stone ON, stone OI	stundar	around ON
steinum	stones ON, stones OI	stundum	sometimes ON, sometimes OI
sterklega	strongly OI		
sterkr	strong ON	styr	Styrr (name) OI
stjórn	stern ON	stýri	steering ON, steering OI
stjórnborða	starboard OI		
stjórnuðu	greatly-ruled-over ON, greatly-ruled-over OI	stýrimenn	steersmen ON, steersmen OI
stóð	stood ON, stood OI, was OI, withstood OI	styrkr	strength ON
		styrkur	steered OI, strength OI
stoða	stand OI	styrr	Styrr (name) ON
stóðst	withstood ON	sú	seen OI, that ON, the ON, the OI, was OI
stokka	stock ON, stock OI		
stokkanesi	Stokkanes (place) ON, Stokkanes (place) OI	suðr	south ON
		suðræn	southern ON
stöng	poles ON	suðrey	Sudrey (place) ON
stönginni	poles ON	suðreyja	Sudreyar (place) ON
stöngum	poles OI	suðreyjar	Sudreyar (place) ON
stopir	stopped ON, stopped OI	suðreyjum	Sudreyar (place) ON
stór	great ON, great OI	suðri	south ON
stórættaða	noble ON, noble OI	suðrland	Sutherland (place) ON
stórar	large ON, large OI	suðu	boiled ON, boiled OI
stórmannliga	great-man-ness ON	suður	south OI
stórmenni	great-men ON, great-men OI	suðurátt	south OI
		suðurey	Sudrey (place) OI
stórmennsku	great-man-ness ON, great-man-ness OI, greatness ON, greatness OI	suðureyja	Sudreyar (place) OI
		suðureyjar	Sudreyar (place) OI
		suðureyjum	Sudreyar (place) OI
		suðurland	Sutherland (place) OI
strandar	shore ON, shore OI	sukku	sank ON, sank OI
strandir	beaches ON, beaches OI	sum	some ON, some OI
strandirnar	beaches ON	sumar	summer ON, summer OI
straumar	a-stream OI, streams ON	sumarið	summer OI
straumey	Straumey (place) ON	sumarit	summer ON
straumfirði	Straumfjord (place) ON	sumir	some ON, some OI
straumfjörð	Straumfjord (place) ON	sumra	some ON, some OI, summer ON, summer OI
straumr	stream ON		
straumsey	Straumsey (place) OI	sumrum	summer ON, summer OI
straumsfirði	Straumfjord (place) OI		
straumsfjörð	Straumfjord (place) OI, Straumsfjord (place) OI	sumt	some ON
		sundr	distribute ON
straumur	a-stream OI	sundur	apart OI
ströndunum	beaches OI		

Word List (Norse to English)

Norse	English
sunnan	from-the-south OI, south ON, south OI
sunnanveður	southern-winds OI
svá	so ON, such ON
svaruð	answered OI
svaraði	answered ON, answered OI
svarar	answered ON, answered OI
svarat	answered ON
svartan	black ON, black OI
svartir	dark ON
svartr	dark ON
svartur	dark OI
svát	so ON
svein	boy OI
sveina	young-men ON
sveinana	young-men ON, young-men OI
sveinanna	young-men OI
sveinbarn	boy ON
sveininn	boy ON, boy OI
sveinn	boy ON, boy OI
sveit	company OI
sveitir	areas ON
sverð	swords ON, swords OI
sverðið	sword OI, the-sword OI
sverðinu	sword ON
sverðit	sword ON
sviku	betrayed ON, betrayed OI
svíney	Sviney (place) ON, Sviney (place) OI
svipu	whip ON, whip OI
svívirða	shame ON, shame OI
svo	so OI, south OI, such OI
syðra	southern ON, southern OI
sýn	seemed ON, seemed OI
sýndi	showed ON, showed OI
sýndist	seemed ON, seemed OI
syni	Son-of (name) ON, Son-Of (name) OI
sýni	showed OI
synir	sons ON, sons OI
sýnir	showed ON
sýnist	seemed ON, seemed OI
systr	sisters ON
systur	sister-of ON, sister-of OI, sisters OI

T, t

Norse	English
táðit	say ON
tæki	take ON, take OI
tækist	takes ON
tækjust	takes OI
taka	take ON, take OI, taken OI
tákna	betoken OI
tal	talked OI
tala	say ON, to-speak ON
talat	told ON
taldi	told OI
talði	told ON
tannbelti	tusk-belt ON, tusk-belt OI
tannskeftan	walrus-tusk ON, walrus-tusk OI
tár	tears ON, tears OI
tauma	reins ON, reins OI
teikna	betoken ON
tekið	taken OI
tekin	taken ON, taken OI
tekit	taken ON
tekr	take ON, takes ON, took ON
tekur	pulled OI, take OI, took OI
tengdir	joined OI
tengðir	joined ON
tíðenda	news ON
tíðinda	news OI
tíðindi	news OI
tigir	ten ON, ten OI, tens ON, tens OI
tigu	ten ON
til	for ON, for OI, to ON, to OI, towards ON, towards OI, until ON, until OI
tillaga	suggested OI
tilskipan	decided OI

Word List (Norse to English)

Norse	English
tíma	time ON, time OI
tinknappar	tin-buttons ON
tíu	ten ON, ten OI
tjóa	avail ON
töfl	table-games OI
töfr	magic ON
töfur	magic OI
tögr	twenty ON
tók	received ON, taken ON, taken OI, took ON, took OI
tókst	took ON, took OI
tóku	taken ON, took ON, took OI, took-to ON, took-to OI
tökum	take ON, take OI
tókust	taken ON, taking OI, took OI
tólf	twelve ON
töluðu	spoke OI, told OI
torflutt	difficult-be ON, difficult-be OI
trausti	trust ON, trust OI
trautt	scarcely ON, scarcely OI
tré	beams OI, tree ON, tree OI, trees ON, trees OI
trjám	poles ON
trjánum	poles ON, poles OI
tröðum	Tradir (place) ON, Tradir (place) OI
trú	faith ON, faith OI
trúðu	believed ON, believed OI
trúna	faith ON, faith OI
trúuð	religious ON, religious OI
tryggvason	Tryggvason (name) ON
tryggvasonar	Tryggvason'S (name) OI, Tryggvason's (name) ON, Tryggvason'S (name) OI
tryggvasyni	Tryggvason (name) ON, Tryggvason (name) OI
tuglamöttul	mantle ON, mantle OI
tuttugu	twenty ON, twenty OI
tvá	two ON
tvær	two ON, two OI
tvau	two ON
tveim	two ON
tveir	two ON, two OI
tvennum	two OI
tvíhólkaðan	two-ringed ON, two-ringed OI
tvo	two OI
tvö	two OI
týna	lose ON, lose OI
týndust	lost ON

Þ, þ

Norse	English
þá	the ON, them ON, them OI, then ON, then OI, there ON, there OI, they ON, they OI, to-them ON, when ON
það	it OI, that OI, that-to OI, the OI, this OI
þaðan	from-there ON, from-there OI, there ON
þær	there ON, there OI, they ON, they OI, those ON, those OI
þætti	seems ON, seems OI
þágu	accepted ON, accepted OI
þakkar	thanked ON, thanked OI
þangað	from-there OI, there OI
þangat	from-there ON, there ON
þann	that ON, that OI, the ON, the OI, then ON, then OI
þar	here OI, that OI, there ON, there OI, therefore OI, they ON, they OI, where ON, where OI
þarf	need ON, needed ON, needed OI
þat	it ON, it ON, ship ON, that ON, that ON, the ON, this ON

Word List (Norse to English)

Norse	English
þau	hers OI, them ON, them OI, there ON, there OI, these ON, these OI, they ON, they OI, those ON, those OI
þegar	as-soon-as ON, when ON, when OI
þeim	that ON, that OI, theirs ON, theirs OI, them ON, them OI, these ON, they ON, they OI, those ON, those OI, to-them ON, to-them OI
þeir	their ON, their OI, theirs OI, them ON, then ON, there ON, there OI, they ON, they OI, this OI, those ON, those OI, you OI
þeira	their ON, theirs ON, there ON, they ON, this ON
þeirar	their ON
þeirra	of-them OI, their OI, theirs OI, them OI, there OI
þeirrar	their OI
þeirri	there OI
þeirs	they ON
þenna	that OI, then ON, this ON, this OI
þér	to-you ON, to-you OI, you ON, you OI
þess	these ON, these OI, this ON, this OI
þessa	these ON, these OI, this ON, this OI
þessara	these OI
þessi	these ON, these OI, this ON, this OI
þessir	these ON, these OI
þessu	his ON, this ON, this OI
þessum	these ON, these OI, this ON, this OI
þetta	that ON, that OI, this ON, this OI
þig	you OI
þiggið	accepted ON, accepted OI
þiggr	accepted ON
þiggur	accepted OI
þik	you ON
þín	your ON, your OI, yours ON
þínir	yours ON, yours OI
þinn	yours ON, yours OI
þinni	yours ON, yours OI
þínum	your ON, your OI
þistils	Thistle (name) ON, Thistle (name) OI
þistilsfjörð	Thistilsfjord (place) ON, Thistilsfjord (place) OI
þjáðir	enslaved ON, enslaved OI
þjóðhildar	Thjodhild (name) ON, Thjodhild (name) OI
þjóðhildarkirkja	Thjodhildakirkja (place) ON, Thjodhildkirkja (place) OI
þjóðhildi	Thjodhild (name) ON
þjóðhildr	Thjodhild (name) ON
þjóðhildur	Thjodhild (name) OI
þó	though ON, though OI, thought OI, yet ON
þokka	thoughts ON
þökkuðu	thanked ON
þolðu	endured ON
þór	Thor (name) ON, Thor (name) OI
þorbirni	Thorbjorn (name) ON, Thorbjorn (name) OI
þorbjargar	Thorbjorg (name) ON, Thorbjorg (name) OI, Thorbjorg's (name) ON, Thorjborn'S (name) OI
þorbjarnar	Thorbjorn (name) OI, Thorbjorn's (name) ON, Thorjborn'S (name) OI
þorbjarnardóttur	Thorbjornadottir (name) OI
þorbjörg	Thorbjorg (name) ON, Thorbjorg (name) OI
þorbjörgu	Thorbjorg (name) ON, Thorbjorg (name) OI
þorbjörn	Thorbjorn (name) ON, Thorbjorn (name) OI

Word List (Norse to English)

Norse	English
þorbrand	Thorbrand (name) OI
þorbrandr	Thorbrand (name) ON
þorbrands	Thorbrand's (name) ON, Thorbrand'S (name) OI
þorbrandsson	Thorbrandson (name) ON, Thorbrandson (name) OI
þórðar	Thord (name) ON, Thord (name) OI
þórðr	Thord (name) ON
þorfinnr	Thorfin (name) ON
þorfinns	Thorfin's (name) ON
þorfinnur	Thorfin (name) OI
þorgeir	Thorgeir (name) OI
þorgeirr	Thorgeir (name) ON
þorgeirsfelli	Thorgeirsfell (place) ON, Thorgeirsfell (place) OI
þorgerði	Thorgerd (name) ON
þorgesti	Thorgest (name) ON, Thorgest (name) OI
þorgestr	Thorgest (name) ON
þorgests	Thorgest's (name) ON, Thorgest'S (name) OI
þorgestur	Thorgest (name) OI
þorgils	Thorgils (name) ON, Thorgils (name) OI
þorgilsson	Thorgilson (name) ON
þórgunna	Thorgun (name) ON, Thorgun (name) OI
þórhall	Thorhall (name) OI
þórhallr	Thorhall (name) ON
þórhalls	Thorhall (name) ON, Thorhall (name) OI
þórhallur	Thorhall (name) OI
þórhildi	Thorhild (name) ON
þóris	Thori's (name) ON
þorkel	Thorkell (name) ON, Thorkell (name) OI
þorkell	Thorkell (name) ON, Thorkell (name) OI
þorláks	Thorlak (name) OI, Thorlak's (name) ON
þórsnessþingi	Thorsnes-Thing (name) ON, Thorsnes-Thing (place) OI
þorstein	Thorstein (name) ON, Thorstein (name) OI
þorsteinn	Thorstein (name) ON, Thorstein (name) OI
þorsteins	Thorstein (name) ON, Thorstein (name) OI, Thorstein's (name) ON, Thorstein'S (name) OI
þórunn	Thorun (name) ON, Thorun (name) OI
þorvald	Thorvald (name) OI
þorvaldi	Thorvald (name) ON, Thorvald (name) OI
þorvaldr	Thorvald (name) ON
þorvaldur	Thorvald (name) OI
þorvarði	Thorvard (name) ON
þorvarðr	Thorvard (name) ON
þorvarður	Thorvard (name) OI
þótt	though ON, though OI, thought ON, thought OI
þótti	think OI, thought ON, thought OI
þóttist	thought ON, thought OI
þóttú	though ON, though OI
þóttust	thought ON, thought OI
þrælana	thralls ON, thralls OI
þrælar	thralls ON, thralls OI
þrælssyni	thrall's-son ON, thrall's-son OI
þrekaðir	exhausted ON, exhausted OI
þrévetr	three-winters ON
þriði	thirty-and ON
þriðja	third ON, third OI
þrír	three ON, three OI
þrívetur	three-winters OI
þrjár	three ON, three OI
þrjú	three ON, three OI
þú	you ON, you OI
þuldi	reciting OI
þulði	rattling-off ON
þungt	unhappy ON, unhappy OI
þurfa	need ON, need OI, needed ON
þurfti	needed ON, needed OI
þurftu	need OI, needed ON, needed OI

Word List (Norse to English)

Norse	English	Norse	English
þuríðar	Thorid (name) ON, Thorid (name) OI	umræður	discussion ON, discussion OI
þurslegur	giant OI	undan	ahead ON, ahead OI, away ON, away OI, away-from OI, from ON, from OI
þursligr	giant ON		
þvengi	tied ON, tied OI		
þverr	decreases ON, decreases OI		
þvers	across ON, across OI	undarlegi	strange OI
þversýningar	illusions OI	undarligi	strange ON
því	according ON, according OI, accordingly ON, accordingly OI, as ON, because ON, because OI, before OI, for ON, for OI, since ON, since OI, that ON, that OI, therefore ON, therefore OI	undir	behind ON, behind OI, near OI, under ON, under OI, up-to ON, up-to OI
		undirförull	scheming OI
		undrast	wonder OI
		undruðust	astonished ON, astonished OI, marvelled ON, marvelled OI
þvílíka	spectacular ON	undu	hoisted ON
þvílíku	likewise ON, likewise OI	ungur	younger OI
		unnið	working OI
þvílíkum	for-like ON, for-like OI	unnit	spared ON
þyki	think OI	unnu	won ON, won OI
þykir	seems OI, think OI, thinking OI, thought OI	uns	until OI
		unz	until ON
þykist	think OI	upp	up ON, up OI, upped ON, upped OI
þykja	valued OI		
þykki	think ON, thought ON	uppi	up ON, up OI
þykkir	seems ON	upplendingakonungs	Opplands-King (name) ON, Opplands-King (name) OI
þykkja	think ON, valued ON		
þykkjast	think ON	urðu	became ON, became OI
þykkjumst	think-us ON		
þyrfti	needed OI	utan	out OI

U, u

Norse	English
uggligt	fearful ON
um	about ON, about OI, around ON, around OI, for ON, for OI, from ON, inclined OI
umbóta	about-further OI
umbótar	about-further ON
umbúningr	clothing ON
umbúningur	clothing OI
umhverfis	around OI

Ú, ú

Norse	English
úlfs	Ulf (name) ON, Ulf (name) OI
úlfssonar	Son-of-Ulf (name) ON, Son-Of-Ulf (name) OI, Ulfson (name) ON, Ulfson (name) OI
úr	from OI, of OI, out OI, out-of OI

Word List (Norse to English)

Norse	English
út	back ON, back OI, back-from ON, back-from OI, from ON, out ON, out OI
útan	out ON, out-of ON, outside-of ON
úti	about ON, about OI, out ON, out OI
útibú	out-houses ON
útibúr	out-house ON, out-house OI
útibúrsdyrin	out-house-door OI
útibúrsdyrrin	out-house-door ON
útidurum	the-out-door ON
útidurunum	the-out-door ON
útidyrum	out-door OI
útivist	out-journey ON, out-journey OI
útróðra	fishing OI, out-rowing ON

V, v

Norse	English
vá	slew ON
vaðmálsmöttul	mantle ON
vænn	a-fair ON, a-fair OI
vænst	fair ON, fair OI
vænt	expected OI
vænti	expect OI, wait ON
væntu	expected OI
væri	was ON, was OI, were ON, were OI, would OI, would-be ON, would-be OI
værir	would-be ON, would-be OI
væru	being OI, were OI, would-be ON, would-be OI
væstir	worn ON
vág	inlet ON
vágskorit	creek-indented ON
vaka	awake ON, awake OI
vakði	awoke ON, woke ON
vakið	awoken OI
vakti	awoke OI, woke OI
valdidida	Avaldidida (name) OI
valslöngur	war-slings ON, war-slings OI
valþjófs	Vallthjof (place) ON, Vallthjof (place) OI
valþjófsstöðum	Vathjolfsstadr (place) ON, Vathjolfsstadr (place) OI
ván	looked ON
vana	custom ON
vanda	accustomed OI, custom OI
vanða	accustomed ON
vandliga	closely ON
vann	won ON, won OI
vánu	hope ON
vápn	weapon ON, weapons ON
var	stayed ON, stayed OI, was ON, was OI, were ON, were OI
vár	been ON, what-was ON
vara	wares ON, wares OI
vára	spring ON
várar	spring ON
varast	avoid ON, avoid OI
varð	became ON, became OI, was ON, was OI, were ON, were OI
varða	concerned ON
varði	expected ON, expected OI
varðlokur	warlock-songs ON, warlock-songs OI
varðveislur	preservation OI
varðveita	supplies ON, supplies OI
varðveitti	preserved ON, preserved OI
vári	spring ON
varir	aware ON, aware OI
várit	spring ON
varla	barely ON, hardly ON, hardly OI, rarely ON
varning	wares ON, wares OI
varningi	wares ON
varninginn	wares OI
varninginum	wares ON, wares OI
varningr	goods ON, wares ON
varningur	goods OI

141

Word List (Norse to English)

Norse	English	Norse	English
varningurinn	wares OI	*veitir*	gave OI
várra	ours ON	*veitt*	given ON
vart	hardly ON, hardly OI, noticed ON, noticed OI	*veitti*	provided-for ON, provided-for OI, supported ON, supported OI
váru	ours ON, was ON, were ON		
vas	was ON	*veittir*	supplied ON, supplied OI
vás	toil ON	*veittr*	given ON
vatn	lake ON, lake OI, water ON, water OI	*veittu*	gave ON, gave OI, supported ON, supported OI
vatni	water ON, water OI		
vatninu	lake ON, lake OI	*veittur*	given OI
vatnshorni	Vatnshorn (place) ON, Vatnshorn (place) OI	*veizla*	feast ON, the-feast ON
		veizlan	the-feast ON
vaxinn	growing ON, growing OI	*veizlu*	feast ON
		veizlum	feasts ON
veðr	wind ON	*veizlunni*	feast ON, the-feast ON
veðrátta	weather ON, weather OI	*vekr*	awoke ON
veðrs	weathered ON, weathered OI	*vekur*	awoke OI
		vel	a ON, well ON, well OI
veður	weather OI, winds OI	*veldr*	brought-about ON, caused ON
vega	ways ON, ways OI		
vegir	way ON, way OI	*veldur*	brought-about OI, caused OI
vegna	ways ON, ways OI		
veiðar	hunting OI	*velja*	will ON, will OI
veiðarnar	fishing ON, hunting OI	*velkði*	drove ON
veiðiferð	hunting OI	*velkti*	drove OI
veiðiferðir	hunting ON	*vella*	boil ON, boil OI
veiðiförum	hunting OI	*vellauðigur*	wealthy OI
veiðimaðr	hunter ON, the-hunter ON	*vér*	we ON, we OI, we-are ON, we-are OI
veiðimaður	hunter OI, the-hunter OI	*vera*	be ON, be OI, being ON, being OI, it-was OI, to-be ON, to-be OI, was ON, was OI
veiðimanns	the-hunter ON, the-hunter OI		
veiðiskap	fishing ON, fishing OI		
veiðum	fishing OI	*verð*	deserve ON, deserve OI
veift	waved ON, waving ON, waving OI	*verða*	be ON, be OI, being OI, to-be ON, to-be OI, was OI, were ON
veisla	feast OI, the-feast OI		
veislan	feast OI	*verði*	will-be ON, will-be OI
veislu	feast OI	*verðr*	become ON, become OI, becomes ON, were ON, worth ON
veislunni	the-feast OI		
veislur	feasts OI		
veit	know ON	*verður*	becomes OI, worth OI
veita	grant ON, grant OI, supplied ON, supplied OI	*verið*	been OI, have-been OI, made OI

142

Word List (Norse to English)

Norse	English
verit	been ON, have-been ON, made ON
verja	protect ON, protect OI
verkstjóri	a-foreman ON, a-foreman OI
verkstjórinn	the-foreman OI
verra	worse ON, worst OI
verri	worse ON, worse OI
vesöld	misery OI
vesölð	misery ON
vestan	west ON, west OI, western ON, western OI
vestanveðr	west-wind ON
vestr	west ON
vestri	western ON, western OI
vestribyggð	Vestribyggd (place) ON, Vestribyggd (place) OI
vestribyggðar	Vestribyggd (place) ON, Vestribyggd (place) OI
vestrvíking	west-raiding ON
vestur	west OI
vesturvíking	west-raiding OI
vethildi	Vethild (name) ON, Vethild (name) OI
vetr	winter ON
vetri	winter ON, winter OI
vetrinn	winter ON
vetrum	winter ON, winter OI, winters ON
vetur	winter OI
veturinn	winter OI
veturnætur	winter OI
veturvistar	winter OI
vexti	grown OI
við	by ON, by OI, in ON, in OI, off ON, off OI, to ON, to OI, we OI, with ON, with OI
víða	widely ON, widely OI
víðar	wide ON
víðara	far-and-wide ON, far-and-wide OI
viðskipti	exchanged OI
viðtaka	taken OI
viðtöku	resistance ON, resistance OI
vífill	Vifil (name) ON, Vifil (name) OI
vífilsdal	Vifilsdal (place) ON, Vifilsdal (place) OI
vífilsson	Vifilson (name) ON, Vifilson (name) OI
víga	killing ON, killing OI
vígðu	ground ON, ground OI
vikur	weeks ON, weeks OI
vil	will ON, will OI
vilda	will ON, wish ON
vildi	will OI, willed ON, willed OI, willing ON, wish OI, wished ON, wished OI
vildu	willed ON, willed OI, willing ON, willing OI, would ON
vili	will ON, wished ON
vilið	will ON
vilir	will-you ON
vilja	he-willed ON, willed ON, willed OI, willing ON, willing OI
vilji	will OI, wished OI
viljið	will OI
viljir	will OI
vill	will ON, will OI, willed ON, willed OI, wills ON, wills OI
vin	friend OI
vín	wine ON, wine OI
vina	friends ON, friends OI
vinaboð	friend-invites ON, friend-invites OI
vinar	friend ON, friend OI
vinátta	friendship ON, friendship OI
vináttu	friendship ON, friendship OI
vínbejaköngul	grape-vines ON
vínber	grapes OI
vinir	friends ON, friends OI
vínlandi	Vinland (place) ON
vínlands	Vinland (place) ON, Vinland (place) OI

143

Word List (Norse to English)

Norse	English
vinnast	go-on ON
vinnur	friend OI
vinr	friend ON
vinsældum	popularity OI
vinsæll	befriended ON, befriended OI, popular ON, popular OI
vinur	friend OI, friend-of OI
vínvið	vines ON
vínviðr	vine-trees ON
vínviður	vines OI, vine-trees OI
virðing	honour ON, honour OI
virðingarráð	worthiness ON, worthiness OI
virðist	seemed OI
vís	aware ON, aware OI
vísendakona	fore-knowing-woman ON
vísendakonunni	wise-woman ON
vísindakona	fore-knowing-woman OI
vísindakonunni	prophetess OI, wise-woman OI
vissi	knew ON, knew OI
vissu	knew ON, knew OI
vist	provisions ON, provisions OI
víst	certain ON, certain OI, made ON, made OI, wise ON, wise OI
vistir	provisions ON, provisions OI, supplies ON
vistuðu	saved ON
vísu	verse ON, verse OI
vit	into ON, known ON, to ON, we ON, with ON
vita	know ON, know OI, knowing ON, knowing OI
vitja	visit ON, visit OI
vó	slew OI
vog	inlet OI
vogskorið	creek-indented OI
vogunum	inlets OI
völdum	doing ON, doing OI
von	looked OI
vonum	hope OI

Norse	English
vopn	weapon OI, weapons OI
vor	gone OI, what-was OI
vora	spring OI
vorar	spring OI
vori	spring OI
vorið	spring OI
voru	was OI, were OI
voruð	were OI
vorum	ours OI
vos	toil OI

Y, y

Norse	English
yðr	you ON
yður	you OI, yours OI
yðvar	you ON, you OI, your OI, yours ON, yours OI
yðvarr	your ON, yours ON
yfir	over ON, over OI
yfirsöngva	burial-service ON, burial-service OI
yfirsöngvar	burial-service ON, burial-service OI
yngveldar	Yngvild (name) OI
yngvildar	Yngvild (name) ON
yrðir	become ON, become OI
yxna-þórissonar	Son-Of-Ox-Thorir (name) OI
yxney	Oxney (place) OI

Ý, ý

Norse	English
ýla	howling ON, howling OI

Word List *(English to Norse)*

OI = Old Icelandic   ON = Old Norse

English	Norse	English	Norse
		afterwards	*eftir* OI, *eftir* ON, *síðan* OI, *síðan* ON, *síðar* OI, *síðar* ON

A, a

English	Norse
a	*at* ON, *einn* OI, *einn* ON, *er* ON, *í* OI, *í* ON, *vel* ON
a-bad	*illa* ON
abode	*bústað* OI, *bústað* ON
about	*á* OI, *í* OI, *í* ON, *of* OI, *of* ON, *um* OI, *um* ON, *úti* OI, *úti* ON
about-further	*umbóta* OI, *umbótar* ON
above	*ofan* OI, *ofan* ON
a-bull	*griðungur* OI
abundance	*gnóttir* OI, *gnóttir* ON
accepted	*þágu* OI, *þágu* ON, *þiggið* OI, *þiggið* ON, *þiggr* ON, *þiggur* OI
accompany	*annan* OI
according	*því* OI, *því* ON
accordingly	*því* OI, *því* ON
account	*frásögnum* OI, *frásögnum* ON
accustomed	*vanda* OI, *vanða* ON
a-company	*liðin* OI
across	*þvers* OI, *þvers* ON
a-cushion	*hægendi* ON
advice	*ráð* OI, *ráð* ON, *ráði* ON, *ráðið* OI, *ráðit* ON, *ráðum* OI, *reiða* OI, *reiða* ON
advisable	*ráðlegra* OI
advise	*ráð* OI, *ráða* OI, *ráða* ON, *ráðið* OI, *ráðs* OI
advised	*ráði* ON
a-fair	*vænn* OI, *vænn* ON
a-farm	*bú* ON
affection	*ástúð* OI, *ástúð* ON
a-foreman	*verkstjóri* OI, *verkstjóri* ON
a-freed-man	*leysingi* OI, *leysingi* ON
after	*áðr* ON, *aftur* OI, *eftir* OI, *eftir* ON, *síðan* OI, *síðan* ON
again	*aftur* OI
against	*móti* OI, *móti* ON
agape	*gapti* OI
age	*aldur* OI
a-girdle	*hnjóskulinda* OI, *hnjóskulinda* ON
a-good	*góðr* ON, *góður* OI
a-great	*mikinn* OI
agreeable	*geðjaðir* ON, *skapfelld* ON, *skapfelldir* OI
ahead	*fyrir* OI, *fyrir* ON, *undan* OI, *undan* ON
a-high-seat	*hásæti* OI, *hásæti* ON
ai	*ái* OI
a-keel	*kjöl* OI
a-knob	*hnappur* OI, *knappr* ON
Alftafjord (place)	*álftafirði* OI, *álftafirði* ON, *álftafirði* ON
a-little	*litlu* ON
all	*á* OI, *allan* ON, *allan* ON, *allar* OI, *allar* ON, *allir* OI, *allir* ON, *allir* ON, *alls* OI, *alls* ON, *alls* ON, *allt* OI, *allt* ON, *allt* ON, *allur* OI, *öll* OI, *öll* ON, *öllu* OI, *öllu* ON, *öllum* OI, *öllum* ON
all-near	*allnær* ON
allow	*leyfa* OI, *leyfa* ON
allowed	*lét* OI
all-very	*allmjök* ON
alone	*ein* OI, *ein* ON, *einni* OI, *einni* ON, *eitt* OI
along	*eftir* OI, *eftir* ON, *ein* OI, *eitt* OI, *eitt* ON, *fyrir* OI, *fyrir* ON, *lengi* OI, *lengi* ON, *með* OI, *með* ON
also	*annars* OI, *og* OI, *ok* ON
altogether	*allt* OI, *allt* ON
always	*hversdaglega* OI
am	*em* ON, *er* OI

Word List (English to Norse)

English	Norse	English	Norse
a-man	maðr ON, maður OI, mann OI	Arnarstapa (place)	arnarstapa OI, arnarstapa ON
ambitious-man	metnaðarmaðr ON, metnaðarmaður OI	Arnarstapi (place)	arnarstapa OI, arnarstapa ON
am-i	er ON	Arnora (name)	arnóru OI, arnóru ON
among	í OI, í ON	around	lit ON, stundar ON, um OI, um ON, umhverfis OI
ample	drjúgari OI, drjúgari ON		
an	ein ON, eitt ON	arrived	kómust ON
an-axe	öx OI	arrow	ör ON, örina ON
ancestry	ætt ON	as	að OI, at ON, er OI, er ON, sem OI, sem ON, því ON
anchor	akkerum OI		
and	en OI, en ON, fyrir OI, og OI, og ON, ok ON		
		as-a-woman	kona ON
an-excellent	ágæts OI	as-big	mikinn ON
animal-hunting	dýraveiðr ON	a-ship	skipi OI
animal-marrow	dýramerg OI, dýramerg ON	as-if	sem OI
		ask	biðja OI, biðja ON
animals	dýra OI, dýra ON	asked	bað OI, bað ON, báðu OI, báðu ON, beðinn OI, beðinn ON, beiddist OI, beiddist ON, biðr ON, spurði OI, spurði ON, spurðu OI, spurðu ON, spurt OI, spurt ON, spyr OI, spyrr ON
an-island	ey OI		
another	annað OI, annar OI, annarr ON, annat ON, öðrum OI, öðrum ON		
answered	segir OI, svarað OI, svaraði OI, svaraði ON, svarar OI, svarar ON, svarat ON		
		a-skin-purse	skjóðupungur OI
anti-sun-wise	andsælis ON, rangsælis OI	a-slab-stone	hellusteinn OI
		Aslak (name)	áslákr ON, áslákur OI
any	enga ON, öngva OI	as-much-as	margar ON
any-of	einnhver OI, einnhverr ON	a-son	son OI, son ON
		a-speck	flekk OI
anyone	nokkur OI, nökkurr ON	as-should-be	skyldi OI, skyldi ON
a-one-footer	einfætingr ON, einfætingur OI	assist	atbeina OI
		assistance	atbeina ON, liðsinni OI, liðsinni ON
apart	sundur OI		
a-pole-axe	bolöxi OI, bolöxi ON	as-soon-as	þegar ON
applied	beita ON, beittu OI	astonished	undruðust OI, undruðust ON
appointed	ráðnir OI, ráðnir ON, réðst OI, réðst ON, réðust OI, réðust ON	a-stream	straumar OI, straumur OI
		Asvald (name)	ásvalds OI
are	búnu OI, búnu ON, er OI, er ON, ert OI, ert ON, eru OI, eru ON, eruð ON, erum OI, erum ON	Asvald's (name)	ásvalds ON
		at	á OI, á ON, að OI, at ON, í OI, í ON
areas	sveitir ON	ate	átu OI, átu ON
are-you	ertu OI, ertu ON	at-sea	hafa OI, hafa ON
Ari (name)	ari ON		
a-ring	hring OI, hring ON		
a-river	á OI		

Word List (English to Norse)

English	Norse	English	Norse
attended	*mannaðr* ON, *mannaður* OI, *sótt* OI, *sótt* ON	bank	*bakkann* OI, *bakkann* ON
Aud (name)	*auðar* OI, *auðar* ON, *auðr* ON, *auður* OI	banned	*bönnuðu* OI, *bönnuðu* ON
aunt	*hímu* ON	banners	*flíkr* ON, *flíkur* OI
autumn	*haust* OI, *haust* ON, *haustið* OI, *haustit* ON	baptised	*skírð* OI, *skírð* ON, *skírðir* OI, *skírðir* ON
avail	*tjóa* ON	bare	*ber* OI, *ber* ON
Avaldamon (name)	*avaldamon* OI, *avaldamon* ON	barely	*varla* ON
		battle	*orrostu* ON, *orustu* OI
Avaldidida (name)	*valdidida* OI	battled	*börðust* ON
avoid	*forðast* OI, *forðast* ON, *varast* OI, *varast* ON	be	*á* ON, *fá* OI, *fá* ON, *vera* OI, *vera* ON, *verða* OI, *verða* ON
awake	*vaka* OI, *vaka* ON	be-able	*mega* ON
aware	*varir* OI, *varir* ON, *vís* OI, *vís* ON	beaches	*strandir* OI, *strandir* ON, *strandirnar* ON, *ströndunum* OI
a-warrior-king	*herkonungur* OI	beams	*tré* OI
away	*braut* ON, *brott* OI, *brott* ON, *brottu* OI, *undan* OI, *undan* ON	bear	*bera* OI, *berum* OI, *berum* ON, *bjarndýr* OI, *björn* ON, *fæða* OI
away-from	*undan* OI	bearded	*skeggjaðr* ON, *skeggjaður* OI
a-whale	*hvalr* ON	beaten	*barðir* OI, *barðir* ON
awhile	*hríð* ON, *stund* OI, *stund* ON	beautiful	*fagrt* ON, *fagurt* OI
a-wife	*konu* OI, *konu* ON	became	*gerðist* OI, *gerðist* ON, *urðu* OI, *urðu* ON, *varð* OI, *varð* ON
awoke	*vakði* ON, *vakti* OI, *vekr* ON, *vekur* OI		
awoken	*vakið* OI	became-a	*gerðist* ON
a-woman	*konu* OI, *konu* ON	because	*því* OI, *því* ON
axe	*öx* ON, *öxin* ON, *öxina* ON	because-of	*fyrir* OI, *fyrir* ON
		become	*orðið* OI, *verðr* OI, *verðr* ON, *yrðir* OI, *yrðir* ON

Á, á

ái	*ái* OI	becomes	*verðr* ON, *verður* OI
		becoming	*gerðist* OI

B, b

		bed-clothes	*klæðin* OI, *klæðin* ON
		been	*vár* ON, *verið* OI, *verit* ON
back	*áður* OI, *aftr* OI, *aftr* ON, *aftur* OI, *baki* OI, *baki* ON, *út* OI, *út* ON	before	*áðr* ON, *áður* OI, *en* ON, *fyrir* OI, *fyrir* ON, *fyrr* OI, *fyrr* ON, *því* OI
back-from	*út* OI, *út* ON	befriended	*vinsæll* OI, *vinsæll* ON
badly	*illa* OI, *illa* ON, *illilega* OI, *illiliga* ON	began	*byrjaði* OI, *byrjaði* ON, *hófust* ON
		behaviour	*athæfi* OI, *athæfi* ON
		be-heard	*hljóðs* OI, *hljóðs* ON
balls	*knött* OI, *knött* ON	behind	*heldur* OI, *seinni* ON, *undir* OI, *undir* ON

Word List (English to Norse)

English	*Norse*	English	*Norse*
behold	*heldr* ON, *heldur* OI	boat	*bát* ON, *báti* ON, *bátinn* OI, *bátinn* ON, *bátrinn* ON, *báturinn* OI, *eftirbát* OI
being	*væru* OI, *vera* OI, *vera* ON, *verða* OI		
believed	*trúðu* OI, *trúðu* ON		
bellowed	*gall* OI, *gellr* ON	boats	*skipunum* OI, *skipunum* ON
belly-fat	*ístruna* ON	body	*lík* ON, *líkin* OI, *líkinu* OI, *líkinu* ON
benefit	*kostum* ON, *njóti* OI, *nýt* ON		
benefits	*hagr* ON, *kosti* OI	boil	*vella* OI, *vella* ON
beside	*hjá* OI, *hjá* ON	boiled	*suðu* OI, *suðu* ON
best	*basta* OI, *bazta* ON, *besta* OI, *besti* OI, *bezta* ON, *bezti* ON	bold	*feitt* OI, *feitt* ON
		boldly	*skörulega* OI, *sköruliga* ON
betoken	*tákna* OI, *teikna* ON	bondsman	*ánauðigr* ON, *ánauðigur* OI
betrayed	*sviku* OI, *sviku* ON		
better	*batna* OI, *batna* ON, *betr* ON, *betur* OI	bondsmen	*ánauðgir* OI, *ánauðgir* ON
		booths	*búðir* ON, *byggðir* OI
bettered	*batnaði* OI, *batnaði* ON	bore	*bar* OI, *bar* ON, *báru* OI, *báru* ON, *ber* OI, *berr* ON
better-than	*batna* OI, *batna* ON		
between	*meðal* ON, *milli* OI, *milli* ON, *millum* OI		
		Borgafjord (place)	*borgarfirði* ON
bid	*beita* OI, *boðit* ON	born	*fæðist* ON
bids-tyr	*beiði-týr* ON	borne	*bornir* OI, *bornir* ON
Bids-Tyr (name)	*beiði-týr* OI	both	*báða* ON, *báðir* OI, *báðir* ON, *báðum* OI, *bæði* OI, *bæði* ON, *beggja* OI, *beggja* ON
birds	*fugl* OI, *fugl* ON		
bishop	*byskups* ON		
Bishop (name)	*byskups* OI		
Bishop'S (name)	*byskups* OI	bought	*kaupir* OI, *kaupir* ON
bit	*bíta* OI, *bíta* ON	bound	*bundu* OI, *bundu* ON
Bjarn (name)	*bjarnar* OI, *bjarnar* ON	boy	*svein* OI, *sveinbarn* ON, *sveininn* OI, *sveininn* ON, *sveinn* OI, *sveinn* ON
Bjarnarhofn (place)	*bjarnarhöfn* OI, *bjarnarhöfn* ON		
Bjarney (place)	*bjarney* OI, *bjarney* ON, *bjarneyja* OI, *bjarneyjar* ON, *bjarneyjum* OI		
		Brand (name)	*brands* OI
Bjarni (name)	*bjarna* OI, *bjarna* ON, *bjarni* OI, *bjarni* ON	Brand's (name)	*brands* ON
		brass	*messingu* OI, *messingu* ON
Bjarn's (name)	*bjarnar* ON	brass-buttons	*látúnshnappar* OI
Bjorn (name)	*birni* OI, *birni* ON	brass-spoon	*messingarspón* OI, *messingarspón* ON
black	*svartan* OI, *svartan* ON		
blamed	*lasta* OI, *lasta* ON	Brattahlid (place)	*brattahlíð* OI, *brattahlíð* ON, *brattahlíð]* ON
Blaserkur (place)	*bláserkr* ON, *bláserkur* OI		
		bravely	*drengiliga* ON
blood	*dreyra* OI, *dreyra* ON	breast	*brjóst* ON, *brjósti* OI, *brjósti* ON, *brjóstið* OI, *brjóstit* ON
blood-letting	*bílds* OI, *bílds* ON		
blue	*blán* OI, *blán* ON	Breidabolstad (place)	*breiðabólstað* OI, *breiðabólstað* ON

Word List (English to Norse)

English	Norse	English	Norse
Breidafjord (place)	*breiðafirði* OI, *breiðafirði* ON, *breiðafjörð* OI, *breiðafjörð* ON, *breiðfirskur* OI, *breiðfirzkr* ON	Caithness (place)	*katanes* OI, *katanes* ON, *katanesi* OI, *katanesi* ON
		calf-skin-shoes	*kálfskinnsskó* OI, *kálfskinnsskúa* ON
bright	*bjartari* ON, *bjartur* OI	call	*kalla* OI, *kalla* ON
bring	*bera* OI, *berim* ON	called	*heita* ON, *heitir* ON, *heitit* ON, *hét* ON, *hétu* ON, *kallað* OI, *kallaði* OI, *kallaði* ON, *kallaðir* OI, *kallaðir* ON, *kallaðr* ON, *kallaður* OI, *kallat* ON, *köllu* OI, *kölluð* OI, *kölluð* ON, *kölluðu* OI, *kölluðu* ON, *krafði* ON, *kvað* OI, *kvaddi* OI
broad	*breiðara* ON, *breiðir* OI, *breiðir* ON, *breitt* OI		
broader	*breiðara* OI		
broke	*braut* OI, *brotna* ON, *brotnaði* OI, *brotnaði* ON		
broken	*brotinn* OI, *brotinn* ON, *brugðist* OI, *brugðizt* ON		
		called-one	*annarr* ON
Brokey (place)	*brokey* OI, *brokey* ON	called-out	*æptu* OI
bronze	*eiri* OI, *eiri* ON	came	*fór* OI, *fór* ON, *kæmi* OI, *kæmi* ON, *kemr* ON, *kemur* OI, *kom* OI, *kom* ON, *koma* OI, *koma* ON, *kominn* OI, *kominn* ON, *komnir* OI, *komnir* ON, *komst* OI, *komu* OI, *kómu* ON
brother	*bróður* OI, *bróður* ON		
brought	*brugðu* OI, *brugðu* ON, *flutti* OI, *flutti* ON		
brought-about	*veldr* ON, *veldur* OI		
brought-out	*brugðið* OI, *brugðit* ON		
buckets	*byttu* OI, *byttu* ON		
bull	*griðungr* ON		
Buna (name)	*bunu* OI, *bunu* ON	can	*get* ON, *geta* ON, *kann* OI, *kann* ON
burial-service	*yfirsöngva* OI, *yfirsöngva* ON, *yfirsöngvar* OI, *yfirsöngvar* ON	can-it	*kann* ON
		captive	*hertekna* OI, *hertekna* ON
		cargo	*farminn* OI
buried	*grafnir* OI, *grafnir* ON	carried	*bar* OI, *báru* OI, *báru* ON, *ber* OI, *borið* OI, *borinn* OI, *borinn* ON, *borit* ON, *flytja* OI, *flytja* ON
burn	*brenna* ON, *láta* OI		
busy	*héldu* OI, *heldu* ON		
but	*an* OI, *at* ON, *en* OI, *en* ON, *enn* OI, *og* OI		
but-for	*en* OI, *en* ON	carry	*bera* OI, *bera* ON, *fættast* ON, *flytja* OI
buy	*kaupa* OI	carrying	*bar* OI, *bar* ON
by	*á* OI, *að* OI, *at* ON, *hjá* OI, *hjá* ON, *við* OI, *við* ON	cast	*kastaði* OI, *köstuðu* OI, *köstuðu* ON
		cat-skin	*kattarskinn* OI, *kattarskinn* ON
Byrdusmjors (name)	*byrðusmjörs* ON	cat-skin-gloves	*kattskinnsglófa* OI, *kattskinnsglófa* ON

C, c

	cattle	*fé* OI, *fé* ON, *fénað* ON, *fénaður* OI
cabins	*skálarnir* OI, *skálarnir* ON
	caught	*fengið* OI, *fengit* ON, *fengu* OI, *fengu* ON
	caused	*veldr* ON, *veldur* OI

Word List (English to Norse)

English	Norse	English	Norse
caves	hellum OI, hellum ON	come	kæmi OI, kæmi ON, kæmir OI, kom OI, koma OI, koma ON, komast OI, komast ON, komat OI, komat ON, komi OI, komið OI, komið ON, kominn OI, kominn ON, komit ON, komk ON
ceremony	atferli OI, atferli ON		
certain	nokkurn OI, nökkurn ON, víst OI, víst ON		
change	skipta OI, skipta ON		
cheeks	kinnum ON, kinnunum OI		
chest	kistil OI, kistil ON		
chief	formaðr ON, formaður OI	comes	komi ON
child	barni OI, barni ON	coming	kemur OI, koma OI, koma ON, komin OI, komin ON, kominn OI, kominn ON, komnir ON
children	börn OI, börn ON		
choice	kostar OI, kostar ON, kostr ON, kostur OI		
choosing	bæði OI	committed	framið ON, framin OI
chosen	kjörin OI, körin ON	companions	föruneyti OI, föruneyti ON
Christ (name)	kristr ON, kristur OI		
Christian (name)	kristin OI, kristin ON, kristinn ON	company	lið ON, liðið OI, liðin ON, liðit ON, líta OI, sveit OI
Christianity (name)	kristni OI, kristni ON	concealed	leyndi OI, leyndi ON
church	kirkju OI, kirkju ON	concerned	varða ON
circumstance	kynni ON, kynnu OI	consider	hirða ON
claimed	heimti OI, heimti ON	considered	kallast ON
clear	allglöggsæ ON, glöggsæ OI	conviction	sakar ON, sakir OI
		corn	korn OI, korn ON
cleared	ruddi OI, ruddi ON	costs	kost OI
clearing	rjóðr ON, rjóðrið OI, rjóðrit ON, rjóður OI	could	geta OI, mun OI, mun ON, mundi OI
cliff-top	hamargnípu OI, hamargnípu ON	could-be	mundi OI
		counsel	ráð OI, ráð ON
closely	vandliga ON	court	hirðar OI, hirðar ON
cloth	klæði OI, klæðið OI, skrúð ON, skrúðit ON	crags	hamra OI, hamra ON
		creatures	kvikindum OI, kykvendum ON
clothes	klæði OI, klæði ON, klæðið OI, klæðum OI, klæðum ON, klæðunum ON	creek-indented	vágskorit ON, vogskorið OI
		creep	krýp OI, krýpk ON
clothing	klæði OI, umbúningr ON, umbúningur OI	cried-out	kvað OI, kvað ON
		crosses	krossa OI, krossa ON
coal	kolum OI, kolum ON	Crow (name)	kráku OI, kráku ON
coffin	kista OI, kista ON	cubits	álna ON
cold	kalt OI, kalt ON	curiosity	forvitni OI
colour	lit OI	curious	forvitni OI, forvitni ON
		custom	siðr ON, siður OI, vana ON, vanda OI
		customs	hattar OI, hattar ON
		cut	skáru OI, skáru ON

Word List (English to Norse)

English	Norse	English	Norse
D, d		Dimunarvog (place)	*dímunarvági* ON, *dímunarvogi* OI
dale-land	*dalalönd* ON	disappeared	*horfinn* OI, *horfinn* ON, *hurfu* OI, *hurfu* ON, *hvarf* OI, *hvarf* ON
Dale-Land (place)	*dalalönd* OI		
danger	*hætta* OI, *hætta* ON		
dark	*ófölvan* OI, *ófölvan* ON, *svartir* ON, *svartr* ON, *svartur* OI	discourage	*letja* OI, *letja* ON
		discussed	*ræða* OI
		discussion	*umræður* OI, *umræður* ON
daughter	*dóttir* OI, *dóttir* ON, *dóttur* OI, *dóttur* ON	disorderly	*illt* OI, *illt* ON
		disposed	*ráðlausir* OI, *ráðstafalausir* ON
daughter-of	*dóttir* OI, *dóttir* ON, *dóttur* OI, *dóttur* ON	distribute	*sundr* ON
		divided	*braut* ON, *brýtur* OI
day	*dægri* OI, *dag* OI, *dag* ON, *degi* OI, *degi* ON	do	*gera* OI, *gera* ON, *get* ON
days	*dægr* ON, *dægur* OI, *dagar* OI	Dogurdara (place)	*dögurðarár* OI, *dögurðarár* ON
day-setting	*dagsetri* OI, *dagsetri* ON	doing	*völdum* OI, *völdum* ON
dead	*dauða* OI, *dauðan* OI, *dauðan* ON, *látin* ON, *önduð* OI	done	*gert* OI
		doorway	*dyrnar* OI, *dyrrin* ON
		down	*niðr* ON, *niður* OI, *ofan* OI, *ofan* ON
death	*dauða* ON	dragged	*dró* OI, *dró* ON
decide	*ráða* OI, *ráða* ON	Drangar (place)	*dröngum* OI, *dröngum* ON
decided	*tilskipan* OI		
declared	*kveðit* ON	drank	*drakk* OI, *drakk* ON
declaring	*kveðið* OI	drew	*brá* ON, *dró* OI, *dró* ON, *drógu* OI
decreased	*minnka* OI		
decreases	*þverr* OI, *þverr* ON	drink	*drukkit* ON, *drykk* OI, *drykk* ON
defeat	*ósigr* ON, *ósigur* OI		
descendents	*ætt* ON, *ættbogi* OI, *átt* OI, *átt* ON	driven	*rak* OI, *rak* ON, *reiddi* OI
		drove	*drífa* OI, *drífa* ON, *drifu* OI, *rak* OI, *velkði* ON, *velkti* OI
deserted-forest	*eyðimerkr* ON, *eyðimerkur* OI		
deserve	*verð* OI, *verð* ON	Dublin (place)	*dyflinnar* ON, *dyflinni* OI, *dyflinni* ON
desire	*fýsa* OI, *fýsa* ON		
desired	*fýsist* OI, *fýsti* OI, *fýsti* ON, *fýstist* OI, *fýstist* ON	Dublinshire (place)	*dyflinnarskíri* OI, *dyflinnarskíri* ON
		during	*leið* OI
did	*gerði* OI, *gerði* ON, *gerðu* OI, *gerðu* ON, *gerir* OI, *gerir* ON	dust	*mold* ON
		dwelled	*dvöldust* OI, *dvölðust* ON
die	*deyja* OI	dwelling	*bæ* OI, *bæ* ON, *búi* OI, *búinu* ON, *bústað* OI, *bústað* ON, *híbýli* OI, *híbýli* ON
died	*andaðist* OI, *andaðist* ON, *andast* OI, *andazt* ON, *dó* ON, *látizt* ON, *lézt* ON, *önduðust* OI, *önduðust* ON		
		dwellings	*bæinn* OI, *bæinn* ON, *bústað* OI, *bústaði* ON, *híbýli* OI, *híbýli* ON
difficult-be	*torflutt* OI, *torflutt* ON		
difficult-of-words	*illorðr* ON		

Word List (English to Norse)

English	*Norse*	English	*Norse*
dwelt	*bjó* OI, *bjó* ON, *bjuggu* OI, *bjuggu* ON, *búið* OI, *búit* ON	entertained	*skemmtu* OI, *skemmtuðu* ON
		equal	*jafn* OI, *jafna* ON, *jafnan* OI, *jafnan* ON, *jafnmikið* OI, *jafnmikit* ON

E, e

English	*Norse*	English	*Norse*
		equal-long	*jafnlangt* OI, *jafnlangt* ON
each	*hver* OI, *hverju* OI, *hverju* ON, *hverr* ON	equally	*jafnan* OI, *jafnan* ON
each-of	*hver* OI	equally-handsome	*jafnmannvænn* ON
each-way	*hvorttveggja* OI	Erik (name)	*eirík* OI, *eirík* ON, *eiríki* OI, *eiríki* ON, *eiríkr* ON, *eiríks* OI, *eiríks* ON, *eiríkur* OI
ear	*eyra* OI, *eyra* ON		
Earl (name)	*jarl* OI, *jarl* ON, *jarli* OI, *jarli* ON		
early	*snemma* OI, *snemma* ON	Erik'S (name)	*eiríks* OI, *eiríks* ON
east	*austri* OI, *austri* ON	Eriksey (place)	*eiríksey* ON, *eiríkseyju* OI
eastern	*eystri* ON	Eriksfjord (place)	*eiríksfirði* OI, *eiríksfirði* ON, *eiríksfjarðar* OI, *eiríksfjarðar* ON, *eiríksfjörð* OI, *eiríksfjörð* ON, *eríksfjörð* OI, *eríksfjörð* ON
east-fjords	*austfirzkr* ON		
East-Fjords (place)	*austfirskur* OI		
eastwards	*austan* OI		
educated	*menntur* OI		
egg-gathering	*eggver* OI	Eriksholmar (place)	*eiríkshólmum* OI, *eiríkshólmum* ON
eggs	*eggjanna* OI, *eggjum* ON, *eggver* ON		
eider-birds	*æðr* ON	Eriksson (name)	*eiríksson* OI, *eiríksson* ON
Einar (name)	*einar* OI, *einar* ON, *einarr* ON	Eriksstadir (place)	*eiríksstöðum* OI, *eiríksstöðum* ON
einar's	*einars* ON	Eriksvog (place)	*eiríksvági* ON, *eiríksvogi* OI
Einar'S (name)	*einars* OI, *einars* ON	errand	*erendi* ON, *erendum* ON, *erindi* OI, *erindum* OI
either	*hvárt* ON, *hvort* OI		
either-side	*hvárirtveggju* ON, *hvorirtveggju* OI	established	*staðfestu* OI, *staðfestu* ON
either-way	*hvorutveggja* OI	estate	*bæ* OI, *bæ* ON
else	*annars* OI, *annars* ON	esteemed	*göfgan* OI, *göfgan* ON
enchantments	*seiðinn* OI, *seiðinn* ON, *seiðsins* ON	evaluate	*met* OI, *meta* ON
encounter	*hitt* OI, *hitt* ON	evening	*kveld* OI, *kveld* ON, *kveldið* OI, *kveldit* ON
encountered	*sótti* OI, *sótti* ON		
end	*enda* OI, *enda* ON, *lauk* OI, *lauk* ON	events	*atburð* OI, *atburð* ON
		ever	*jafnan* ON
ended	*lauk* OI, *lauk* ON	every	*hver* OI, *hverr* ON
ends	*endunum* OI, *endunum* ON, *lýkr* ON, *lýkur* OI	excellent	*ágæti* OI, *ágæti* ON, *ágæts* ON
		exchange	*skiptumst* OI
endured	*þolðu* ON	exchanged	*skipti* ON, *skiptust* OI, *viðskipti* OI
enjoy	*njóta* ON		
enslaved	*þjáðir* OI, *þjáðir* ON	exchanges	*skipti* OI, *skipti* ON

Word List (English to Norse)

English	Norse
exerted	*kostaði* OI, *kostaði* ON
exhausted	*þrekaðir* OI, *þrekaðir* ON
expect	*vænti* OI
expected	*allvænt* ON, *vænt* OI, *væntu* OI, *varði* OI, *varði* ON
expenses	*gjalda* OI, *gjalda* ON
experienced	*reyndi* OI, *reyndi* ON, *reynt* OI, *reynt* ON
explore	*kanna* OI, *kanna* ON, *könnuðu* ON
explored	*könnuðu* OI
exploring	*kanna* OI
extraordinary	*kynjalaust* OI, *kynjalaust* ON
eyed	*eygðir* ON
eyes	*augum* OI, *augum* ON, *eygðir* OI
Eyolf (name)	*eyjólf* OI, *eyjólf* ON, *eyjólfr* ON, *eyjólfur* OI
Eyolf'S (name)	*eyjólfs* OI, *eyjólfs* ON
Eystein (name)	*eysteins* OI, *eysteins* ON
Eyvind (name)	*eyvindar* OI, *eyvindar* ON

F, f

English	Norse
fair	*fagra* OI, *fagra* ON, *vænst* OI, *vænst* ON
fair-wind	*byri* OI, *byri* ON
faith	*trú* OI, *trú* ON, *trúna* OI, *trúna* ON
fall	*fall* OI, *fall* ON, *fallinn* OI, *fallinn* ON
falls	*fellr* ON, *fellur* OI
family	*ættkvíslum* OI, *kynkvíslum* ON
family-good	*ættgóður* OI
famine	*hallæri* OI, *hallæri* ON
famous-man	*sómamaðr* ON, *sómamaður* OI
far-and-wide	*víðara* OI, *víðara* ON
farm	*bæ* OI, *bæ* ON, *bær* OI, *bær* ON, *bú* OI, *búi* OI, *búi* ON
farmer	*bónda* OI, *bóndi* OI, *bóndi* ON
farms	*bæjum* OI, *bæjum* ON, *bóndum* ON
fastened	*hneppt* OI, *kneppt* ON
fastening	*hnappur* OI, *knappi* ON
faster-than	*skjótari* OI, *skjótari* ON
father	*faðir* OI, *faðir* ON, *föður* OI, *föður* ON
father's	*föður* ON
father-and-son	*feðga* OI, *feðga* ON, *feðgar* OI, *feðgar* ON, *feðgum* OI, *feðgum* ON
father-of	*faðir* ON
father-to	*faðir* OI
favourable	*hagstætt* OI
fear	*ótta* OI, *ótta* ON, *ótti* OI, *ótti* ON
feared	*óttast* ON
fearful	*uggligt* ON
feast	*veisla* OI, *veislan* OI, *veislu* OI, *veizla* ON, *veizlu* ON, *veizlunni* ON
feasts	*veislur* OI, *veizlum* ON
feed	*fæða* OI, *fæða* ON
feet	*fæti* OI, *fætr* ON, *fætur* OI, *fóta* OI, *fóta* ON, *fótum* OI, *fótum* ON, *iljar* OI
fell	*féll* OI, *fell* ON, *felldu* OI, *felldu* ON, *féllu* OI, *fellu* ON
few	*fátt* OI, *liðfáir* OI, *liðfáir* ON
few-words	*fámálugur* OI
fifteen	*fimmtán* ON
fight	*berjast* OI, *berjast* ON
finances	*fjárhagur* OI
financial-cost's	*fjárkosta* OI, *fjárkosta* ON
find	*finna* OI, *finna* ON, *finnið* OI, *finnið* ON, *fund* OI, *fund* ON
finding	*finnst* ON, *finnur* OI
finger	*fingrar* OI, *fingrar* ON
finger-gold	*fingrgull* ON, *fingurgull* OI
fire	*báli* OI, *báli* ON
first	*fyrra* OI, *fyrra* ON, *fyrst* OI, *fyrst* ON, *fyrsta* OI, *fyrsta* ON

Word List (English to Norse)

English	*Norse*	English	*Norse*
fish	*fiskar* OI, *fiskar* ON, *fiskum* OI, *fiskum* ON	fortune	*auðnumann* OI, *auðnumann* ON, *forlög* OI, *forlög* ON, *forlögum* OI, *forlögum* ON
fishing	*fiski* ON, *útróðra* OI, *veiðarnar* ON, *veiðiskap* OI, *veiðiskap* ON, *veiðum* OI	fortunes	*forlög* OI, *forlög* ON
		forty	*fjóra* ON
five	*fimm* OI, *fimm* ON	foster	*fóstra* OI, *fóstra* ON, *fóstri* OI, *fóstri* ON
fixed	*festar* ON	foster-child	*fóstra* OI, *fóstra* ON
fjord	*firðinum* OI, *firðinum* ON, *fjörð* ON, *fjörðinn* OI	fought	*börðust* OI, *börðust* ON
fjords-carving	*fjarðskorið* OI	found	*fann* OI, *fann* ON, *fengið* OI, *fengit* ON, *finna* OI, *finna* ON, *fundið* OI, *fundit* ON, *fundu* OI, *fundu* ON, *fundust* OI, *fyndi* OI, *fyndi* ON
flat	*helgir* OI, *helgir* ON		
Flat-Nose (name)	*flatnefs* OI, *flatnefs* ON		
flat-stones	*hella* OI, *hella* ON		
fleeing	*flýja* ON		
flew	*fleygðu* ON, *fló* OI		
flows	*flytist* ON	four	*fjórir* OI, *fjórir* ON
folk	*fólki* ON	fourteen	*fjórtán* ON
follow	*fylgdar* OI, *fylgi* OI, *fylgja* ON	fourth	*fjórða* OI
		free	*frjálsa* OI, *frjálsa* ON
followed	*fylgdi* OI, *fylgði* ON, *fylgdu* OI, *fylgðu* ON, *fylgir* OI, *fylgt* OI, *fylgt* ON	Freydis (name)	*freydís* OI, *freydís* ON, *freydísi* OI, *freydísi* ON
		Fridgerdar (name)	*friðgerðar* ON
		friend	*vin* OI, *vinar* OI, *vinar* ON, *vinnur* OI, *vinr* ON, *vinur* OI
following	*áliðnum* OI, *áliðnum* ON		
food	*matar* OI, *matar* ON, *matarins* OI	friend-invites	*vinaboð* OI, *vinaboð* ON
food-prepared	*matbúið* OI, *matbúin* ON, *matbúit* ON	friendliness	*blíðu* ON
		friend-of	*vinur* OI
for	*á* OI, *á* ON, *að* OI, *af* OI, *at* ON, *er* ON, *fyr* OI, *fyr* ON, *fyrir* OI, *fyrir* ON, *fyrr* OI, *fyrr* ON, *því* OI, *því* ON, *til* OI, *til* ON, *um* OI, *um* ON	friends	*vina* OI, *vina* ON, *vinir* OI, *vinir* ON
		friendship	*vinátta* OI, *vinátta* ON, *vináttu* OI, *vináttu* ON
		frightened	*fælast* OI, *fælast* ON
foraging	*rekum* OI	from	*á* OI, *á* ON, *af* OI, *af* ON, *at* ON, *farm* ON, *frá* OI, *frá* ON, *fram* OI, *fram* ON, *ór* ON, *um* ON, *undan* OI, *undan* ON, *úr* OI, *út* ON
foreclose	*bregða* OI, *bregða* ON		
fore-knowing-woman	*vísendakona* ON, *vísindakona* OI		
foremost	*framast* OI, *framast* ON		
foresight	*forsjá* OI, *forsjá* ON	from-going	*framgengt* ON
forest	*skógi* OI, *skóginum* ON, *skógur* OI	from-there	*þaðan* OI, *þaðan* ON, *þangað* OI, *þangat* ON
forest-grown	*skógvaxit* ON	from-the-south	*sunnan* OI
forests	*skógurinn* OI	full	*fullr* ON, *fullur* OI
for-her	*hennar* OI, *hennar* ON	full-come	*fullkomna* OI, *fullkomna* ON
for-like	*þvílíkum* OI, *þvílíkum* ON		

Word List (English to Norse)

English	*Norse*	English	*Norse*
full-knowing	*fjölkunnig* OI, *fjölkunnig* ON	glass-beads	*glertölur* OI, *glertölur* ON
fur	*loðna* ON	glittered	*glitraði* OI, *glitraði* ON
Furdustrandir (place)	*furðustrandir* OI, *furðustrandir* ON, *furðuströndum* OI, *furðuströndum* ON	glory	*dýrð* OI, *dýrð* ON
		Glumra (name)	*glumru* OI, *glumru* ON
		go	*fær* ON, *far* OI, *far* ON, *fara* OI, *fara* ON, *förum* OI, *förum* ON, *gakk* ON, *ganga* OI, *ganga* ON, *gangi* OI, *gangi* ON
furry	*loðnir* OI, *loðnir* ON		
further	*firr* OI, *firr* ON, *lengra* OI, *lengra* ON		
		god	*guð* ON, *guðs* ON
		God (name)	*guð* OI

G, g

English	*Norse*	English	*Norse*
		God'S (name)	*guð* OI, *guð* ON, *guðs* OI, *guðs* ON
Gamlason (name)	*gamlason* OI, *gamlason* ON	goes	*fer* OI, *ferr* ON
gaping	*gapði* ON	going	*fer* OI, *förum* OI, *förum* ON, *gekk* OI, *gekk* ON
Gardar (place)	*garða* OI, *garðar* ON		
garden	*garði* OI, *garði* ON, *garðs* OI	going-from	*gagnvart* OI, *gagnvart* ON
Gardi (name)	*garðarr* ON, *garði* OI	going-out	*fært* ON
gathered	*fengu* OI	gold	*goldið* OI, *goldit* ON, *gull* OI, *gull* ON
gave	*gæfi* OI, *gæfi* ON, *gaf* OI, *gaf* ON, *gáfu* OI, *gáfu* ON, *gifti* OI, *gifti* ON, *veitir* OI, *veittu* OI, *veittu* ON	gone	*farið* OI, *farit* ON, *förum* OI, *förum* ON, *vor* OI
		good	*góð* OI, *góð* ON, *góða* OI, *góða* ON, *góðan* OI, *góðan* ON, *góðar* OI, *góðar* ON, *góðir* OI, *góðir* ON, *góðr* ON, *góðra* ON, *góðs* OI, *góðu* ON, *góður* OI, *gott* OI, *gott* ON
Gellir (name)	*gellis* OI, *gellis* ON		
Gellis (name)	*gellis* ON		
generosity	*rausn* OI, *rausn* ON, *rausnarveislu* OI		
generous	*rausn* ON	good-man-like	*góðmannlega* OI, *góðmannliga* ON
Gerstein (name)	*geirsteinn* OI, *geirsteinn* ON	goodness	*gæsku* OI
get	*fá* OI, *fá* ON	goods	*varningr* ON, *varningur* OI
giant	*þurslegur* OI, *þursligr* ON		
		good-will	*góðvilja* OI, *góðvilja* ON
gift	*gæfa* OI	good-words-man	*goðorðsmaður* OI
gifted	*gæfu* ON	go-on	*vinnast* ON
gifts	*gjafar* ON, *gjafir* OI	got	*fékk* OI, *fekk* ON, *fengu* OI, *náði* OI, *náði* ON
give	*gefa* OI, *gefa* ON, *gifta* OI, *gifta* ON		
given	*gefið* OI, *gefið* ON, *gefin* OI, *gefin* ON, *gefit* ON, *gjaforð* OI, *veitt* ON, *veittr* ON, *veittur* OI	grant	*veita* OI, *veita* ON
		grapes	*vínber* OI
		grape-vines	*vínbejaköngul* ON
		grass	*grös* OI
glacier	*jökli* OI, *jökli* ON		
gladly	*gjarna* OI		
gladness	*gleði* OI, *gleði* ON		

Word List (English to Norse)

English	Norse
great	*mikil* OI, *mikil* ON, *mikill* OI, *mikill* ON, *mikinn* OI, *mikinn* ON, *mikla* ON, *miklar* OI, *miklar* ON, *miklir* OI, *miklir* ON, *stór* OI, *stór* ON
greatest	*mestr* ON, *mestur* OI
great-estate	*rausnarbú* OI, *rausnarráð* ON
greatly	*drjúgum* ON, *stæra* OI, *stæra* ON
greatly-ruled-over	*stjórnuðu* OI, *stjórnuðu* ON
great-man-ness	*stórmannliga* ON, *stórmennsku* OI, *stórmennsku* ON
great-men	*stórmenni* OI, *stórmenni* ON
greatness	*stórmennsku* OI, *stórmennsku* ON
green	*grön* OI, *grön* ON
Greenland (place)	*grænland* OI, *grænland* ON, *grænlandi* OI, *grænlandi* ON, *grænlands* OI, *grænlands* ON
Greenlander (place)	*grænlenskir* OI, *grænlenskum* OI, *grænlenzkum* ON
Greenland-Sea (place)	*grænlandshaf* OI
greenland-skin	*grænlenzkan* ON
Greenland-Skin (place)	*grænlenskan* OI
greetings	*kveðjur* OI, *kveðjur* ON
Grelod (name)	*grélaðar* OI, *grélaðar* ON
grew	*óxu* OI, *óxu* ON
grey	*algrá* ON
Grimolfson (name)	*grímólfsson* OI, *grímólfsson* ON
gripped	*lesti* OI, *lesti* ON
Gro (name)	*gró* ON
Groa (name)	*gró* OI
ground	*mold* OI, *moldu* OI, *moldu* ON, *vígðu* OI, *vígðu* ON
group	*hópit* ON
growing	*vaxinn* OI, *vaxinn* ON

English	Norse
grown	*vexti* OI
guess	*get* OI, *get* ON
guests	*boðsmanna* OI, *boðsmanna* ON
Gunnbjarnarsker (place)	*gunnbjarnarsker* OI, *gunnbjarnarsker* ON
Gunnbjorn (name)	*gunnbjörn* OI, *gunnbjörn* ON
Guthrid (name)	*guðríðar* OI, *guðríðar* ON, *guðríði* OI, *guðríði* ON, *guðríðr* ON, *guðríður* OI

H, h

English	Norse
habitable	*byggjanda* OI, *byggjanda* ON
had	*átti* OI, *átti* ON, *áttu* OI, *áttu* ON, *hafa* OI, *hafa* ON, *hafði* OI, *hafði* ON, *hafi* OI, *hafi* ON, *haft* OI, *haft* ON, *hefða* ON, *hefði* OI, *hefði* ON, *hefir* OI, *hefir* ON, *hefr* ON, *hefur* OI, *höfðu* OI, *höfðu* ON
had-been	*hafði* OI, *hafði* ON
hair	*hár* OI, *hár* ON, *loðna* OI
Haki (name)	*haki* OI, *haki* ON
half	*hálfan* OI, *hálfan* ON, *helming* OI, *helming* ON, *helmingr* ON, *helmingur* OI
half-of	*hálfr* ON, *hálft* OI, *hálft* ON
Halldis (name)	*halldís* OI, *halldís* ON
Hallfrid (name)	*hallfríðr* ON, *hallfríður* OI
Hallveig (name)	*hallveig* OI, *hallveig* ON
hand	*hendi* OI, *hendi* ON, *hendr* ON, *hendur* OI, *hönd* OI, *hönd* ON, *höndina* ON, *höndum* OI, *höndum* ON
hands	*höndum* OI, *höndum* ON
handsome	*mannvænn* OI
happened	*gerðist* OI, *gerðist* ON
happy	*sælir* OI, *sælir* ON

Word List (English to Norse)

English	*Norse*	English	*Norse*
hard	*harða* OI, *harða* ON, *hörð* OI, *hörð* ON	hearth	*hjörð* ON, *hjú* OI
hardened	*herðir* OI, *herðir* ON	hearts	*hjörtu* OI, *hjörtu* ON
hardly	*varla* OI, *varla* ON, *vart* OI, *vart* ON	heathenry	*heiðni* OI
		heed	*gaum* OI, *gaum* ON
harm	*mein* OI, *mein* ON	heeded	*gáðu* ON
harried	*herjaði* OI, *herjaði* ON	Hekja (name)	*hekja* OI, *hekja* ON
harvest	*árangr* ON, *árangur* OI	held	*heldi* ON, *heldr* ON, *héldu* OI, *heldu* ON, *heldur* OI, *hélt* OI, *helt* ON
harvest-feast	*haustboð* OI, *haustboð* ON		
has	*hefir* OI, *hefir* ON	Heldr'S (name)	*heldr* OI, *heldr's* ON
Haukadal (place)	*haukadal* OI, *haukadal* ON, *haukdælski* OI, *haukdælski* ON	Helga (name)	*helga* ON
		Helgason (name)	*helgasonar* OI
		Helgi (name)	*helga* OI
hauntings	*aftrgöngum* ON, *afturgöngum* OI, *fróðárundr* ON, *fróðárundur* OI	Hellisvellir (place)	*hellisvöllum* OI, *hellisvöllum* ON
		Helluland (place)	*helluland* OI, *helluland* ON
have	*átt* ON, *hafa* OI, *hafa* ON, *hafði* OI, *hafðir* OI, *hafðir* ON, *hafi* OI, *hafi* ON, *hafið* OI, *hafið* ON, *halda* OI, *hefi* OI, *hefi* ON, *hefir* OI, *hefir* ON, *höfum* OI, *höfum* ON, *leggur* OI	help	*hjálp* OI, *hjálp* ON, *hjálpa* OI, *hjálpar* ON, *liði* OI, *liði* ON
		hen's-feathers	*hænsafiðri* OI, *hænsafiðri* ON
		her	*hana* OI, *hana* ON, *hennar* OI, *hennar* ON, *henni* OI, *henni* ON, *honum* OI, *hún* OI, *sér* OI, *sér* ON, *sínu* ON, *sínum* OI, *sínum* ON
have-been	*hafa* OI, *verið* OI, *verit* ON		
have-you	*áttu* OI, *áttu* ON		
having	*hafa* ON		
having-like	*höfðinglegt* OI, *höfðingligt* ON	herd	*hjörð* OI, *hjú* ON
		herding	*gæsla* OI, *gæzla* ON
he	*hana* OI, *hann* OI, *hann* ON, *henni* OI, *honum* OI, *honum* ON, *sér* OI, *sér* ON, *sinn* OI, *sinn* ON	here	*hér* OI, *hér* ON, *hingað* OI, *hingat* ON, *þar* OI
		Herjolfsnes (place)	*herjólfsnes* OI, *herjólfsnes* ON, *herjólfsnesi* OI, *herjólfsnesi* ON
head	*höfði* OI, *höfði* ON		
headland	*nes* OI, *nes* ON, *nesi* ON, *nesið* OI, *nesinu* ON, *nesit* ON	hers	*hennar* OI, *hennar* ON, *henni* OI, *henni* ON, *sér* OI, *sér* ON, *sín* ON, *sínar* OI, *sínar* ON, *sínu* OI, *sínu* ON, *sínum* OI, *sínum* ON, *þau* OI
heads	*höfði* OI, *höfði* ON, *höfðu* OI, *höfuð* OI, *höfuð* ON		
hear	*heyr* ON, *heyra* OI, *heyra* ON, *heyrðu* OI	herself	*sér* OI, *sér* ON, *sig* OI, *sik* ON
heard	*frétti* OI, *frétti* ON, *heyrðu* ON, *heyrt* OI, *heyrt* ON, *hjá* ON, *spurðist* ON	he-saw	*sjá* OI
		he-was	*hann* ON
		hewed	*höggr* ON, *höggur* OI
heard-of	*spurði* OI, *spurði* ON	he-willed	*vilja* ON

Word List (English to Norse)

English	Norse	English	Norse
hid	*fal* OI, *fal* ON	honourable	*sæmilegar* OI, *sæmilegast* OI, *sæmilegur* OI, *sæmiligar* ON, *sæmiligast* ON, *sæmiligr* ON, *sæmiligsta* ON, *sköruleg* OI
hidden	*duldið* ON, *duldir* OI, *fólgið* OI, *fólgit* ON		
highest	*efst* OI, *ofast* ON		
high-family	*ættstór* OI, *ættstórr* ON		
high-tide	*háflæðum* OI, *háflæðum* ON		
hills	*holta* OI, *holta* ON	hood	*höttr* ON
him	*hann* OI, *hann* ON, *hans* OI, *hans* ON, *henni* ON, *honum* OI, *honum* ON, *sér* OI, *sér* ON	hoods	*hötturinn* OI
		Hop (place)	*hópi* OI, *hópi* ON
		hope	*vánu* ON, *vonum* OI
		Hornstrandir (place)	*hornströndum* OI, *hornströndum* ON
himself	*hann* ON, *sér* OI, *sér* ON, *sig* OI	horrible	*hörmung* OI, *hörmung* ON
hindered-knowledge	*hindrvitni* ON	Horse-Head (name)	*hesthöfða* OI, *hesthöfði* ON
hired	*laun* OI, *laun* ON		
his	*hans* OI, *hans* ON, *honum* OI, *honum* ON, *síðunni* ON, *sín* OI, *sín* ON, *sína* OI, *sína* ON, *sínar* OI, *sinn* OI, *sinn* ON, *sinna* OI, *sinna* ON, *sinnar* OI, *sinnar* ON, *sinni* OI, *sinni* ON, *síns* OI, *síns* ON, *sínum* OI, *sínum* ON, *sitt* OI, *sitt* ON, *þessu* ON	house	*bús* OI, *hús* OI, *hús* ON
		households	*heimilis* ON, *heimkynna* OI
		housemen	*heimamönnum* OI, *heimamönnum* ON
		houses	*hús* OI, *hús* ON
		housewife	*húsfreyja* OI, *húsfreyja* ON
		how	*hvé* ON, *hversu* OI, *hversu* ON
		howling	*ýla* OI, *ýla* ON
Hitardal (place)	*hítardal* OI, *hítardal* ON	Hrafnsfjord (place)	*hrafnsfjörð* OI, *hrafnsfjörð* ON
Hofda (place)	*höfða* ON	Hraunhafnaros (place)	*hraunhafnarósi* OI, *hraunhafnarósi* ON
Hofdastrond (place)	*höfðaströnd* ON		
hoisted	*undu* ON	hundred	*hundrað* ON, *hundraðs* OI
hold	*halda* OI, *haldast* OI, *haldast* ON	hunt	*matfanga* OI
holding	*halda* ON	hunter	*veiðimaðr* ON, *veiðimaður* OI
holes	*holum* OI, *holum* ON		
Holmlatr (place)	*hólmlátri* OI, *hólmlátri* ON	hunting	*veiðar* OI, *veiðarnar* OI, *veiðiferð* OI, *veiðiferðir* ON, *veiðiförum* OI
homage	*hlýðni* OI, *hlýðni* ON		
home	*heim* OI, *heim* ON, *heima* OI, *heima* ON, *heiman* OI, *heiman* ON	hurt	*meiðar* OI, *meiðar* ON
		husband	*bónda* OI, *bóndi* OI, *bóndi* ON, *mannvönd* OI, *mannvönd* ON
homes	*heim* ON, *heima* ON		
honour	*drengskap* ON, *sæmd* OI, *sæmðinni* ON, *virðing* OI, *virðing* ON	Hvamm (place)	*hvammi* OI, *hvammi* ON
		Hvarfsgnipu (place)	*hvarfsgnípu* OI, *hvarfsgnípu* ON

Word List (English to Norse)

English	Norse	English	Norse
I, i		intercourse	samfarar OI, samræði ON
		into	í OI, í ON, vit ON
i	eg OI, ek ON, mér OI, mér ON, mig OI, mik ON	invited	bauð OI, bauð ON, buðu OI, buðu ON, býðr ON, býður OI, láð OI, láð ON
Iceland (place)	ísland OI, ísland ON, íslandi OI, íslandi ON, íslands OI, íslands ON		
		Ireland (place)	írland OI, írland ON, írlandi OI, írlandi ON
Icelander (place)	íslenskur OI, íslenzkr ON	Ireland-King (name)	írakonungs ON
if	ef OI, ef ON, hvárt ON, sem OI	Ironside (name)	járnsíðu ON
		is	er OI, er ON
ill	illt OI, illt ON	island	ey ON, eyna OI, eynni OI, eynni ON
illegitimate	laungetna OI, laungetna ON	islands	eyjar OI, eyjarnar OI, eyjarnar ON, eyrar ON
ill-looking	illilegir OI, illiligir ON	Islands (place)	eyrar OI
Illugi (name)	illugi OI, illugi ON	it	að OI, at ON, hana OI, hana ON, hann OI, hann ON, hon ON, hún OI, í OI, í ON, kann OI, það OI, þat ON
illusions	sjónhverfingar ON, þversýningar OI		
important	ráðabreytni ON, ráðagerð OI		
impression	leist OI	it-ends	lýkr ON
imprint	merki OI, merki ON	itself	sjálfan OI, sjálfan ON, sjálfar OI
in	á OI, á ON, að OI, at ON, eg OI, hin OI, hinn OI, í OI, í ON, in ON, inn OI, inn ON, innan OI, innan ON, inum ON, við OI, við ON		
		it-was	vera OI
		J, j	
		Jaeren (place)	jaðri OI, jaðri ON
inclined	hallat ON, um OI	jewelled-man	skartsmaðr ON, skartsmaður OI
increased	aukin OI, aukin ON		
indebted	skuldalið ON	joined	festi ON, hent OI, hent ON, tengdir OI, tengðir ON
indebted-to	skuldalið OI		
Ingjald'S (name)	ingjalds OI, ingjalds ON		
Ingolf (name)	ingólfi OI, ingólfi ON	Jorfi (name)	jörva ON
inhabitants	bjuggu OI, bjuggu ON	Jorfi (place)	jörva OI
inlet	ósinn ON, vág ON, vog OI	Jorund (name)	jörundar OI, jörundar ON
inlets	vogunum OI	journey	ferð OI
inside	inn OI, innan OI, innan ON	journeyed	ferr ON, fór OI
intend	ætla OI, ætla ON, ætlar OI, ætlar ON	**K, k**	
intended	ætlaði OI, ætlaði ON, ætlar ON, ætluðu OI, ætluðu ON	Karlsefni (name)	karlsefni OI, karlsefni ON
intends	ætlað OI	Karlsefni'S (name)	karlsefnis OI, karlsefnis ON
interaction	samfarar OI, samfarar ON		

Word List (English to Norse)

English	Norse
Karlsefnison (name)	*karlsefnissonar* OI, *karlsefnissonar* ON
keel	*kjöl* ON
Ketil (name)	*ketils* OI
Ketil's (name)	*ketils* ON
kid's-milk	*kiðjamjólk* OI, *kiðjamjólk* ON
kill	*drepa* OI, *drepa* ON
killed	*drap* OI, *drap* ON, *drápu* OI, *drápu* ON
killing	*víga* OI, *víga* ON
kind	*háttar* OI, *háttar* ON
kind-of	*konar* OI
kinds	*konar* OI, *konar* ON
king	*konungi* OI, *konungi* ON, *konungr* ON, *konungs* OI, *konungs* ON, *konungur* OI
King (name)	*konungr* ON, *konungur* OI
kings	*konungar* OI, *konungar* ON
kinsman	*frændi* OI, *frændi* ON, *frændur* OI
kinsmen	*frænda* OI, *frænda* ON
kjafal	*kjafal* OI, *kjafal* ON
Kjalarnes (place)	*kjalarnes* OI, *kjalarnes* ON
Kjarval (name)	*kjarvals* ON
Knarrarbringu (name)	*knarrarbringu* OI, *knarrarbringu* ON
knee	*hné* ON, *hneig* OI
knew	*kenndi* OI, *kenndi* ON, *kenndu* OI, *kunni* OI, *kynni* OI, *kynni* ON, *kynnu* OI, *vissi* OI, *vissi* ON, *vissu* OI, *vissu* ON
knife	*hníf* OI, *hníf* ON
knob	*hnappinn* OI, *knappinn* ON
know	*kann* OI, *kann* ON, *veit* ON, *vita* OI, *vita* ON
know-choose	*kenni-val* OI, *kenni-val* ON
know-how	*kunna* OI, *kunna* ON
knowing	*kunna* OI, *kunnandi* OI, *vita* OI, *vita* ON
knowledge	*fræði* OI, *fróðleiks* OI, *fróðleiks* ON
known	*kann* ON, *kunnigt* OI, *kunnigt* ON, *vit* ON
Krossholar (place)	*krosshólum* OI, *krosshólum* ON

L, l

English	Norse
laid	*lagði* OI, *lagði* ON, *lagt* OI, *lagt* ON, *lágu* OI, *lágu* ON, *láta* ON, *legið* OI, *legit* ON, *lét* OI, *lögð* OI, *lögð* ON, *lögðu* OI, *lögðu* ON
lake	*vatn* OI, *vatn* ON, *vatninu* OI, *vatninu* ON
lamb-skin-hood	*lambskinnskofra* OI, *lambskinnskofra* ON
land	*jörð* ON, *land* OI, *land* ON, *landar* OI, *landar* ON, *landi* OI, *landi* ON, *landið* OI, *landinu* OI, *landinu* ON, *landit* ON, *lands* OI, *lands* ON, *lendur* OI, *lönd* OI, *lönd* ON
land-benefits	*landkosta* ON, *landskosta* OI, *landskosta* ON, *landskosti* OI, *landskostir* OI, *landskostir* ON, *landsnytja* OI
landowner	*bóndi* OI, *bóndi* ON
lands	*landa* OI, *landa* ON, *lands* OI, *lands* ON, *landsins* ON, *lönd* OI, *lönd* ON
landscape	*landsleg* ON
landslide	*skriðu* OI, *skriðu* ON
landsmen	*landsmenn* OI, *landsmenn* ON
Langadal (place)	*langadal* OI, *langadal* ON
language	*mál* OI, *mál* ON
lap	*skaut* OI, *skaut* ON
larboard-side	*bakborða* OI, *bakborða* ON
large	*mikill* OI, *mjög* OI, *stórar* OI, *stórar* ON

160

Word List (English to Norse)

English	*Norse*	English	*Norse*
last	*síðast* ON	liquidity	*lausafé* OI, *lausafé* ON
late	*sein* OI, *seint* OI, *seint* ON	liquidity's	*lausafjár* OI, *lausafjár* ON
later	*síðar* OI, *síðar* ON	little	*lítið* OI, *lítils* OI, *lítils* ON, *lítit* ON, *litla* OI, *litla* ON, *litlu* ON, *lítt* OI, *lítt* ON
Laugarbrekka (place)	*laugarbrekku* OI, *laugarbrekku* ON		
launched	*skaust* OI, *skauzt* ON, *skutu* ON	Little (name)	*litlu* OI
launching	*skothríð* OI, *skothríð* ON	Little-Prophetess (name)	*lítilvölva* OI, *lítilvölva* ON
law	*lög* ON	little-with	*lítt* OI
lay	*lá* OI, *lá* ON, *lágu* OI, *lágu* ON, *legði* OI, *legðir* OI, *legðir* ON, *leið* OI, *lét* OI, *lét* ON, *liggja* OI, *liggja* ON	live	*fjörsins* ON
		lived	*bjó* OI, *bjó* ON, *lifað* OI
		livestock	*búfé* OI, *búfé* ON
		living	*lífi* OI, *lífi* ON
		living-space	*híbýlabótar* OI
laying	*lá* ON, *lágu* OI, *lágu* ON	loan	*launa* OI, *launa* ON
leaf	*laufa* OI, *laufa* ON	long	*langa* OI, *langa* ON, *langæðar* OI, *langæðar* ON, *langar* OI, *langar* ON, *langt* OI, *langt* ON, *lengi* OI, *lengi* ON, *lengja* OI, *lengst* OI, *löngum* OI, *löngum* ON
Lean (name)	*magra* OI, *magra* ON		
leave	*brottu* OI, *brottu* ON, *hætta* OI, *hætta* ON, *láta* OI, *láta* ON, *legði* ON, *leyfis* OI, *leyfis* ON		
led	*leiddi* OI, *leiddi* ON		
left	*látið* OI, *létu* OI, *létu* ON, *skildu* OI	longer	*lengr* ON, *lengur* OI
		long-spanning	*spannarlangt* ON
Leif (name)	*leif* OI, *leif* ON, *leifi* ON, *leifr* ON, *leifur* OI	look	*líta* OI, *litast* OI
		looked	*gáðu* OI, *horfði* OI, *horfðu* ON, *litast* ON, *lituðust* OI, *lituðust* ON, *sjá* OI, *sjá* ON, *sóttu* OI, *ván* ON, *von* OI
Leikskalar (place)	*leikskálum* OI, *leikskálum* ON		
lent	*léði* OI, *léði* ON		
less	*laust* OI, *laust* ON, *síðr* ON, *síður* OI		
let	*brenna* OI, *lætr* ON, *láta* OI, *láta* ON, *lét* OI, *lét* ON, *létta* OI, *létta* ON, *létu* OI, *létu* ON	looked-like	*leizt* ON
		looking	*horfði* ON
		lose	*týna* OI, *týna* ON
		lost	*lét* ON, *týndust* ON
let-us	*látum* OI, *látum* ON	lot	*hlaut* OI, *hlaut* ON, *hluta* ON, *hlutr* ON, *hlutur* OI
lies	*liggja* OI, *liggja* ON, *liggr* ON, *liggur* OI		
life	*ævi* OI, *ævi* ON, *líf* OI, *líf* ON, *lífs* OI	Lothbrok (name)	*loðbrókar* ON
		lots	*hlotist* OI, *hluta* OI, *hlutaðir* ON, *hlutaðist* OI, *hlutuðu* ON
like	*leikr* ON, *leikur* OI, *líkar* ON, *líkast* OI, *líkast* ON		
liked	*leist* OI, *líkaði* OI, *líkaði* ON	lot-taking	*hlutföllum* OI
likely	*líklegt* OI	loud	*hátt* ON
likewise	*eins* OI, *eins* ON, *þvílíku* OI, *þvílíku* ON	loudly	*hátt* OI, *hátt* ON
		low-ground	*lægðir* OI, *lægðir* ON
lineage	*ætt* OI, *ætt* ON	luck	*giftu* OI, *giftu* ON

Word List (English to Norse)

English	*Norse*	English	*Norse*
lucky	*heppni* OI, *heppni* ON	Markland (place)	*markland* OI, *markland* ON
lucky-wise	*happfróð* ON	marriage-offer	*gjaforðs* OI, *gjaforðs* ON
lying	*liggja* ON	marriage-proposal	*ráðahag* OI
Lysufjord (place)	*lýsufirði* OI, *lýsufirði* ON, *lýsufjörð* OI, *lýsufjörð* ON	married	*átti* OI, *átti* ON, *fékk* OI, *fekk* ON, *gjaforð* OI, *gjaforð* ON, *kvæntir* ON, *kvángaðist* ON, *kvongaðir* OI, *kvongaðist* OI

M, m

made	*ger* OI, *ger* ON, *gera* OI, *gera* ON, *gerðist* ON, *gerðu* OI, *gerðu* ON, *gerr* ON, *gert* OI, *gert* ON, *gervir* OI, *gervir* ON, *verið* OI, *verit* ON, *víst* OI, *víst* ON	marry	*eiga* OI, *eiga* ON, *gefin* OI, *giftast* OI, *giftast* ON
		marvelled	*undruðust* OI, *undruðust* ON
		matter	*mál* OI, *mála* ON, *máli* OI, *máli* ON
magic	*töfr* ON, *töfur* OI	matters	*mál* OI
mainland	*meginlandinu* OI	may	*heimilt* OI, *má* OI, *má* ON, *mætti* OI, *mætti* ON, *mættið* ON, *mættist* OI, *mættist* ON, *mættuð* OI, *mátti* OI, *mátti* ON, *máttu* OI, *megum* ON
maintain	*óhægjast* OI, *óhægjast* ON		
make	*gera* OI, *gera* ON, *gerið* OI, *gerið* ON		
malt	*malt* OI, *malt* ON		
man	*at* ON, *maðr* OI, *maðr* ON, *maður* OI, *mann* OI, *mann* ON, *manns* OI, *manns* ON, *menn* OI, *og* OI	me	*mér* OI, *mér* ON, *mig* OI, *mik* ON
		meal	*mjöl* OI
		measured	*atmælasamur* OI
		meet	*mót* OI, *mót* ON, *móti* OI, *móti* ON, *móts* ON
manner	*hættir* ON	meeting	*móti* ON
mannered	*hættir* OI	melrakka	*melrakka* ON, *melrakkar* OI
mantle	*möttul* OI, *tuglamöttul* OI, *tuglamöttul* ON, *vaðmálsmöttul* ON	men	*háseta* ON, *karla* OI, *karla* ON, *mann* ON, *manna* OI, *manna* ON, *manni* OI, *menn* OI, *menn* ON, *mennina* ON, *mönnum* OI, *mönnum* ON
many	*fjölda* OI, *fjölða* ON, *fjöldi* OI, *fjölði* ON, *fjölmenni* OI, *fjölmenni* ON, *fjórir* OI, *marga* OI, *marga* ON, *margar* OI, *margar* ON, *margir* OI, *margir* ON, *margt* OI, *margt* ON, *margur* OI, *mjög* OI, *mörg* OI, *mörg* ON, *mörgu* ON		
		men's	*manna* OI
		Men's (name)	*manna* ON
		menservants	*karlmaðrinn* ON
		merchant-ship	*kaupskipinu* OI, *knarrar* ON
many-knowing	*margkunnig* ON	mercy	*miskunn* OI, *miskunn* ON, *miskunnar* OI
many-men	*fjölmenna* OI, *fjölmenna* ON		
many-people	*allfjölmennt* ON, *fjölmenn* OI	merrier	*kátari* OI, *kátari* ON
maple	*mösur* OI, *mösurr* ON		

162

Word List (English to Norse)

English	Norse	English	Norse
message	*orðsending* ON, *orðsendingar* OI	much	*mikið* OI, *mikil* OI, *mikill* OI, *mikill* ON, *mikilli* OI, *mikilli* ON, *mikinn* OI, *mikinn* ON, *mikit* ON, *mikla* OI, *mikla* ON, *miklar* OI, *miklar* ON, *miklu* OI, *miklu* ON, *miklum* OI, *miklum* ON, *mjög* OI, *mjök* ON
met	*fundust* ON, *hitti* OI, *hitti* ON, *hittir* ON, *hittu* OI, *hittu* ON, *móti* OI, *móti* ON		
metal-assemblies	*málmþings* OI, *malmþings* ON		
middle	*miðri* OI		
mind	*hug* OI, *hug* ON, *minni* ON	muck-encrusted	*mykiskán* OI, *mykiskán* ON
mine	*mín* OI, *mín* ON, *mína* OI, *minn* OI, *minn* ON, *minni* OI, *míns* OI, *mínu* OI, *mínum* OI, *mínum* ON, *mitt* OI, *mitt* ON	my	*mig* OI, *mik* ON, *míns* OI, *míns* ON, *mitt* ON
		myself	*mér* OI, *mér* ON

N, n

English	Norse
misery	*vesöld* OI, *vesölð* ON
mixed	*blandast* OI, *blandinn* OI, *blandinn* ON
month	*mánuð* OI, *mánuð* ON
months	*mánuði* OI, *mánuði* ON
mood	*skapi* OI, *skapi* ON
Moray (place)	*meræfi* OI, *meræfi* ON
more	*fleira* OI, *fleiri* ON, *meir* OI, *meir* ON, *meira* OI, *meira* ON, *mér* OI
more-beautiful	*fegri* OI, *fegri* ON
morning	*morgin* ON, *morgininn* ON, *morginn* ON, *morgun* OI, *morguninn* OI, *morgunn* OI, *myrgin* ON
most	*flestra* OI, *flestra* ON, *megin* ON, *mest* OI, *mest* ON, *mesta* ON, *mesti* OI, *mesti* ON, *mestu* OI, *mestu* ON
mostly	*flestir* OI
mother	*móðir* OI, *móðir* ON, *móður* OI, *móður* ON
mother-of	*móðir* OI, *móðir* ON, *móður* OI, *móður* ON
mother-to	*móðir* OI
mountains	*fjöll* OI, *fjöll* ON
mouth	*munni* OI, *munni* ON
move	*færast* OI, *færast* ON
moved	*réðst* OI, *réðst* ON

English	Norse
name	*nafn* OI, *nafn* ON
named	*heita* OI, *heitir* OI, *heitir* ON, *hét* OI, *héti* OI, *héti* ON, *hétu* OI, *nafn* OI, *nefndist* OI, *nefndist* ON, *nefndu* OI, *nefndu* ON
namesake	*nafna* OI, *nafna* ON
near	*allnær* OI, *hjá* OI, *hjá* ON, *nær* OI, *nær* ON, *undir* OI
nearly	*nær* ON
neck	*hálsi* OI, *hálsi* ON
need	*þarf* ON, *þurfa* OI, *þurfa* ON, *þurftu* OI
needed	*þarf* OI, *þarf* ON, *þurfa* ON, *þurfti* OI, *þurfti* ON, *þurftu* OI, *þurftu* ON, *þyrfti* OI
neither	*hvárki* ON, *hvárkis* ON, *hvergi* OI, *hvergi* ON, *hvorgis* OI, *hvorki* OI
nettle	*nesla* OI, *nezlu* ON
news	*frétt* OI, *frétt* ON, *tíðenda* ON, *tíðinda* OI, *tíðindi* OI
next	*annað* OI, *annat* ON, *næst* OI, *næst* ON
night	*nætrnar* ON, *næturnar* OI, *nóttina* OI, *nóttina* ON
nine	*níu* OI, *níu* ON

163

Word List (English to Norse)

English	*Norse*	English	*Norse*
no	*eigi* OI, *eigi* ON, *engan* ON, *engar* OI, *engar* ON, *engi* OI, *engi* ON, *engin* ON, *enginn* ON, *engum* ON, *nei* OI, *nei* ON, *öngu* OI, *öngvan* OI	of	*á* OI, *á* ON, *að* OI, *af* OI, *af* ON, *at* ON, *hinn* OI, *í* OI, *í* ON, *inn* ON, *ofan* OI, *ofan* ON, *og* OI, *ok* ON, *ór* ON, *sonr* ON, *úr* OI
noble	*ættstór* OI, *ættstór* ON, *göfgir* OI, *göfgir* ON, *göfugmenni* OI, *göfugmenni* ON, *kvenskörungr* ON, *skörungr* ON, *skörungur* OI, *stórættaða* OI, *stórættaða* ON	of-exchange	*skipta* OI
		off	*af* ON, *ofan* OI, *ofan* ON, *við* OI, *við* ON
		of-the	*inni* ON
		of-them	*þeirra* OI
		oh	*ó* OI
		Olaf (name)	*ólafi* OI, *óláfi* ON, *óláfr* ON, *ólafs* OI, *óláfs* ON, *óleifur* OI
none	*eigi* OI, *eigi* ON, *enga* ON, *engan* ON, *engi* OI, *engi* ON, *engu* ON, *öngva* OI, *öngvan* OI, *öngvir* OI	on	*á* OI, *á* ON, *af* OI, *af* ON, *í* OI, *í* ON, *ofan* OI, *ofan* ON
		once	*eitt* OI, *eitt* ON
		one	*annað* OI, *annar* OI, *annat* ON, *eina* OI, *eina* ON, *einn* OI, *einn* ON, *einni* ON, *einu* OI, *einu* ON, *eitt* OI, *eitt* ON
no-one	*engi* ON		
nor	*né* OI, *né* ON		
north	*norðan* OI, *norðan* ON, *norðr* ON, *norður* OI		
Norway (place)	*noreg* OI, *nóreg* ON, *noregi* OI, *nóregi* ON, *noregs* OI, *nóregs* ON	one-footer	*einfæting* OI, *einfæting* ON, *einfætingi* OI, *einfætingr* ON, *einfætingurinn* OI
nose	*nösum* OI, *nösum* ON	One-Footer-Land (place)	*einfætingaland* OI, *einfætingaland* ON
not	*eigi* OI, *eigi* ON, *ekki* OI, *ekki* ON, *engi* ON		
nothing	*einskis* OI, *einskis* ON, *ekki* OI, *ekki* ON, *engu* ON, *öngu* OI, *öngvum* OI	only	*eina* ON, *einar* OI, *einar* ON, *einskis* OI
		open	*beru* ON
		opened	*opið* OI, *opit* ON
		open-sea	*hafvillur* ON
noticed	*vart* OI, *vart* ON	Opplands-King (name)	*upplendingakonungs* OI, *upplendingakonungs* ON
not-popular	*óvinsæll* OI		
not-without-obstacle	*ógreitt* OI, *ógreitt* ON		
now	*nú* OI, *nú* ON		
		opposite	*gegnt* OI, *gegnt* ON
		or	*eða* OI, *eða* ON

O, o

		Orkney (place)	*orkneyjar* OI, *orkneyjar* ON
obliged	*ráð* OI, *ráð* ON, *skyldir* OI, *skyldir* ON	Orm (name)	*orm* OI, *orm* ON, *ormi* OI, *ormi* ON, *ormr* ON, *ormur* OI
Odd (name)	*oddr* ON, *oddur* OI		

164

Word List (English to Norse)

English	Norse
other	*aðrar* ON, *aðrir* OI, *aðrir* ON, *annað* OI, *annarr* ON, *annars* OI, *annars* ON, *annat* ON, *hitt* ON, *öðru* OI, *öðru* ON, *öðrum* OI, *öðrum* ON
others	*aðra* OI, *aðra* ON, *aðrir* OI, *aðrir* ON, *annan* ON, *hinir* OI, *hinir* ON, *öðrum* OI, *öðrum* ON, *órir* OI, *órir* ON
other-side	*öðrumegin* OI
otherwise	*öðru* ON
our	*okkur* OI
our-places	*rúmunum* OI
ours	*okkar* OI, *okkarr* ON, *okkr* ON, *várra* ON, *váru* ON, *vorum* OI
out	*á* OI, *af* OI, *brott* OI, *brott* ON, *ór* ON, *úr* OI, *út* OI, *út* ON, *utan* OI, *útan* ON, *úti* OI, *úti* ON
out-door	*dyrunum* OI, *útidyrum* OI
outhouse	*náðahúss* ON
out-house	*útibúr* OI, *útibúr* ON
out-house-door	*útibúrsdyrin* OI, *útibúrsdyrrin* ON
out-houses	*útibú* ON
out-journey	*útivist* OI, *útivist* ON
outlawed	*sekir* OI, *sekir* ON
outnumbered	*ofrliði* ON, *ofurliði* OI
out-of	*af* OI, *af* ON, *úr* OI, *útan* ON
out-rowing	*útróðra* ON
outside-of	*útan* ON
Ovaegi (name)	*óvægi* OI, *óvægi* ON
over	*ofan* OI, *yfir* OI, *yfir* ON
owned	*áttu* OI, *áttu* ON
Oxney (place)	*öxney* ON, *yxney* OI

P, p

English	Norse
part	*hluta* OI
partakers	*bellendr* OI, *bellendr* ON
parting	*skilnaðr* ON, *skilnaður* OI
Part's (name)	*hluta* ON
passed	*leið* OI, *leið* ON, *liðin* OI, *liðin* ON, *liðnir* OI
paternity	*faðerni* OI, *faðerni* ON
patron	*fulltrúann* OI, *fulltrúann* ON
peace	*kyrrt* OI, *kyrrt* ON
peaceful	*fríð* OI
peace-mark	*friðarmark* ON, *friðartákn* OI
pelts	*belg* OI, *belg* ON
people	*fólk* OI, *fólk* ON, *fólkit* ON, *lýðum* OI, *lýðum* ON, *manna* OI, *manna* ON, *menn* OI, *menn* ON, *mönnum* OI, *mönnum* ON, *mönnunum* OI
people's	*manna* ON
people's	*manna* OI, *manna* ON
perform	*fremja* OI, *fremja* ON
performed	*flutt* ON
perished	*létist* OI
pierce	*smjúgi* OI
pillows	*hægindi* OI
pinched	*klípti* OI
place	*stað* ON, *staðar* ON, *stæðist* OI, *stæðist* ON
place-names	*örnefni* OI, *örnefni* ON
places	*rúmunum* OI, *staðar* OI, *staðar* ON
plans	*ráðs* OI, *ráðs* ON
played	*léku* OI
pledged	*hétu* OI
poem	*kvæði* ON, *kvæðið* OI, *kvæðit* ON, *kveðið* OI
poetry	*skáldskap* OI, *skáldskap* ON
poles	*stangir* OI, *stangir* ON, *staur* OI, *staur* ON, *staurinum* ON, *staurnum* OI, *stöng* ON, *stönginni* ON, *stöngum* OI, *trjám* ON, *trjánum* OI, *trjánum* ON
poor	*fátæku* ON, *fátækum* OI, *fátækum* ON
popular	*vinsæll* OI, *vinsæll* ON
popularity	*vinsældum* OI
porridge	*grautr* ON, *grautur* OI

Word List (English to Norse)

English	Norse	English	Norse
position	*lags* OI, *lags* ON	protect	*verja* OI, *verja* ON
possessions	*föng* OI, *föng* ON	provide	*framt* OI, *fremi* ON
possible	*að* OI	provided	*kost* ON
power	*forræði* OI, *forræði* ON	provided-for	*veitti* OI, *veitti* ON
praised	*lofa* OI, *lofa* ON	provisions	*fang* ON, *föng* OI, *vist* OI, *vist* ON, *vistir* OI, *vistir* ON
prayer-holdings	*bænahald* OI, *bænahald* ON		
prayers	*bænir* OI, *bænir* ON	pulled	*dró* ON, *kippa* OI, *kippa* ON, *tekur* OI
preach	*boða* OI, *boða* ON		
preached	*boðaði* OI, *boðaði* ON	purchase	*kaupa* OI, *kaupa* ON
preferably	*helst* OI, *helzt* ON	purpose	*ætlat* ON
preparations	*búið* OI, *búit* ON	pursued	*eltu* OI, *eltu* ON
prepared	*bjó* OI, *bjó* ON, *bjóst* ON, *bjuggu* OI, *bjuggu* ON, *bjuggust* OI, *bjuggust* ON, *búið* OI, *búin* OI, *búinn* ON, *búit* ON, *býr* OI, *býr* ON, *býst* OI, *býst* ON		

Q, q

English	Norse
quickly	*skjótast* OI, *skjótast* ON, *skjótt* OI, *skjótt* ON
quiet	*hljóðlyndr* ON, *hljóðlyndur* OI
quietly	*hljótt* OI, *hljótt* ON

English	Norse
prepared-with	*búinn* OI
present	*fyrir* ON
preservation	*varðveislur* OI
preserved	*varðveitti* OI, *varðveitti* ON
priest	*kennimenn* ON
priests	*kennimenn* OI, *kennimönnum* OI, *kennimönnum* ON
promised	*hést* OI, *hézt* ON
promising	*efnilegir* OI, *efnilegur* OI, *efniligir* ON, *efniligsti* ON
properly	*almennilega* OI, *almenniliga* ON
prophetess	*spákona* OI, *spákona* ON, *spákonan* ON, *spákonu* OI, *spákonunni* OI, *spákonunni* ON, *vísindakonunni* OI
Prophetess (name)	*spákona* OI
prophetesses	*spákonur* OI, *spákonur* ON
proposal	*bónorð* OI, *bónorð* ON, *bónorðið* OI, *bónorðit* ON, *ráð* OI, *ráð* ON
proposals	*beðið* OI, *beðit* ON
propose	*biðja* OI, *biðja* ON
prospects	*efni* ON

R, r

English	Norse
raise	*reisa* ON
raised	*reisa* OI
ran	*hlaupa* OI, *hlaupa* ON, *hleypr* ON, *hleypur* OI, *hljóp* OI, *hljóp* ON, *hljópu* OI, *hljópu* ON
rank	*mannvirðingu* ON, *mannvirðingum* OI
rarely	*varla* ON
rather	*heldr* ON, *heldur* OI, *helzt* ON
rattling-off	*þulði* ON
Raven-The-Dueller (name)	*hólmgöngu-hrafn* OI, *hólmgöngu-hrafn* ON
rays	*geislar* ON, *geisli* OI
ready	*búin* OI, *búin* ON, *búinn* OI, *búnir* OI, *búnir* ON
received	*tók* ON
recently	*skömmu* OI, *skömmu* ON
recited	*kvæðit* ON
reciting	*þuldi* OI
recognise	*kenni* OI, *kenni* ON

Word List (English to Norse)

English	*Norse*	English	*Norse*
reconciled	*sættir* OI, *sættir* ON	run	*hlaupa* OI, *hlaupa* ON, *renna* OI, *renna* ON, *rennið* OI, *rennið* ON
red	*rauða* OI, *rautt* OI, *rautt* ON	running	*hlupu* ON
Red (name)	*rauða* ON, *rauðan* ON, *rauði* ON	Runolfsson (name)	*runólfssonar* OI
Redbeard (name)	*rauðskeggjaði* ON	rushed	*rásar* OI, *rásar* ON
red-bearded	*rauðskeggjaði* OI		

S, s

English	*Norse*
reins	*tauma* OI, *tauma* ON
released	*leysti* OI, *leysti* ON
relieve	*létta* OI, *létta* ON
religious	*trúuð* OI, *trúuð* ON
remained	*eftir* OI, *eftir* ON
repay	*launa* OI, *launa* ON
resistance	*viðtöku* OI, *viðtöku* ON
return	*aftr* ON, *aftur* OI
returned	*áðr* ON, *áður* OI, *aftr* ON, *aftur* OI, *fór* OI
returning	*aftr* ON, *aftur* OI, *komnir* OI
Reynines (place)	*reynines* OI, *reynines* ON, *reyninesi* OI
rib	*rifin* ON
ribs	*rif* OI
rich	*ríka* OI
Rich (name)	*ríka* ON
riding	*reið* ON
river	*á* ON, *ána* OI, *ána* ON, *ánni* ON
river-bank	*árbakkann* OI, *árbakkann* ON
river-mouth	*árósinn* OI, *árósinn* ON, *árósinum* OI, *áróssins* OI
Rjupa (name)	*rjúpu* ON
Roaldsson (name)	*hróaldssonar* ON
rocks	*björg* OI
rode	*réðst* OI, *réðst* ON, *reið* OI, *reið* ON
rose	*reistist* OI
Ross (place)	*ross* OI, *ross* ON
rough	*hart* OI, *hart* ON
route	*leiðar* OI, *leiðar* ON
routes	*slóðir* OI, *slóðir* ON
row	*róa* OI, *róa* ON
rowed	*reru* OI, *reru* ON
rowing	*reri* OI, *reri* ON
sadness	*fæð* ON, *ógleði* OI, *ógleði* ON
saga	*sögu* OI, *sögu* ON
said	*kvað* OI, *kvað* ON, *kváðu* OI, *kváðu* ON, *kveðst* OI, *kveðst* ON, *mælt* OI, *mælt* ON, *mælti* OI, *mælti* ON, *sagði* OI, *sagði* ON, *sagðir* ON, *sagt* OI, *sagt* ON, *seggir* OI, *seggir* ON, *segir* OI, *segir* ON, *segja* OI, *segja* ON, *sögðu* OI, *sögðu* ON, *sögn* OI, *sögn* ON
said-of	*sögn* OI
sail	*sigla* OI, *sigla* ON
sailed	*sigldi* OI, *sigldi* ON, *sigldu* OI, *sigldu* ON, *sigldum* ON, *siglt* OI, *siglt* ON, *sildu* ON, *silgdu* ON
sailing	*siglingu* OI, *siglingum* ON
sails	*segl* ON, *seglið* OI
sake	*sakar* ON, *sakir* OI
same	*ein* OI, *ein* ON, *sama* OI, *sama* ON, *samir* OI, *samir* ON, *samt* OI
same-summer	*samsumars* OI
sand-heaven's	*sandhimins* OI, *sandhimins* ON
sands	*sandar* OI
sandy	*sandar* ON
sank	*sökk* ON, *sukku* OI, *sukku* ON
sat	*sat* OI, *sat* ON, *settist* ON
saved	*bjargaði* OI, *vistuðu* ON

Word List (English to Norse)

English	*Norse*	English	*Norse*
saw	sá OI, sá ON, sáu OI, sjá OI, sjá ON	seen	sáit ON, séð OI, sét ON, sjá OI, sjá ON, sú OI
say	sé OI, segðu OI, segðu ON, segi OI, segi ON, segja OI, segja ON, táðit ON, tala ON	seldom	sjaldan OI, sjaldan ON
		self-sowing	sjálfsáið OI, sjálfsáit ON, sjálfsána OI, sjálfsána ON, sjálfsánir OI, sjálfsánir ON
saying	kvað OI, kvað ON, kveðst OI, kveðst ON	send	senda OI, senda ON, sendi OI
scarcely	trautt OI, trautt ON	sent	sendi OI, sendi ON, sendr ON, sendur OI, sent OI, sent ON
scarcity	óárani OI, óárani ON		
scheming	undirförull OI		
Scotland (place)	skotland OI, skotland ON	separate	skilja OI, skilja ON, skiljast OI, skiljast ON
Scots (name)	skotar ON	separated	skildu OI, skildum OI, skilðum ON, skilðust ON, skilja OI, skilja ON
Scots (place)	skotar OI		
Scottish (place)	skoska OI, skosku OI, skozka ON, skozku ON		
scratched	klóraði OI	servants	karlmaðurinn OI
Scull-Cleaver (name)	hausakljúfr ON, hausakljúfur OI	set	setja OI, setja ON, settr ON, settur OI
sea	haf OI, haf ON, hafi OI, hafi ON, sjó OI, sjó ON, sjónum OI, sjónum ON, sjórinn ON, sjóvar OI, sjóvar ON	settle	byggja OI, byggja ON, byggva ON
		settled	biðuðu ON, bjó ON, bjuggust ON, byggðu ON
seal-fat	seltjöru OI, seltjöru ON, seltjörunni OI	settlement	búða OI, búða ON, byggð OI, byggð ON, byggðinni OI, byggðum OI, byggðum ON, óbyggð OI, óbyggð ON
search	leita OI, leita ON		
sea-scattered	sæhafa OI, sæhafa ON		
season	árferð OI, árferð ON		
seat	sætis OI, sætis ON	shall	mun OI, mun ON, muni OI, muni ON, munt ON, muntu OI, skal OI, skal ON
seat-posts	setstokka OI, setstokka ON, setstokkana OI, setstokkana ON		
		shall-you	skaltu OI, skaltu ON
sea-worms	sjómaðkr ON	shame	svívirða OI, svívirða ON
second	annað OI, annan OI, annan ON, önnur OI, önnur ON	she	hana ON, hann OI, hennar OI, hennar ON, henni OI, henni ON, hér ON, hon ON, hún OI
see	sé OI, sé ON, sjá OI, sjá ON	sheathed-sword	skeið OI, skeið ON
seek	leita OI, leita ON, leitað OI, leitaðir ON, leitat ON, sækja ON	shed	felldi OI, felldi ON
		sheep's-stomach	sauðarvömb ON
		shell-worms	skelmaðkurinn OI
seemed	sýn OI, sýn ON, sýndist OI, sýndist ON, sýnist OI, sýnist ON, virðist OI	shield	skjöld OI, skjöld ON
		shields	skjöld ON, skjöldu OI, skjöldum OI, skjöldum ON
seems	þætti OI, þætti ON, þykir OI, þykkir ON	shine	skína OI, skína ON

Word List (English to Norse)

English	Norse	English	Norse
ship	*knarrar* OI, *knörr* OI, *knörr* ON, *skip* OI, *skip* ON, *skipi* OI, *skipi* ON, *skipið* OI, *skipinu* OI, *skipinu* ON, *skipit* ON, *skipum* ON, *skipunum* OI, *skipunum* ON, *þat* ON	sickness	*sótt* OI, *sótt* ON, *sóttarfar* OI, *sóttarfar* ON
		side	*megin* ON
		sideboards	*rekkjustokkinn* OI, *rekkjustokkinn* ON
		sides	*hliðum* OI, *hliðunum* ON
ships	*skip* OI, *skip* ON, *skipa* OI, *skipa* ON, *skipi* ON, *skips* OI, *skips* ON, *skipum* OI, *skipum* ON, *skipunum* OI, *skipunum* ON	sign-herself	*sig* OI
		Sigrid (name)	*sigríðr* ON, *sigríður* OI
		Sigurd (name)	*sigurði* OI, *sigurði* ON
		silent	*fámálug* OI, *fámálug* ON
		silver	*silfr* ON, *silfur* OI
		since	*sem* OI, *sem* ON, *síðan* OI, *síðan* ON, *síðar* OI, *síðar* ON, *því* OI, *því* ON
ship's-company	*förunautur* OI, *skipverjum* OI, *skipverjum* ON	single	*eitt* ON
ship's-cook	*matsveinar* OI, *matsveinar* ON	sister-of	*systur* OI, *systur* ON
ships-ports	*skipshöfnum* ON, *skipverjunum* OI	sisters	*systr* ON, *systur* OI
		sitting	*setu* OI, *setu* ON
ship-worms	*maðksjá* OI, *maðksjó* ON	Skagafjord (place)	*skagafirði* OI
shipwreck	*skipflaki* OI, *skipflaki* ON	Skeidsbrekkur (place)	*skeiðsbrekkum* OI, *skeiðsbrekkum* ON
shirt	*serkinum* OI	skin-boats	*húðkeipa* OI, *húðkeipa* ON
shore	*strandar* OI, *strandar* ON	skin-purse	*skjóðupungr* ON
short	*skammt* OI, *skammt* ON	skins	*skinn* ON
shortage	*skorti* OI, *skorti* ON, *skortir* OI, *skortir* ON	skin-sacks	*skinnhjúpum* OI, *skinnhjúpum* ON
shortly	*skammt* OI, *skjótt* OI, *skjótt* ON	skin-wares	*skinnavöru* ON
		Skraelings (name)	*skrælinga* ON, *skrælingar* ON, *skrælingaskipa* ON, *skrælingja* OI, *skrælingjar* OI, *skrælingjarnir* OI, *skrælingjum* OI, *skrælingum* ON
short-stories	*sagnaskemmtan* OI		
shot	*skaut* OI, *skaut* ON		
should	*lézt* ON, *mun* OI, *mun* ON, *mundi* OI, *mundu* OI, *muni* ON, *muntu* OI, *muntu* ON, *mynda* ON, *myndi* ON, *skylda* ON, *skyldi* OI, *skyldi* ON, *skyldu* OI, *skyldu* ON, *skylt* OI, *skylt* ON		
		Skraelings (place)	*skrælingjalandi* OI
		Skraumuhlaupsa (place)	*skraumuhlaupsár* OI, *skraumuhlaupsár* ON
		sky	*loft* OI, *loft* ON
should-be	*skyldi* OI, *skyldi* ON	slabs	*hellur* OI, *hellur* ON
shoulder	*axlarliðnum* ON, *öxl* OI	slab-stone	*hellusteinn* ON
shouted	*æpðu* ON, *æptu* OI	slapped	*slettir* OI, *slettir* ON
showed	*sýndi* OI, *sýndi* ON, *sýni* OI, *sýnir* ON	sleep	*sofa* OI, *sofa* ON
shown	*auðsýnir* OI, *auðsýnir* ON	sleeping	*sofnaða* OI, *sofnaða* ON
		sleeves	*ermar* OI, *ermar* ON

169

Word List (English to Norse)

English	Norse	English	Norse
slept	*sofið* OI, *sofit* ON, *sofnar* OI	Son-Of-Gudrod (name)	*guðröðarsonar* OI, *guðröðarsonar* ON
slew	*vá* ON, *vó* OI	Son-Of-Halfdan (name)	*hálfdanarsonar* OI, *hálfdanarsonar* ON
slighting	*sleitum* OI	Son-of-Helga (name)	*helgasonar* ON
small	*smáir* OI, *smátt* ON	Son-of-Karlsefni (name)	*karlsefnissonar* ON
small-intestine	*smáþarma* OI, *smáþarma* ON	Son-Of-Ketil (name)	*ketilssonar* OI, *ketilssonar* ON
smoothly	*greiðleg* OI, *greiðlig* ON	Son-Of-Olaf (name)	*ólafssonar* OI, *óláfssonar* ON
Snaefell (place)	*snæfells* OI, *snæfells* ON	Son-of-Ox-Thorir (name)	*öxna-þórissonar* ON, *yxna-þórissonar* OI
Snaefellsjokli (place)	*snæfellsjökli* OI, *snæfellsjökli* ON	Son-of-Ragnar (name)	*ragnarssonar* ON
Snaefellstrond (place)	*snæfellsnesi* OI, *snæfellströnd* ON	Son-of-Runolf (name)	*runólfssonar* ON
Snorrason (name)	*snorrason* OI, *snorrason* ON	Son-Of-Sigmund (name)	*sigmundarsonar* OI, *sigmundarsonar* ON
Snorri (name)	*snorra* OI, *snorra* ON, *snorri* OI, *snorri* ON	Son-Of-Ulf (name)	*úlfssonar* OI, *úlfssonar* ON
Snorri'S (name)	*snorra* OI	sons	*sonu* OI, *sonu* ON, *synir* OI, *synir* ON
snow	*snjár* OI, *snjór* ON	son's-property	*sonareignin* OI, *sonareignin* ON
so	*sá* OI, *sá* ON, *sé* OI, *sé* ON, *sem* ON, *svá* ON, *svát* ON, *svo* OI	soon	*brátt* OI, *brátt* ON, *fljótlega* OI, *fljótliga* ON
sold	*selr* ON, *selur* OI	sooner	*bráðara* OI, *bráðara* ON
solution	*bragð* OI, *bragð* ON	sought	*leitaði* OI, *leituðu* OI, *leituðu* ON, *sækja* OI, *sækja* ON, *sóttu* OI
some	*eitthvert* OI, *nokkuð* OI, *nokkur* OI, *nökkur* ON, *nokkurir* OI, *nökkurir* ON, *nökkurn* ON, *nokkurra* OI, *nökkurra* ON, *nökkut* ON, *sum* OI, *sum* ON, *sumir* OI, *sumir* ON, *sumra* OI, *sumra* ON, *sumt* ON	south	*suðr* ON, *suðri* ON, *suður* OI, *suðurátt* OI, *sunnan* OI, *sunnan* ON, *svo* OI
		south-east	*landsuðr* ON, *landsuðrs* ON, *landsuður* OI
something	*nokkuð* OI, *nokkurra* OI, *nökkurra* ON, *nökkut* ON	southern	*suðræn* ON, *syðra* OI, *syðra* ON
sometime	*nokkuru* OI, *nökkuru* ON	southern-winds	*sunnanveður* OI
sometimes	*stundum* OI, *stundum* ON	sown	*sáð* OI
somewhat	*nokkuru* OI	space	*bilstyggir* OI, *bilstyggvir* ON
son	*son* OI, *sonr* ON	spanning-long	*spannarlangt* OI
Son-Of (name)	*son* OI, *sonr* ON, *sonur* OI, *syni* OI, *syni* ON	spared	*unnit* ON
		speak	*mæla* OI, *mæla* ON, *máli* OI, *máli* ON
Son-of-Aslak (name)	*áslákssonar* ON	spears	*spjót* OI, *spjót* ON
Son-Of-Bjorn (name)	*bjarnarsonar* OI, *bjarnarsonar* ON	speck	*flekk* ON
Son-Of-Erik (name)	*eiríksson* OI, *eiríksson* ON	spectacular	*þvílíka* ON

Word List (English to Norse)

English	*Norse*	English	*Norse*
speed	*skjótleiks* OI	straw-staves	*hálmþúst* ON, *hálmþústum* OI
spell-platform	*seiðhjallinum* OI	stream	*lækr* ON, *lækur* OI, *straumr* ON
spirits	*náttúrur* OI, *náttúrur* ON	streams	*straumar* ON
spoke	*er* OI, *mælti* OI, *mælti* ON, *mæltu* OI, *mæltu* ON, *töluðu* OI	strength	*styrkr* ON, *styrkur* OI
		strong	*sterkr* ON
spread	*bræddr* ON, *bræddur* OI, *brætt* OI	strongly	*sterklega* OI
		struck	*hjó* OI, *hjó* ON, *sló* OI, *sló* ON, *slógu* OI, *slógu* ON
spring	*vára* ON, *várar* ON, *vári* ON, *várit* ON, *vora* OI, *vorar* OI, *vori* OI, *vorið* OI	Styrr (name)	*styr* OI, *styrr* ON
		submerge	*kaf* ON
staff	*staf* OI, *staf* ON	such	*slík* OI, *slík* ON, *slíka* OI, *slíkra* OI, *slíkra* ON, *slíkt* OI, *slikt* ON, *slíkt* ON, *slíku* ON, *slíkum* OI, *svá* ON, *svo* OI
stand	*stað* OI, *stað* ON, *standa* OI, *standa* ON, *stoða* OI		
starboard	*stjórnborða* OI		
state	*hagi* OI, *hagi* ON	Sudrey (place)	*suðrey* ON, *suðurey* OI
stayed	*var* OI, *var* ON	Sudreyar (place)	*suðreyja* ON, *suðreyjar* ON, *suðreyjum* ON, *suðureyja* OI, *suðureyjar* OI, *suðureyjum* OI
staying	*haldið* OI		
steady	*stæði* OI, *stæði* ON		
steered	*styrkur* OI		
steering	*stýri* OI, *stýri* ON		
steersmen	*stýrimenn* OI, *stýrimenn* ON	suggested	*tillaga* OI
		suits	*hentar* OI, *hentar* ON
stern	*stjórn* ON	summer	*sumar* OI, *sumar* ON, *sumarið* OI, *sumarit* ON, *sumra* OI, *sumra* ON, *sumrum* OI, *sumrum* ON
steward	*bryti* ON		
still	*enn* ON		
stirred	*hrærðist* OI, *hrærðist* ON		
stock	*stokka* OI, *stokka* ON	sung	*kveðið* OI, *kveðit* ON
Stokkanes (place)	*stokkanesi* OI, *stokkanesi* ON	sun-wise-motion	*sólarsinnis* OI, *sólarsinnis* ON
stone	*stein* OI, *stein* ON	supplied	*veita* OI, *veita* ON, *veittir* OI, *veittir* ON
stones	*grjótinu* OI, *grjótit* ON, *steinum* OI, *steinum* ON	supplies	*birgðir* OI, *föng* ON, *varðveita* OI, *varðveita* ON, *vistir* ON
stood	*staðið* OI, *staðit* ON, *stóð* OI, *stóð* ON		
stopped	*stopir* OI, *stopir* ON	supported	*veitti* OI, *veitti* ON, *veittu* OI, *veittu* ON
strange	*undarlegi* OI, *undarligi* ON	supposed	*ætla* OI, *ætla* ON, *ætlaði* OI, *ætluðu* OI, *ætluðu* ON
Straumey (place)	*straumey* ON		
Straumfjord (place)	*straumfirði* ON, *straumfjörð* ON, *straumsfirði* OI, *straumsfjörð* OI	supposing	*ætlan* ON
		suspect	*grunar* OI, *grunar* ON
		Sutherland (place)	*suðrland* ON, *suðurland* OI
Straumsey (place)	*straumsey* OI		
Straumsfjord (place)	*straumsfjörð* OI	Sviney (place)	*svíney* OI, *svíney* ON

Word List (English to Norse)

English	Norse
sword	*sverðið* OI, *sverðinu* ON, *sverðit* ON
swords	*sverð* OI, *sverð* ON

T, t

English	Norse
table	*borð* OI, *borð* ON
table-games	*töfl* OI
tables	*borð* OI, *borð* ON
take	*tæki* OI, *tæki* ON, *taka* OI, *taka* ON, *tekr* ON, *tekur* OI, *tökum* OI, *tökum* ON
take-advantage	*nýta* OI
taken	*færð* OI, *færð* ON, *höfð* OI, *nema* OI, *numið* OI, *numit* ON, *taka* OI, *tekið* OI, *tekin* OI, *tekin* ON, *tekit* ON, *tók* OI, *tók* ON, *tóku* ON, *tókust* ON, *viðtaka* OI
takes	*tækist* ON, *tækjust* OI, *tekr* ON
taking	*nema* OI, *tókust* OI
talked	*tal* OI
taught	*kenndi* OI, *kenndi* ON, *kenndu* OI, *kenndu* ON
team	*lið* OI, *lið* ON, *liði* OI, *liði* ON, *liðið* OI, *liðit* ON, *liðs* ON
teams	*liðin* OI
tears	*tár* OI, *tár* ON
temperamental	*skapstór* OI, *skapstórr* ON
ten	*tigir* OI, *tigir* ON, *tigu* ON, *tíu* OI, *tíu* ON
tens	*tigir* OI, *tigir* ON
than	*en* OI, *en* ON
thanked	*þakkar* OI, *þakkar* ON, *þökkuðu* ON
that	*á* OI, *á* ON, *að* OI, *at* ON, *en* OI, *en* ON, *er* OI, *er* ON, *hana* OI, *hin* OI, *sá* OI, *sá* ON, *sem* OI, *sem* ON, *sú* ON, *það* OI, *þann* OI, *þann* ON, *þar* OI, *þat* ON, *þeim* OI, *þeim* ON, *þenna* OI, *þetta* OI, *þetta* ON, *því* OI, *því* ON
that-might	*mátti* OI
that-to	*það* OI
the	*á* OI, *að* OI, *at* ON, *er* OI, *hið* OI, *hin* OI, *hina* OI, *hinn* OI, *hinni* OI, *hins* OI, *hinu* OI, *hinum* OI, *í* OI, *in* ON, *ina* ON, *inn* ON, *inni* ON, *ins* ON, *inum* ON, *it* ON, *sér* OI, *sér* ON, *sinn* OI, *sinn* ON, *sú* OI, *sú* ON, *þá* ON, *það* OI, *þann* OI, *þann* ON, *þat* ON
the belly	*ístruna* OI
the people	*manna* OI
the-alternative	*liggja* ON
the-arrow	*örina* OI
the-axe	*öxin* OI, *öxina* OI
the-bishop	*byskups* ON
the-boat	*bátinn* OI, *bátinn* ON, *bátum* OI, *báturinn* OI
the-bodies	*líkinu* ON, *líkunum* OI
the-bottom-of	*botn* OI, *botn* ON
the-breast	*brjóstið* OI
the-church	*kirkju* ON
the-company	*liðit* ON
the-company-of	*lið* OI
the-dead	*dauða* ON
the-deep-minded	*djúpúðgu* ON
The-Deep-Minded (name)	*djúpúðgu* OI
the-door	*durunum* ON, *dyrunum* OI
the-earth	*jörð* OI
The-Easterner (name)	*austmanns* OI
the-easternman	*austmanns* ON
the-farmer	*bóndi* ON
The-Farmer (name)	*bóndi* OI

Word List (English to Norse)

English	Norse	English	Norse
the-feast	veisla OI, veislunni OI, veizla ON, veizlan ON, veizlunni ON	then	á OI, á ON, en OI, en ON, er OI, er ON, inn OI, inn ON, sem OI, sem ON, síðan OI, síðan ON, sinn OI, sinn ON, skip ON, þá OI, þá ON, þann OI, þann ON, þeir ON, þenna ON
the-foreman	verkstjórinn OI		
The-Foul (name)	saur OI, saur ON, saurr ON		
the-headland	nesið OI, nesinu OI		
the-house	húsunum OI, húsunum ON		
the-hunter	veiðimaðr ON, veiðimaður OI, veiðimanns OI, veiðimanns ON	the-one-footer	einfætingr ON
		the-out-door	útidurum ON, útidurunum ON
their	sér OI, sér ON, sinna OI, sins ON, síns ON, sínu OI, sínu ON, sitt OI, sitt ON, þeir OI, þeir ON, þeira ON, þeirar ON, þeirra OI, þeirrar OI	the-people	manna OI
		the-platform	hjallinn ON
		there	þá OI, þá ON, þaðan ON, þær OI, þær ON, þangað OI, þangat ON, þar OI, þar ON, þau OI, þau ON, þeir OI, þeir ON, þeira ON, þeirra OI, þeirri OI
the-Irish-Sea (place)	írlandshaf ON		
theirs	sér OI, sér ON, sín OI, sín ON, sína OI, sína ON, sínar OI, sínar ON, sinna OI, sinna ON, sinnar OI, sinnar ON, sínu OI, sínu ON, sínum OI, sínum ON, sitt OI, sitt ON, þeim OI, þeim ON, þeir OI, þeira ON, þeirra OI	The-Red (name)	rauða OI, rauða ON, rauði OI, rauði ON, rauðr ON, rauður OI
		The-Red'S (name)	rauðs OI
		The-Red'S (name)	rauða OI, rauða ON, rauðs ON
		therefore	at ON, fyrir OI, þar OI, því OI, því ON
		the-river	ánni OI
the-island	eyna OI	the-sad	hryggs ON
the-king	konungr ON	the-same	sama OI, sama ON
The-King (name)	konungs OI, konungs ON, konungur OI	these	þau OI, þau ON, þeim ON, þess OI, þess ON, þessa OI, þessa ON, þessara OI, þessi OI, þessi ON, þessir OI, þessir ON, þessum OI, þessum ON
the-land	landið OI, landinu OI, landit ON		
them	sér OI, sér ON, þá OI, þá ON, þau OI, þau ON, þeim OI, þeim ON, þeir ON, þeirra OI		
		the-sea	sjó OI
		the-ship	skipi ON, skipið OI, skipinu OI, skipinu ON, skipum OI
the-matter	mál OI, máli OI, máli ON		
the-men	manna ON		
the-middle	miðri ON	The-Skraelings (name)	skrælingjar OI
the-mouth-of	mynni OI, mynni ON		
themselves	sér OI, sér ON, sjálfala OI, sjálfala ON	the-sword	sverðið OI
		the-team	lit OI, lit ON
		the-way	háttr ON, háttur OI, leið OI
		the-wedding	brúðkaupið OI
		The-White (name)	hvíti OI, hvíti ON

173

Word List (English to Norse)

English	Norse	English	Norse
the-woman	*konan* OI	Thorbjorg's (name)	*þorbjargar* ON
the-woods	*skóginn* OI	Thorbjorn (name)	*þorbirni* OI, *þorbirni* ON, *þorbjarnar* OI, *þorbjörn* OI, *þorbjörn* ON
the-worm-sea	*maðksjónum* ON		
The-Worm-Sea (place)	*maðkahafinu* OI		
they	*af* OI, *hitt* OI, *sér* OI, *síns* OI, *síns* ON, *sínu* ON, *þá* OI, *þá* ON, *þær* OI, *þær* ON, *þar* OI, *þar* ON, *þau* OI, *þau* ON, *þeim* OI, *þeim* ON, *þeir* OI, *þeir* ON, *þeira* ON, *þeirs* ON	Thorbjornadottir (name)	*þorbjarnardóttur* OI
		Thorbjorn's (name)	*þorbjarnar* ON
		Thorbrand (name)	*þorbrand* OI, *þorbrandr* ON
		Thorbrand'S (name)	*þorbrands* OI, *þorbrands* ON
		Thorbrandson (name)	*þorbrandsson* OI, *þorbrandsson* ON
they-saw	*sjá* OI	Thord (name)	*þórðar* OI, *þórðar* ON, *þórðr* ON
thick	*gildir* OI, *gildir* ON		
things	*hluti* OI, *hluti* ON, *hlutir* OI, *hlutir* ON	Thorfin (name)	*þorfinnr* ON, *þorfinnur* OI
think	*þótti* OI, *þyki* OI, *þykir* OI, *þykist* OI, *þykki* ON, *þykkja* ON, *þykkjast* ON	Thorfin's (name)	*þorfinns* ON
		Thorgeir (name)	*þorgeir* OI, *þorgeirr* ON
		Thorgeirsfell (place)	*þorgeirsfelli* OI, *þorgeirsfelli* ON
thinking	*þykir* OI		
think-us	*þykkjumst* ON	Thorgerd (name)	*þorgerði* ON
third	*þriðja* OI, *þriðja* ON	Thorgest (name)	*þorgesti* OI, *þorgesti* ON, *þorgestr* ON, *þorgestur* OI
thirty-and	*þriði* ON		
this	*í* ON, *sé* OI, *það* OI, *þat* ON, *þeir* OI, *þeira* ON, *þenna* OI, *þenna* ON, *þess* OI, *þess* ON, *þessa* OI, *þessa* ON, *þessi* OI, *þessi* ON, *þessu* OI, *þessu* ON, *þessum* OI, *þessum* ON, *þetta* OI, *þetta* ON	Thorgest'S (name)	*þorgests* OI, *þorgests* ON
		Thorgils (name)	*þorgils* OI, *þorgils* ON
		Thorgilson (name)	*þorgilsson* ON
		Thorgun (name)	*þórgunna* OI, *þórgunna* ON
		Thorhall (name)	*þórhall* OI, *þórhallr* ON, *þórhalls* OI, *þórhalls* ON, *þórhallur* OI
Thistilsfjord (place)	*þistilsfjörð* OI, *þistilsfjörð* ON	Thorhild (name)	*þórhildi* ON
Thistle (name)	*þistils* OI, *þistils* ON	Thorid (name)	*þuríðar* OI, *þuríðar* ON
Thjodhild (name)	*þjóðhildar* OI, *þjóðhildar* ON, *þjóðhildi* ON, *þjóðhildr* ON, *þjóðhildur* OI	Thori's (name)	*þóris* ON
		Thorjborn'S (name)	*þorbjargar* OI, *þorbjarnar* OI
		Thorkell (name)	*þorkel* OI, *þorkel* ON, *þorkell* OI, *þorkell* ON
Thjodhildakirkja (place)	*þjóðhildarkirkja* ON	Thorlak (name)	*þorláks* OI
Thjodhildkirkja (place)	*þjóðhildarkirkja* OI	Thorlak's (name)	*þorláks* ON
Thor (name)	*þór* OI, *þór* ON	Thorsnes-Thing (name)	*þórsnessþingi* ON
Thorbjorg (name)	*þorbjargar* OI, *þorbjargar* ON, *þorbjörg* OI, *þorbjörg* ON, *þorbjörgu* OI, *þorbjörgu* ON	Thorsnes-Thing (place)	*þórsnessþingi* OI

Word List (English to Norse)

English	*Norse*	English	*Norse*
Thorstein (name)	þorstein OI, þorstein ON, þorsteinn OI, þorsteinn ON, þorsteins OI, þorsteins ON	to-another	annars ON
		to-be	vera OI, vera ON, verða OI, verða ON
		to-bear	berja ON
Thorstein'S (name)	þorsteins OI, þorsteins ON	to-bear-to	berja OI
		to-follow	fylgja OI
Thorun (name)	þórunn OI, þórunn ON	together	saman OI, saman ON, samt OI, samt ON
Thorvald (name)	þorvald OI, þorvaldi OI, þorvaldi ON, þorvaldr ON, þorvaldur OI	to-go	fara OI
		to-her	henni OI, henni ON
Thorvard (name)	þorvarði ON, þorvarðr ON, þorvarður OI	to-him	hans ON, honum OI
		toil	vás ON, vos OI
those	þær OI, þær ON, þau OI, þau ON, þeim OI, þeim ON, þeir OI, þeir ON	told	sagði OI, sagði ON, sögðu ON, talat ON, taldi OI, talði ON, töluðu OI
though	þó OI, þó ON, þótt OI, þótt ON, þóttú OI, þóttú ON	told-of	getið OI, getit ON
		to-lie	leggjast OI, leggjast ON
thought	hyggja OI, hyggja ON, íhuga OI, íhuga ON, þó OI, þótt OI, þótt ON, þótti OI, þótti ON, þóttist OI, þóttist ON, þóttust OI, þóttust ON, þykir OI, þykki ON	to-me	mér OI, mér ON
		took	nam OI, nam ON, námu OI, námu ON, sótti OI, sótti ON, tekr ON, tekur OI, tók OI, tók ON, tókst OI, tókst ON, tóku OI, tóku ON, tókust OI
thoughts	alendu OI, hug OI, hug ON, þokka ON	took-to	tóku OI, tóku ON
thralls	þrælana OI, þrælana ON, þrælar OI, þrælar ON	to-preach	boða OI
		to-sell	selja OI, selja ON
thrall's-son	þrælssyni OI, þrælssyni ON	to-sign	signa ON
		to-speak	mæla OI, tala ON
three	þrír OI, þrír ON, þrjár OI, þrjár ON, þrjú OI, þrjú ON	to-that	hvað OI
		to-the-land	landinu OI
		to-them	þá ON, þeim OI, þeim ON
three-winters	þrévetr ON, þrívetur OI	to-travel	fara OI
tidal-pool	hópi OI, hópi ON	touch	spyrnast OI
tide	flóðið OI, flóðit ON	towards	á OI, á ON, að OI, at ON, mót OI, móti OI, móti ON, til OI, til ON
tied	þvengi OI, þvengi ON		
time	frá OI, frá ON, stund OI, stund ON, tíma OI, tíma ON	town	bæ OI, bæ ON
		to-you	þér OI, þér ON
tin-buttons	tinknappar ON	trading	keipana OI, keipana ON
tip	oddrinn ON, oddurinn OI		
to	á OI, á ON, að OI, at ON, er OI, er ON, fyrir ON, í OI, í ON, it ON, signa OI, til OI, til ON, við OI, við ON, vit ON	trading-journeys	kaupferðum OI, kaupferðum ON

175

Word List (English to Norse)

English	Norse	English	Norse
trading-men	kaupmenn OI, kaupmenn ON, kaupmönnum OI, kaupmönnum ON	two	tvá ON, tvær OI, tvær ON, tvau ON, tveim ON, tveir OI, tveir ON, tvennum OI, tvo OI, tvö OI
trading-posts	kaupstefna OI, kaupstefna ON, kaupstefnu OI, kaupstefnu ON	two-ringed	tvíhólkaðan OI, tvíhólkaðan ON

U, u

English	Norse
Tradir (place)	tröðum OI, tröðum ON
tradition	sið OI, sið ON
transferred	fluttr ON, fluttur OI
travel	fara OI, fara ON, farir OI, fer OI, ferð OI, ferð ON, ferðar OI, ferðar ON
travelled	farið OI, farit ON, fer OI, ferr ON, fór OI, fór ON, fóru OI, fóru ON, fóruð OI
traveller-generous	fardreng OI, fardreng ON
travelling	fara OI, fara ON, fór OI
travelling-companion	fardrengr ON, fardrengur OI
travel-we	förum OI, förum ON
treasure	féið OI, féit ON, gersemi OI, gersimi ON
tree	tré OI, tré ON
trees	tré OI, tré ON
trenches	grafar ON, grafir OI, gröfunum OI, gröfunum ON
tried	reynt OI
true	
true	
true	
trust	trausti OI, trausti ON
Tryggvason (name)	tryggvason ON, tryggvasyni OI, tryggvasyni ON
Tryggvason'S (name)	tryggvasonar OI
Tryggvason'S (name)	tryggvasonar OI, tryggvasonar ON
turn	snúast OI
turned	hverfr ON, hverfur OI, sneru OI
tusk-belt	tannbelti OI, tannbelti ON
twelve	tólf ON
twenty	tögr ON, tuttugu OI, tuttugu ON

English	Norse
Ulf (name)	úlfs OI, úlfs ON
Ulfson (name)	úlfssonar OI, úlfssonar ON
unconsecrated	óvígðri OI, óvígðri ON
un-consecrated	óvígða OI, óvígða ON
uncovered	bert ON
under	undir OI, undir ON
understanding	skyn OI
understood	skilði ON
uneasiness	óró ON
un-glad	óglaðari ON
unhappy	þungt OI, þungt ON
unknown	ókunnu OI, ókunnu ON
unmarried	kvonlausir OI, ókvæntir ON
unruly	ódæll OI
unsettled-land	óbyggðum OI, óbyggðum ON
until	áðr ON, áður OI, til OI, til ON, uns OI, unz ON
unwisely	óhyggilega OI, óvarliga ON
un-worthy-men	auvirðismönnum OI, auvirðismönnum ON
up	upp OI, upp ON, uppi OI, uppi ON
upped	upp OI, upp ON
up-to	undir OI, undir ON
urged	eggjaði ON, fýstu OI
us	okkr ON, okkur OI, oss OI, oss ON
use	nýt OI, nýt ON, nytjum OI, nytjum ON
useful	nytjumaður OI

V, v

176

Word List (English to Norse)

English	Norse	English	Norse
Valdidida (name)	*avaldidida* ON	war-taken	*hertekinn* OI, *hertekinn* ON, *herteknir* OI, *herteknir* ON
Vallthjof (place)	*valþjófs* OI, *valþjófs* ON	was	*er* OI, *er* ON, *gerist* OI, *hét* ON, *stóð* OI, *sú* OI, *væri* OI, *væri* ON, *var* OI, *var* ON, *varð* OI, *varð* ON, *váru* ON, *vas* ON, *vera* OI, *vera* ON, *verða* OI, *voru* OI
valued	*þykja* OI, *þykkja* ON		
Vathjolfsstadr (place)	*valþjófsstöðum* OI, *valþjófsstöðum* ON		
Vatnshorn (place)	*vatnshorni* OI, *vatnshorni* ON		
verse	*kviðling* OI, *kviðling* ON, *vísu* OI, *vísu* ON		
very	*mjög* OI, *mjök* ON	was-called	*hét* ON
Vestribyggd (place)	*vestribyggð* OI, *vestribyggð* ON, *vestribyggðar* OI, *vestribyggðar* ON	was-carried	*bar* ON
		was-done	*gert* ON
		was-named	*hét* OI, *hét* ON
		was-not	*eigi* OI, *eigi* ON
Vethild (name)	*vethildi* OI, *vethildi* ON	water	*vatn* OI, *vatn* ON, *vatni* OI, *vatni* ON
Vifil (name)	*vífill* OI, *vífill* ON		
Vifilsdal (place)	*vífilsdal* OI, *vífilsdal* ON	waved	*veift* ON
Vifilson (name)	*vífilsson* OI, *vífilsson* ON	waving	*veift* OI, *veift* ON
vines	*vínvið* ON, *vínviður* OI	way	*háttr* ON, *háttur* OI, *leið* ON, *leiðar* OI, *leiðar* ON, *vegir* OI, *vegir* ON
vine-trees	*vínviðr* ON, *vínviður* OI		
Vinland (place)	*vínlandi* ON, *vínlands* OI, *vínlands* ON	ways	*megin* OI, *megin* ON, *vega* OI, *vega* ON, *vegna* OI, *vegna* ON
visit	*vitja* OI, *vitja* ON		
voice	*raust* OI, *rödd* ON	we	*vér* OI, *vér* ON, *við* OI, *vit* ON

W, w

English	Norse	English	Norse
		wealth	*fé* OI, *fé* ON, *féið* OI, *féit* ON
wait	*bíða* OI, *bíða* ON, *vænti* ON	wealthy	*auðigr* ON, *auðigur* OI, *vellauðigur* OI
walk	*ganga* ON	weapon	*vápn* ON, *vopn* OI
walked	*gekk* OI, *gekk* ON	weapons	*vápn* ON, *vopn* OI
walrus-tusk	*tannskeftan* OI, *tannskeftan* ON	we-are	*vér* OI, *vér* ON
wares	*vara* OI, *vara* ON, *varning* OI, *varning* ON, *varningi* ON, *varninginn* OI, *varninginum* OI, *varninginum* ON, *varningr* ON, *varningurinn* OI	wearied	*mæddir* OI
		weather	*veðrátta* OI, *veðrátta* ON, *veður* OI
		weathered	*veðrs* OI, *veðrs* ON
		wedding	*brúðkaup* ON, *brullaup* OI, *brullaup* ON
		weeks	*vikur* OI, *vikur* ON
		welcomed	*fagnat* ON
warlock-songs	*varðlokur* OI, *varðlokur* ON	well	*heil* OI, *heil* ON, *með* ON, *vel* OI, *vel* ON
warrior-king	*herkonungr* ON	well-educated	*menntr* ON
war-slings	*valslöngur* OI, *valslöngur* ON	wellspring	*keldu* OI, *keldu* ON

Word List (English to Norse)

English	Norse	English	Norse
went	færðu OI, færðu ON, fara OI, fer OI, fór OI, fór ON, fórst OI, fórst ON, fóru OI, fóru ON, gekk OI, gekk ON, gengr ON, gengu OI, gengu ON, gengur OI, kómust ON	white	hvít ON, hvítan OI, hvítan ON, hvítir OI, hvítir ON, hvítt OI, hvítum OI, hvítum ON
		White-Leg (name)	hvítbeins OI, hvítbeins ON
		White-Man-Land (place)	hvítramannaland OI, hvítramannaland ON
were	að OI, at ON, er OI, er ON, eru OI, eru ON, væri OI, væri ON, væru OI, var OI, var ON, varð OI, varð ON, váru ON, verða ON, verðr ON, voru OI, voruð OI	who	er OI, er ON, hver OI, hver ON, sem OI, sem ON
		whole	heil OI, heil ON
		who-was	er ON
		why	hví OI, hví ON
		wide	breiðu OI, breiðu ON, víðar ON
were-found	fundust ON	widely	víða OI, víða ON
west	vestan OI, vestan ON, vestr ON, vestur OI	wife	kona OI, kona ON, konu OI, konu ON
western	vestan OI, vestan ON, vestri OI, vestri ON	wild-animals	dýr OI, dýr ON, dýrin OI, dýrin ON, dýrum OI, dýrum ON
west-raiding	vestrvíking ON, vesturvíking OI		
west-wind	vestanveðr ON	wild-birds	fugl OI
whale	hval OI, hval ON, hvala ON, hvalinn ON, hvalur OI	wilderness	öræfi OI
		will	mun ON, velja OI, velja ON, vil OI, vil ON, vilda ON, vildi OI, vili ON, vilið ON, vilji OI, viljið OI, viljir OI, vill OI, vill ON
whales	hvalnum OI		
what	að OI, hvað OI, hvað ON, hvat ON, hvert OI		
what-was	vár ON, vor OI	will-be	hallist OI, verði OI, verði ON
wheat	hveiti OI, hveitiax ON		
wheat-acres	hveitiakra OI, hveitiakra ON, hveitiakrar OI, hveitiakrar ON	willed	vildi OI, vildi ON, vildu OI, vildu ON, vilja OI, vilja ON, vill OI, vill ON
		willing	fús OI, fúss ON, vildi ON, vildu OI, vildu ON, vilja OI, vilja ON
when	en OI, en ON, er OI, er ON, hvenær OI, þá ON, þegar OI, þegar ON		
		wills	vill OI, vill ON
where	er OI, er ON, es ON, sem OI, sem ON, þar OI, þar ON	will-you	vilir ON
		wind	veðr ON
		winds	veður OI
wherever	sem OI, sem ON	wine	vín OI, vín ON
whether	hvort OI	winter	vetr ON, vetri OI, vetri ON, vetrinn ON, vetrum OI, vetrum ON, vetur OI, veturinn OI, veturnætur OI, veturvistar OI
which	að OI, at ON, en OI, er OI, er ON, es ON, sé ON, sem OI, sem ON		
while	en OI, en ON, meðan OI, meðan ON, sem OI, stund OI, stund ON		
		winters	vetrum ON
whip	svipu OI, svipu ON	wisdom	fræði OI, fræði ON

Word List (English to Norse)

English	Norse	English	Norse
wise	*fróðr* ON, *fróður* OI, *víst* OI, *víst* ON	would-be	*mundi* OI, *mundu* OI, *mundu* ON, *væri* OI, *væri* ON, *værir* OI, *værir* ON, *væru* OI, *væru* ON
wiser	*fróðari* OI		
wise-woman	*vísendakonunni* ON, *vísindakonunni* OI		
wish	*vilda* ON, *vildi* OI	wound	*sári* ON
wished	*skyldi* OI, *vildi* OI, *vildi* ON, *vili* ON, *vilji* OI	wounds	*sár* ON
		wrote	*orta* ON, *orti* OI
wishing	*annt* OI		
with	*á* OI, *með* OI, *með* ON, *við* OI, *við* ON, *vit* ON	**Y, y**	
withdrawn	*fálátari* OI		
within	*innan* OI, *innan* ON	yet	*á* OI, *á* ON, *enn* OI, *enn* ON, *þó* ON
without-gladness	*óglaðari* OI, *óglaðari* ON	Yngvild (name)	*yngveldar* OI, *yngvildar* ON
without-peace	*ófriðr* ON, *ófriður* OI	you	*þeir* OI, *þér* OI, *þér* ON, *þig* OI, *þik* ON, *þú* OI, *þú* ON, *yðr* ON, *yður* OI, *yðvar* OI, *yðvar* ON
withstood	*stóð* OI, *stóðst* ON		
woke	*vakði* ON, *vakti* OI		
woman	*kona* OI, *kona* ON, *konan* ON, *konu* OI, *konu* ON, *konum* ON, *kvenna* OI, *kvenna* ON		
		younger	*ungur* OI
		young-men	*sveina* ON, *sveinana* OI, *sveinana* ON, *sveinanna* OI
women	*konur* OI, *konur* ON		
won	*unnu* OI, *unnu* ON, *vann* OI, *vann* ON	your	*þín* OI, *þín* ON, *þínum* OI, *þínum* ON, *yðvar* OI, *yðvarr* ON
wonder	*undrast* OI		
wonderful	*kynlegr* OI, *kynligr* ON	yours	*þín* ON, *þínir* OI, *þínir* ON, *þinn* OI, *þinn* ON, *þinni* OI, *þinni* ON, *yður* OI, *yðvar* OI, *yðvar* ON, *yðvarr* ON
woods	*skógi* OI, *skógi* ON, *skóginn* ON		
word	*orð* OI, *orð* ON		
words	*orð* OI, *orð* ON, *orða* OI, *orða* ON, *orðum* ON		
		Yule (name)	*jól* OI, *jól* ON, *jólin* OI, *jólin* ON, *jólum* OI, *jólum* ON
working	*unnið* OI		
worm-eaten	*maðksmogið* OI		
worn	*væstir* ON	yule-feast	*jólaveizlu* ON
worse	*verra* ON, *verri* OI, *verri* ON	Yule-Feast (name)	*jólaveislu* OI
worst	*verra* OI		
worth	*verðr* ON, *verður* OI		
worthiness	*virðingarráð* OI, *virðingarráð* ON		
would	*mun* OI, *mun* ON, *mundi* OI, *mundi* ON, *mundu* OI, *mundu* ON, *myndi* ON, *myndu* OI, *skyldu* OI, *skyldu* ON, *væri* OI, *vildu* ON